Peter Berger and the Study of Religion

Peter Berger is the most influential and the most cited contemporary sociologist of religion, who has been writing on this subject for over forty years. Yet until now there has been no in-depth study of Berger's contribution to the study of religion. A collection of essays by leading scholars in the study of religion and theology, *Peter Berger and the Study of Religion* is a comprehensive introduction to both the work of Peter Berger and to current thought on the central issues and ideas in the study of religion. The themes and subjects addressed in this volume include:

- Berger on religion and theology
- Religion, spirituality and the discontents of modernity
- Secularization and sacralization
- Signals of transcendence.

A postscript by Peter Berger himself, responding to the essays, completes this definitive overview of a major figure's work in a diverse and complex discipline.

Linda Woodhead is Senior Lecturer in Religious Studies at Lancaster University. She is the editor of Routledge's forthcoming *Religion in the Modern World* and editor (with Paul Heelas) of *Religion in Modern Times: An Interpretive Anthology* (2000). **Paul Heelas** is Professor in Religion and Modernity at Lancaster University. **David Martin** is a Visiting Professor at Lancaster University and Professor Emeritus of Sociology at the London School of Economics.

Peter Berger and the Study of Religion

Edited by Linda Woodhead
with Paul Heelas and David Martin

London and New York

First published 2001
by Routledge
11 New Fetter Lane, London EC4P 4EE

Simultaneously published in the USA and Canada
by Routledge
29 West 35th Street, New York, NY 10001

Routledge is an imprint of the Taylor & Francis Group

© 2001 Linda Woodhead, Paul Heelas and David Martin

Typeset in Sabon by Rosemount Typing Services, Thornhill, Dumfriesshire
Printed and bound in Great Britain by TJ International Ltd, Padstow, Cornwall

British Library Cataloguing in Publication Data
A catalogue record for this book is available from the British Library

Library of Congress Cataloguing in Publication Data

ISBN 0–415–21532–3 (pbk)
ISBN 0–415–21531–5 (hbk)

Contents

Notes on contributors

Steve Bruce is Professor of Sociology at the University of Aberdeen. He was previously lecturer, reader and professor at The Queen's University of Belfast. His works include *Conservative Protestant Politics* (1998), *Choice and Religion: A Critique of Rational Choice Theory* (1999), and *Fundamentalism* (2001).

Colin Campbell is Professor of Sociology at the University of York. He has written on irreligion, the cult and the cultic milieu, and superstition, while his books include *The Romantic Ethic and the Spirit of Modern Consumerism* (1987) and *The Myth of Social Action* (1996).

Grace Davie is Reader in the Sociology of Religion, University of Exeter. Recent publications include *Religion in Britain since 1945: Believing without Belonging* (1994) and *Religion in Modern Europe: A Memory Mutates* (2000).

Gary Dorrien is Ann V. and Donald R. Parfet Distinguished Professor at Kalamazoo College, Michigan. His most recent book is *The Barthian Revolt in Modern Theology: Theology without Weapons* (1999). Parts of his essay in this volume are adapted from Dorrien (1993), with permission.

Richard K. Fenn is Maxwell Upson Professor of Christianity and Society at Princeton Theological Seminary. Recent publications include *The Persistence of Purgatory* (1996), *The Blackwell Companion to the Study of Religion* (edited, 2000) and *Time Exposure: The Personal Experience of Time in Secular Societies* (2001).

Paul Heelas is Professor in Religion and Modernity at the Department of Religious Studies, Lancaster University. Recent publications include *The New Age Movement* (1996) and, with Linda Woodhead, *Religion in Modern Times: An Interpretive Anthology* (2000).

Danièle Hervieu-Léger is Professor at the École des Hautes Études en Sciences Sociales (Paris), and director of the Centre d'Études Interdisciplinaires des Faits Religieux (CEIFR, EHESS/CNRS). Recent publications include *La Religion pour Mémoire* (1993) (translated in English as *Religion as a Chain of Memory*, 1999), *Identités religieuses en Europe* (edited with G. Davie) (1996), and *Le Pèlerin et le Converti. La Religion en Mouvement* (1999).

David G. Horrell is Senior Lecturer in New Testament Studies in the Department of Theology, University of Exeter. Recent publications include *The Social Ethos of the Corinthian Correspondence* (1996), *An Introduction to the Study of Paul* (2000) and an edited collection entitled *Social-Scientific Approaches to New Testament Interpretation* (1999).

Thomas Luckmann is Professor Emeritus at the University of Constance, Honorary Professor at the University of Salzburg, formerly Visiting Professor at Harvard Divinity School and the Universities of Wollongong and Vienna. Recent publications include *Modernity, Pluralism and the Crisis of Meaning* (1995) (with Peter Berger) *Morals in Everyday Life* (1980) and *The Communicative Construction of Morals* (1999) (with Jörg Bergmann and others) (in German).

Bernice Martin is Reader Emeritus in Sociology at the University of London (Royal Holloway College). Her best known publication is *A Sociology of Contemporary Cultural Change* (1981).

David Martin is Professor Emeritus of Sociology at the London School of Economics, University of London, and Honorary Professor in the Department of Religious Studies at Lancaster University. Recent publications include *Does Christianity Cause War?* (1997) and *Reflections on Theology and Sociology* (1997).

Linda Woodhead is Senior Lecturer in Christian Studies in the Department of Religious Studies, Lancaster University. Recent publications include *Diana: The Making of a Media Saint* (edited with Jeffrey Richards and Scott Wilson, 1999), *Reinventing Christianity: Nineteenth-century Contexts* (edited, 2001) and, with Paul Heelas, *Religion in Modern Times: An Interpretative Anthology* (2000).

Introduction

Linda Woodhead

> Here I want to see those men of hard voice.
> Those that break horses and dominate rivers;
> those men of sonorous skeleton who sing
> with a mouth full of sun and flint
>
> Federico Garcia Lorca
> Used as the epigraph of *The Homeless Mind*
> (Berger and Kellner, 1973)

When Paul Heelas and I recently put together a reader on *Religion in Modern Times* there were a handful of authors whose work we found ourselves using again and again. Try as we might to find alternatives, there was no getting away from the fact that these were the writers responsible for a disproportionate number of the key formulations in the study of religion. If we take the Second World War as a watershed, the prewar authors we used the most were Weber, Troeltsch, Durkheim, Marx and Simmel. No big surprises there – our work merely confirmed an informal canon which is already widely accepted. But a canon in the postwar study of religion is not yet as clearly defined, and it was therefore with genuine interest that we discovered that the authors from whom we had extracted the most were David Martin, Robert Bellah, Robert Wuthnow – and Peter Berger.

In varying degrees and in different ways, all four of these authors combine high-level theorizing with close attention to empirical evidence. Arguably, it is Berger who has contributed the most to the study of religion at the level of what might be called 'meta-theory'. The essentials of Berger's theoretical framework were laid down early in his career, particularly through his collaboration with Thomas Luckmann on *The Social Construction of Reality* (1966). This foundational text in the sociology of knowledge explored and exposed the linkages between conviction, commitment, and social reality. Berger applied the arguments of this book to the religious realm in *The Sacred Canopy* (1967). His unique insight –

which he now modestly refers to as his one truly original idea – was that pluralism undermines stable belief. Under the pressure of the pluralizing forces of modernity the 'sacred canopy' becomes the 'precarious vision'. A central conclusion was that pluralism leads inevitably to secularization. Berger's version of secularization theory endorsed the view that there is an intrinsic link between modernization and secularization, but found in pluralism the missing link which made the connection clear.

The power of this early theoretical framework is proven by the way in which it yielded rich insights in the many different spheres to which Peter Berger applied it in subsequent work. To 'the modern condition' in *The Homeless Mind* (1973) and *Facing up to Modernity* (1979); to the family in *The War over the Family* (1983); to economic cultures and development in books such as *Pyramids of Sacrifice* (1974a) and *The Capitalist Revolution* (1987). The history of its continuing application to religion is particularly interesting and revealing. Berger's interest in religion has continued throughout his career. His initial focus on the fate of religion (particularly Christianity) in America and Europe has continued, but quickly broadened to take account of global religious developments, not least the spread of Islam and Charismatic Christianity. It is testament to Peter Berger's openness to empirical evidence that such developments have led him to revise his earlier views on secularization (see, for example, *The Desecularization of the World*, 1999). While he believes that his insights into the cognitively corrosive effects of pluralism still stand, he is prepared to admit that he may have misconceived the relation between pluralism and secularization. As he puts it in the postscript to this volume: 'I would say now that pluralism affects the *how* of religious belief, but not necessarily the *what*.' In other words, it is still possible to hold religious beliefs even though they have ceased to be taken-for-granted certainties – but it is impossible to hold them in the same way. People continue to be religious in most modern societies (with the possible exception of Europe), but are religious in new ways – even when the new ways present themselves as a return to the old ways.

Peter Berger's interest in religion – particularly but not exclusively Christianity – has always been from the inside as well as from the outside. (Again, interesting parallels could be drawn with the work of David Martin, Robert Wuthnow and Robert Bellah.) Even before he and Luckmann had written *The Social Construction of Reality*, Berger had published *The Precarious Vision: A Sociologist Looks at Social Fictions and the Christian Faith* (1961a) and *The Noise of Solemn Assemblies: Christian Commitment and the Religious Establishment* (1961b). While Berger seems coy about the designation 'theologian', there is no doubting the passionate commitments and revulsions which the contemporary churches provoke in him, nor his continuing interest in 'the transcendent'. Both *A Rumour of Angels* (1969a) and *The Heretical Imperative* (1979a) have had a profound influence within the churches, and are still frequently cited. His recent *Redeeming Laughter* (1997a) stands in the same tradition. The appeal of these books to a wide audience seems to lie not only in the clarity of Berger's prose, but in their empirical starting point: instead of beginning with revealed dogma taken on faith, Berger starts from the 'signals of transcendence' which he believes we can discern amid the ambiguities of everyday experience. Though he distinguishes this theological method from the deductive method of traditional and neo-orthodox theology and the 'reductive' method of much modern liberal theology (1979a), Berger's approach allies him more closely with the latter than with the former. Yet he retains a Barthian impatience with the dilutions of transcendence which result from what he sees as liberal Christianity's misguided attempts at modernization. In his theology as in his politics, Berger jousts with both conservatives and liberals, often managing to discomfit both.

Peter Berger's publications now span more than four decades. This volume attempts to take stock of this enormous achievement, and in particular of his work in the study of religion. At the same time, it seeks to give an impression of the living and continuing tradition of such study and of Berger's place within it. To this end we have commissioned a number of leading scholars in the field to reflect upon Berger's legacy from the standpoint of their own work. Contributors were deliberately chosen to reflect both different generations and different specialisms. The intention was to produce a volume which could highlight both continuities and new developments in the study of religion, while retaining a central focus on Berger's work.

The first section, 'Berger on religion and theology', serves as an introduction to Peter Berger's contribution to the study of religion. David Martin offers an overview and appreciation, while Thomas Luckmann reflects on the nature of the scholarly collaboration which is such a striking feature of Berger's career. Gary Dorrien offers a critical analysis of the development of Berger's theology, and relates it to Berger's wider convictions and commitments in sociology and politics.

The dominance of secularization theory in the sociology of religion has often inhibited study of the nature, survival, and transformations of religion in modern societies. Despite his massive contribution to secularization theory, Peter Berger has never ceased paying attention to the fate of religion on the ground. What is more, his contributions to a sociology of modernity have significant implications for our understanding of religion in modern contexts – and vice versa. The section on 'Religion, spirituality and the discontents of modernity' takes these contributions as its starting point. Paul Heelas and Linda Woodhead consider the implications of Berger's magisterial characterization of modernity in terms of 'homelessness' for an understanding of the fate of religion and spirituality today, and investigate the way in which the proliferation of secondary institutions in the economic and religious spheres (among others) may have served to counteract homelessness. Colin Campbell considers another aspect of Berger's work: his Weberian exploration of religion in terms of its ability to generate and sustain meaning. Campbell develops this theoretical approach in relation to the 'theodicy' of the contemporary New Age movement.

In the section on 'Secularization and sacralization' which follows, Steve Bruce accuses Peter Berger of an unnecessary recantation of secular- ization theory. *Contra* Berger, Bruce defends the 'strong' version of secularization theory which holds that modernization inevitably involves secularization. It is a measure of the sea-change which has recently taken place in the sociology of religion that Bruce's position is now unusual and unfashionable. The chapters by Grace Davie and Danièle Hervieu-Léger are more representative of current priorities in the field in their attempt to look beyond secularization theory to the more complex patterns of secularization and de-secularization (or sacralization) on the ground. While Berger admits the reality of secularization in Europe, he argues that this should be treated as the exceptional rather than the typical case of religion in the modern world. It is this exceptionalism which both Davie and Hervieu-Léger explore, each author suggesting that the secularity of Europe needs to be qualified in important ways.

The final section of the book, 'Signals of transcendence', considers Berger's contribution to theology (in its broadest sense, including both systematic theology and Biblical Studies). Richard Fenn argues that the 'sociological imagination' has become a common inheritance of symbolically and cognitively sophisticated modern societies, and that the fact that we can now all see through the 'sacred canopy' to the 'precarious vision' which it once veiled has the most profound implications for modern theology and religiosity. David Horrell considers the far-reaching impact of Peter Berger's sociology within New Testament Studies, where it has helped to engender a new interest in the social world of early Christianity. While endorsing this development, Horrell also makes some sharp comments about its tendency to underestimate the importance of power relations in the social construction of reality. Bernice Martin offers the first detailed exposition and analysis of Peter Berger's little-known novel, *Protocol of a Damnation* (1975). She teases out the 'anthropological theology' of the novel, and relates it to Berger's wider theological scheme developed in works such as *A Rumour of Angels*. Bernice Martin also suggests that gender emerges as an unexamined but nevertheless key structuring theme of the novel.

In his postscript Peter Berger responds to each of these contributions in turn. He listens attentively to the interpretations and criticisms offered and – while defending his theories with vigour – indicates a number of issues on which he has modified his views or changed his mind. The reader is left with a sense of the richness and vitality of the corpus of guiding theories, formulations, metaphors, and perspectives which Berger has developed over the years; its continuing power to illuminate; and its continuing genesis in collaboration and dialogue with others. Some of Berger's sticking points also emerge very clearly. The notion of a 'gendered perspective' (introduced in different ways in the chapter by Paul Heelas and Linda Woodhead and in that by Bernice Martin) calls forth a 'polite dissent'; likewise, Berger is 'unable to follow' Richard Fenn's claims about the sacralization of everyday life; and he believes that Fenn, and also Heelas and Woodhead, are guilty of overestimating and probably over-egging the cultural transformation of recent decades. Berger's harshest comments are reserved for 'postmodernism', which he charges with a relativistic, solipsistic constructivism that amounts to 'a recipe for the self-liquidation of science and, beyond that and far more dangerously, a politics of fanaticism'.

Something of the nature and extent of Berger's contribution to the study of religion emerges from each section of this volume. Clearly his influence has been profound within many of the most central areas of research and debate in the study of religion: the sociological nature of religious commitment; the transformations of religion in modern times; the relations between religion and the economic realm; secularization theory and its revision; Biblical Studies; the interface between theology and sociology.

Though Peter Berger's career began more than four decades ago, it is interesting to note the way in which many topics on which he has been writing for much of this time have only recently been taken up into the mainstream of the study of religion. A good example is de-secularization, on which Berger began to write as early as 1977. Similarly, he has long been interested in the topic of religion and globalization, which again has become widely fashionable only in the past decade or so. Equally, Berger's long-standing and foundational interest in the topic of religion and pluralization has recently become such a central topic in the sociology of religion that in 1993 Stephen Warner claimed that it had become a 'new paradigm' within the discipline, rivalling that of secularization (Warner, 1993). While the topic of religion and pluralism may have been taken in directions with which he has little sympathy (not least by the rational choice theorists), there is no doubting Berger's pioneering role in this as in so many other areas of debate.

One of the most concrete ways in which Peter Berger has shaped the field has been in his role as Director of the Institute for the Study of Economic Culture in Boston, a position he has held since 1985. ISEC institutionalizes Berger's long-standing (Weberian) interest in the interaction of culture and economics. Beginning with *Pyramids of Sacrifice* (1974a), this interest fanned out to take in developments in Latin America, the Pacific (Indonesia, Hong Kong, Taiwan and elsewhere), and led into a particular concern with development in South Africa. At the same time Berger's interest in the changing face of capitalism in the developed world, the rise of a 'new economy' and 'new class', and the cultural and religious dimensions of this development, has remained constant. The work of ISEC has reflected and furthered these interests, and even a very selective list of the scholars and projects it has supported gives some impression of how wide-ranging and influential its work has been. These include:

- research by David Martin and Bernice Martin on the Charismatic upsurge in Latin America (published as *Tongues of Fire*, David Martin, 1990), and currently on the life-worlds of global Pentecostalism;
- research by Robert Hefner on 'liberal' forms of Islam, particularly Islam in Indonesia (published (for example) as *Civil Islam* (2000));
- research by Joan Estruch on Opus Dei and economic culture, published as *Saints and Schemers. Opus Dei and its Paradoxes* (1995);
- research by Hansfried Kellner and Frank Heuberger on recent developments in capitalism, published as *Hidden Technocrats. The New Class and New Capitalism* (1992);
- research by Nancy Ammerman and others on American congregations, published as *Congregation and Community* (1997);
- a project on religion and tolerance undertaken by Adam Seligman;
- a ten-country study entitled 'Globalization and Culture', currently being sponsored.

It is from one of the above projects that my favourite recollection of Peter Berger comes. At the beginning of *Congregation and Community* (1997), Nancy Ammerman acknowledges Berger's crucial role in the project, and offers up thanks for 'his insistent "So what?"' (p. xiii). To anyone who has met Peter Berger, the anecdote will have the ring of truth. What is more, these two words seem to offer an interpretative key to much that is distinctive about his remarkable contribution.

'So what?' So you have all these rich and fascinating data, so what? What do they tell us? What is there of generalizable significance about the data? In this context, the question is a reminder of the importance of theory in the social sciences. Without downplaying the essential place of empirical research, Peter Berger continues to remind us of the importance of theory as the engine of responsible thought and agency. Data must be theorized in order to have relevance to anything but themselves. The reminder is important at a time when certain tendencies in the social sciences generate anxiety and suspicion about the possibilities of generalizing beyond the particular case.

'So what?' So you have all these theories and ideas, so what? What practical implications might they have? Again, Berger rides over many common hesitancies in his insistence that sociology can and should make a difference. This seems to be grounded in his work on social construction, where he exposes the given as the created. It is because society is a human construction that it is amenable to human reason and enquiry and capable of being shaped by human agency. Berger does not overlook the extent to which we humans are ourselves social constructions: rather, he tries to balance an awareness that society is a human product with an awareness that humans are social products. It is precisely in this balance that sociology's potential – and duty – to inform, empower, and liberate is located. Berger does not believe that the sociologist can be or should become a political or social visionary; rather, the duty of the sociologist is to be clear-sighted about the pretensions, ironies, contradictions, constraints, and opportunity costs involved in all social choices.

'So what?' What does it all mean? While it would be easy, even natural, for a sociologist to evade this question, Berger does not. It is the 'big' question which has repeatedly drawn him into theological territory. While he does not believe we can start anywhere other than with the empirical, it is 'in, with and under' human experience that he discerns 'rumours of angels' and 'signals of transcendence'. These he finds in the fundamental experiences of love, play, laughter, outrage at evil, hope in adversity. All, in Berger's view, reveal an awareness of a deep order in the structure of things. The basic human responsibility is to strain to discern such order, to live in responsiveness to it, and to preserve the fragile but essential structures which are all that stands between us and ever-threatening collapse into meaninglessness and disorder.

Uncertainty, fragmentation, disorder: these themes lie at the heart of Berger's work and link his theological and sociological contributions. In Berger's analysis they form the inescapable but uncomfortable context in which all modern men and women must live out their lives. Both the flight to ideological or religious certainties on the one hand and that to 'radical' anarchic or relativistic disorder on the other are evasions. 'Soft' options. For Berger the 'harder', nobler, calling of the modern-day warrior is to dwell with integrity in the difficult, dangerous, and uncomfortable territory which lies between.

Part I

Berger on religion and theology

1 Berger: an appreciation

David Martin

I want to begin with some features of Peter Berger's writing and intellectual personality, and to do so through my personal encounter with his work. I think I was initially intrigued about a third of a century ago by his talent for the unexpected. Flicking the pages of a new book *The Precarious Vision* (1961a) in the recent acquisitions section of the LSE library, I was brought up short by his imagining a possible future dominated by Islam. The idea was bizarre since everybody in those days assumed the only possible future was under the aegis of the secular politics of the left. Peter Berger's interesting madness made me think again.

My next fragment of memory is of a Marxist student leader, Robin Blackburn, telling me in the tones of one who knew where the wires twanged in avant-garde London, that I should read Peter Berger's article on marriage in *Diogenes* (reprinted in Berger, 1979b, pp. 27–47). I did so and recognized a talent for turning the everyday into something rich and strange. I saw how we, out of our shared devices and desires, create common worlds. The weight of the given freshly emerged as a case of world-maintenance.

It was precisely that talent for revising everyday perceptions which I encountered again in *Invitation to Sociology* (1966d; orig. 1963b), and it led me to recommend the book to intending students. However, it was important they read something else more boring. You might just as well treat Peter Brown's *Augustine of Hippo* (1967) as an introduction to theology, and get all fired up for further stirrings in 'the cauldron of boiling loves'. Here in the *Invitation* were the structures of recognizably human experience presented by somebody who sounded as if he had tasted some of it himself. The writing jettisoned all our evasive passives and dehydrated abstractions to grasp the objects of our study, or rather the *subjects* of our study, each after its kind.

Not merely was Berger's prose seductive; it was also almost damagingly lucid. Its special merit was well-placed concreteness, perhaps because Berger's curiosity about the world far outweighed his interest in abstract intellection. Though an intensely private individual, he wanted most of all to communicate his fascination with the taken-for-granted recipes which shape our social activity rather than to deal in pregnant tautologies and tortuous renaming of the familiar. Yet if a fresh analytic move or coinage were really required he immediately invented it or else redeployed classical resources: *nomoi, cosmoi,* sacred canopies, plausibility structures. Given that American sociological English has been infected by Germanic constructions – piled up agglomerations and multiple hyphenation – it was a singular grace that a migrant from Austria to the English-speaking world could write such lucid prose. Maybe he took his favourite P. G. Wodehouse as his model.

I will mention just one other virtue, and one he shares with Thomas Luckmann: a readiness to change his mind. Maybe as you constantly rotate all the facets of the diamond of the given a new light will strike you. Take, for example, his approach to secularization. Readers will recollect the role played in his theory of secularization by pluralism as it corrodes and relativizes our commitments. When Peter Berger became doubtful about that he said so. More recently he has taken up the theme of 'European exceptionalism', not in the spirit of holding a brief for a position but curious to see how things might look when you treat European irreligion as the odd man out rather than treat religion in America or the rest of the world as retarded.

So far I have referred only tangentially to the sociology of religion, which is the strict focus of our concern. After all, the virtues just mentioned are present equally in his general sociology as in his sociology of religion. Yet even as we adhere to that focus we ought to remember that the sociology of religion is just one set of opus numbers in a very extensive opera. Berger's concerns have included a prolonged commitment to studies of economic and social development, most notably in *Pyramids of Sacrifice* (1974a) dealing with the differing costs of the capitalist and communist alternatives, and in *The Capitalist Revolution* (1987; orig. 1986a), but also in the scenarios he devised for possible solutions in South Africa. These apart, he has co-authored and edited books on differential economic advance especially as affected by varied cultural contexts, and has created 'The Institute for the Study of Economic Culture' to help finance others, myself included, to pursue cognate studies. There has been a major work on *The War over the Family* (1983) with Brigitte Berger, and one of his most influential works written with Brigitte and Hansfried Kellner, *The Homeless Mind* (1974; orig. 1973).

Beginning with his path-breaking and classic cooperation with Thomas Luckmann, in which they worked from a joint indebtedness to Alfred Schutz, he has been prescient and lucky in his collaborators, above all that very special collaboration with Brigitte, from whom he has received in his own words 'critical support' in both senses of the adjective 'critical'.

Here I interpose an anecdote. The particular occasion it relates was close to a turning point in Peter Berger's career, which came quite soon after setting aglow the hearts of people such as Robin Blackburn. It has always seemed to me that with titles such as *The Social Construction of Reality* (1966a) and *The Social Reality of Religion* (1973) (originally published as *The Sacred Canopy* (1967)), Berger gave the impression of being ready for some active deconstruction and subversion. To the casual reader here was the theory of a practice of changing the world. With that object in mind, students one day entered his office asking for further enlightenment on direct action. It had not occurred to them that their hero entertained a mild nostalgia for the benefits of multi-ethnic empires. Their disappointment was great when he pointed to a picture of the Emperor Franz Joseph and invited them to depart.

Something similar occurred when I chaired a lecture he gave at the LSE in the lateish 1960s on the double nature of sociology, radical and conservative. The Old Theatre buzzed with revolutionary and anarchic anticipations – though no one streaked for Berger as they did for Parsons, since no such adventitious aids to attention were needed. For the first half-hour fervour reigned. Then, as Berger proceeded in praise of apathy the audience became ever more hyperactive until at question time they were convulsed. Peter Berger then recommended European manners to them and publicly consoled himself with the thought that they all needed sleep some time or other and would one day be constrained by progeny. He had written about the social location of prophecy but not, I think, about the fate of prophets who go 'off message'. Maybe that is the point: would he ever want to speak according to script or be the leader of a crowd? His recent disagreement with some old colleagues in arms over their absolutist attitude to abortion is a case in point.

Peter Berger's talent for the unexpected confirms him as a heretic sceptical of conventional heresies. That does not make him an ordinary conservative for whom semblance is solidity, but aligns him with all those who are wary of our social precariousness, knowledgeable as Macchiavelli was about the universality of corruption in all its fascinating detail. He is not even a standard anti-intellectual intellectual but one who will use the hermeneutic of suspicion on its Western-educated practitioners. Berger does not expect to descry the deep currents in generalized notions such as postmodernism, but by patient observation of whatever is the case. The world out there is more instructive than the *Dictionnaire des Idées Reçues*.

Some theologians – not all – have found Berger as discomfiting as the radicals. Not quite perhaps, because theologians recognize a friend to their enterprise as well as a critic of the way they go about it. A title such as *The Heretical Imperative* (1979a) sounds promising, and Berger's openness to Benares as well as to Jerusalem can count for virtue, but still they poke about for that disreputable clue to unmask just how it is a man who sounds so right can be so wrong. (That hunting for clues confirms that we are all sociologists now.) For quite a number the natural attitude is conservatism in religion, liberalism in politics, and the reverse is unconscionable.

Sociology ought to be the amenable tool of a social agenda and correct thinking, not a school of hard choices, opportunity costs and escalating ironies. It was Berger's bad habit to suggest that sociology was not as they construed it.

Some, perhaps the more evangelical, were also unhappy about his 'methodological atheism' as if one could somehow give a systematic account of the divine activity in our world. For Berger, however, the principle of *Etsi Deus non daretur* in sociological enquiry was not negotiable.

This mismatch of aims, expectations and understandings is quite frequent between Christians who are sociologists and clerical intellectuals, especially maybe those in the religious bureaucracies whom Berger suspects of peddling a contemporary credulity. Relativism is one issue where mismatch may occur, along with views of 'modern man', and acculturation. On relativism philosophical conclusions masquerade as sociology and one of Berger's projects has been 'to relativize the relativizers'. He also in some of his earlier work sought to undermine those who in Barthian manner sought to fence off the Word proclaimed in the church behind an unassailable palisade.

One has to sympathize with learned theologians who did their reading and found that, whatever they wrote, some sociologist would declare them deluded adepts of a mistaken fashion. It made some more than ready to believe that John Milbank's *Theology and Social Theory* (1993) had caught all those disagreeable bees in a single sack. But others did not. Reactions have been varied. Perhaps this is the point at which to recollect Pope Paul VI's courteous and measured response when Peter Berger brought a bevy of us sociologists to Rome in 1968 – Bellah, Parsons, Wilson, Cox and others – under the auspices of the Secretariatus pro non Credentibus.

Whatever one's position on this, I suspect that distrust of theologians pushed Peter Berger to become his own theologian. Though his early works such as *The Noise of Solemn Assemblies* (1961b) and *The Precarious Vision* (1961a) indicate theological commitments, it was in *A Rumour of Angels* (1969a) that he embarked on theological construction and added 'signals of transcendence' to our vocabulary. As his sociology is humanist so his theology begins with the human, above all the implications of our gestures. Berger is a Christian humanist, understanding society without reduction as of human devising, and incarnational in finding the manifestation of God in the lineaments of the human face, in the gestures of the body, in the incongruity of our condition.

Berger's theological liberalism is clear from his response to other religious revelations in *The Heretical Imperative* (1979a) and in *A Far Glory* (1992). This latter book is *Echt* Berger and too little known. At one level it offers a thematic index to his whole repertoire: relativity, pluralism, plausibility, meaningful *cosmoi*, the occlusion of our own projections, cognitive contamination and bargaining, as well as contemporary homelessness and uncertainty about who we are. (Not that Berger has any doubts about who *he* is: a Lutheran rabbi.) There is also his analysis of the passage through the fiery brook of Feuerbach and how to reverse it; the imperialism of the international 'knowledge class' and how to challenge it; and the genuine relevance of the secularization thesis as well as how to take into account 'European exceptionalism' and the global import of Islam and evangelicalism.

However, *A Far Glory* (1992) combines sociology and theology in a way which would make some, such as Bryan Wilson, feel uneasy. For myself I believe it is possible to devise a mixed text, just as literary criticism may switch to philosophy or sociology. We all of us deploy rhetorical genres with their varied resonances, and in sociology we even have a weakness for the rhetorical stance of the legal brief. What we find in the mixed text of *A Far Glory* is direct commitment and a clear theological profile. Given my own battles with clerical intellectuals over liturgy, I cannot help regretting that Berger has not pursued further the incipient critique of liturgical reform which we find here in his espousal of 'I believe' rather than 'We believe'.

Fundamentally in *A Far Glory* Peter Berger seeks a Christian theory of revelation to include the Mahayana texts, mystical writing and the gods of Greece as sought after in Hölderlin. As Schiller put it in 'Die Götter Griechenlands', 'Schöne Welt, wo bist du?'. He wants a less specific understanding (I quote) of 'how the community of worship of the galaxies and all the archangels may find a habitation in the world of men'. He asks how he, a German-speaking Lutheran, *simul iustus et peccator*, makes his obeisance to Apollo.

Berger's theory of divine plenitude and of revelation appears in paragraphs on pages 160 and 165–6 of *A Far Glory*. The first stands Feuerbach on his head: the empirical world is itself a gigantic, though fragmented, symbol of the face of God. The second is a search under all forms for the analogues of the logos, the cosmic Christ. Read those passages and gauge what the pulpit lost when Peter Berger the ordinand felt scruples more exacting than those of his compeers concerning the Augsburg Confession.

If I were Peter Berger I would end with a joke or invent an Analect of Confucius. Instead I borrow from Bernice Martin to suggest that what for some is the epiphany of music or poetry is found for Berger in the incongruities of the comic story. That is all explored in his *Redeeming Laughter* (1997a). We only laugh because we are at once greatly rude and rudely great. Our genuine dignity uncovers our primal absurdity and we howl in derision and delight. In a very Lutheran way we are double natured, lost and found, but Peter Berger's expression of that manifests a long Jewish genealogy in Central European Jewry. The Jews, through long historical experience, know only too well the unexpected punch line, and the impact of life's gentle or terrible ironies. It has always seemed to me that the conversion of the Jews is a risky business, and a far more frequent risk than

Andrew Marvell realized when apostrophizing his coy mistress for delay. Such *conversos* as St John of the Cross and Torquemada – or Gustav Mahler – illustrate my point. But it is not simply Jewish intelligence that suggests that within a generation or two they will come up with wry and creative observations about Christianity. We must be more sociological than that. It is their capacity to stand both within and without while migrating about our global society. It is that, together with passionate commitments, and a desire to communicate out of momentary silences and a loneliness, that has provided a context for Berger to refresh our vocabulary, renew our frameworks, and alter our perceptions. In my experience that is self-evident from examining theses in the hundreds over thirty-five years. The trouble is that in characteristically Bergerian mode we may occlude how and when that happened, why that was so salutary, and by what human agency it was produced. This, then, is our anamnesis as a scholarly community, and if in what follows we have sundry reservations or criticisms they come in the context of our gratitude.

2 Berger and his collaborator(s)

Thomas Luckmann

Introduction – quasi-systematic

It would be an exaggeration to say that I was eager to accept the invitation to contribute to this volume. In spite of some clarifying words from the editors, I was uncertain precisely what was expected of me. What could I say about Peter Berger and his collaborators? Collaborators? What worried me was not the well-known fact of historical semantics that the term collaborateur had lost its innocence during the Second World War, together with the fact that I doubted that the passing years had succeeded in wiping out the obloquy which the quislings had conferred upon it at that time. As the word is used here, however, it surely does not carry a suggestion that Berger's collaborators should undergo a process of debergerization? What did worry me were other matters, among them the plural form of the expectation. I shall come back to that.

In any case, the difficulty was not only that at first I did not know what to write. I could see that even if I were to find something to add to the volume, not perhaps about a multitude of collaborators, but at least about a collaborator in the singular, I would have some difficulty in deciding how to write it. Was there a literary form, a genre, that was clearly appropriate for the task? Evidently, the occasion did not demand a laudatio, nor, most happily, an epitaph. Another, weightier possibility presented itself. Should I try to produce a theoretical essay, extracting a social psychology of collaboration (scholarly collaboration, to be sure) from the narrowly circumscribed example of the books and articles – two and three, if I counted correctly – which we wrote together? I might have been willing to risk the ire of our confrères in the sociological mainstream (is it still flowing or has it turned into a braided river, to borrow a term from my angling friends?) by daring to generalize from a non-representative sample. But I did not feel that I had the necessary qualifications for the task, among which objectivity is not the least.

As one of the collaborators, and as one of the earliest ones at that, I was understandably tempted to indulge in reminiscences. Should posterity be interested to hear about the breathtaking speed with which my friend hammered away at the typewriter when, in the grip of inspiration, he put to paper a formulation to be used in one of our joint texts? I was in doubt whether it would it be proper to add such anecdotal marginalia to a volume with scholarly intentions. Would anyone but co-reminiscers be interested in them?

Having seen the list of the other contributors (collaborators?) to the volume, and the titles of their contributions, I felt reassured that all serious theoretical issues connected with Berger's *opus* in the general theory and sociology of religion – and beyond – will be most adequately covered. I therefore no longer hesitated to accept the invitation and committed myself to contribute a rather different, minor introductory chapter to the volume: a few personal observations on our collaboration, adding a few scattered reflections on its outcome. To be sure, I must do without an established *genre* to serve as a mould for the words that follow. Perhaps one should consider them a hybrid of anecdotal *reminiscences* on collaborating and unsystematic *paralipomena* on the results of one particular instance of scholarly collaboration.

I just wrote 'a few personal observations on our collaboration' because I wish to disclaim any competence for saying anything substantial about Berger's other collaborative enterprises. True, I do know most of his collaborators, the lady, his wife and the men who worked with Berger on books and investigations of various kinds. Many I know well, some are good friends of mine. But I do not have much of an idea how Brigitte Berger and Hansfried Kellner collaborated with him on *The Homeless Mind* (1973) (I *did* read that book), and I have even less of a notion how, for example, his collaboration went in the old days with Richard Neuhaus, and more recently with David Martin, for instance; or Hans-Georg Soeffner, and all the others. There was only one instance, beyond our joint undertakings, when I was a witness to, and marginal participant in, an entirely different kind of large-scale collaboration. That was the project which was sponsored by the Bertelsmann Foundation in the middle 1990s and presented as a report to the Club of Rome. It was planned and directed by Berger and involved collaborators from Europe, North and South America, Asia and Africa.

This means that my knowledge of Berger's collaborations is essentially limited to what I remember of our excursions into thinking and writing – and getting older – together. This also means that I cannot pretend to have an objective perspective on the matter. What follows is to be read with that reservation in mind.

Unsystematic observations on thinking and writing together

In the beginning was shared boredom. Berger and I were both students at the Graduate Faculty for Political and Social Science of the New School for Social Research in New York. Karl Löwith – whom I consider to have been not only one of the most important philosophers of the last century but also one of the most underestimated – gave a seminar on religion at that institution in the early 1950s. Great philosopher he was, and a most honourable man in difficult times. From that seminar, however, I remember little but that he read monotonously from one of his essays that treated the dilemma of being both a Christian and a gentleman. In order to keep awake, I started to doodle on paper. I know not what, nor do I remember in which language or script. Another student did the same. Berger and I became friends. I may add that we two disrespectful students developed great respect for Löwith, and formed a sort of personal attachment to him in later years.

Berger and I found that we came from partly very similar, partly quite dissimilar milieus from the same background. Our families were rooted in the Austro-Hungarian monarchy and we came from its successor states. In a manner of speaking, we talked the same language whether in German or English. Furthermore, in our conversations it became obvious that we thought in a similar way on many matters. For one, we shared the suspicion that some of the reigning intellectual emperors and rulers of social science wore no clothes. Although the happy circumstance of intellectual affinity was serendipitous with regard to our friendship, it was, of course, a necessary condition, first for conceiving the idea that we might engage in joint writing, and then for actually doing so. Another condition for collaboration, although I cannot say whether necessary or merely very helpful, was that for several years in the early 1960s we both taught at the Graduate Faculty of the New School. We had returned to our *alma mater* after having started our teaching careers at different colleges and universities in the late 1950s. By that time we had both published several articles in various journals, Berger also had brought out a book or two (I remember his *The Noise of Solemn Assemblies* (1961b), and I was about to publish the early German version of *The Invisible Religion*.

As students at the Graduate Faculty of the New School, Berger and I had been influenced by Carl Mayer,[1] a precise and conscientious Weberian sociologist of religion, and Albert Salomon whose intellectual enthusiasm for returning to the sources directed us to look back to the early history of social thought and to the forefathers of sociology. But the most important influence on our thinking, certainly on mine, had come from Alfred Schutz. Schutz's attempt to provide a solid phenomenological foundation for the theory of action upon which Max Weber had built a historical sociology of institutions and cultural formations seemed to us a project well worth taking up and continuing. It seemed logical to approach this project from the vantage point of Schutz's own conception of a sociology of knowledge which went well beyond the traditional and increasingly sterile epistemological and ideological preoccupations of that discipline.

At the early stages of thinking and talking about the project Berger and I were not alone. Several colleagues, former graduate students at the New

School and some present ones whom we met in its unique intellectual climate, shared many of our theoretical interests, aversions and philosophical and sociological dispositions. The notion of a common undertaking may have been in the air, but I am pretty sure that it was Berger who gave concrete shape to the idea that he and I, together with some of these 'fellow travellers' – Maurice Natanson, Hansfried Kellner and Stanley Pullberg – should form the core of a group which might try to pursue our Schutz-inspired project. For various reasons the envisioned team fell apart before it was properly constituted.[2] None the less, Berger and I remained committed to the project and planned it in more detail when we met in the Austrian Alps for several days during the summer vacation. If memory serves, we started to work on it seriously at the beginning of the following fall term.

I have already alluded to the fact that Berger and I had some earlier practice in joint authorship. Before starting on the book we came to call *The Social Construction of Reality* (1966a) – not *The Construction of Social Reality*, the title of another book by another author – we had written a paper on the sociology of religion and the sociology of knowledge, another on secularization and pluralism, and one on social mobility and personal identity. I do not recall the details of those earlier collaborative efforts. There certainly were no heated arguments. The few – perhaps not entirely unimportant – issues on which we held different opinions, such as the most appropriate way to define the nature of religion, could be, and were, bracketed for later debate.

In later years I fielded many questions about one aspect of our collaboration, especially with regard to *The Social Construction of Reality*: who wrote what? This was something that seemed to interest both colleagues and students, and the questions were asked both in formal discussions and in ordinary conversations. However, neither Berger nor I gave much thought to the matter at the time of writing the book nor did we talk about it afterwards. Now, so many years later, writing about our collaboration, I tried to recollect how things went in this respect and if there were any differences between the early jointly written papers (Berger and Luckmann, 1963, 1966; Luckmann and Berger, 1964) and *The Social Construction of Reality* (1966a) and the recent book(let) we wrote together (Berger and Luckmann, 1995).

As far as I can remember, the initiative for the first two papers mentioned above came from Berger. The paper on the sociology of religion and sociology of knowledge (1963) represents joint authorship both in the ideas and in the writing; in a manner of speaking it was also an apprenticeship for the book. The paper on secularization and pluralism (1966) owes substantially more to Berger's ideas than to mine. The paper on social mobility and personal identity(1964) originated in a somewhat different way. I had conceived the main idea for the paper and talked about it with Berger. Eventually, after I had procrastinated with the writing for some time, Berger became impatient with the slow rate of progress I had made in writing that paper on my own. It held up our starting on what to both of us was a more important project – *The Social Construction of Reality*. He joined me as co-author, probably did most of the writing, and greatly speeded up the completion of the work.

This little item from the history of the early days of our thinking and writing together intimates something about an aspect of our collaboration which is relevant to the question who wrote what. Berger wrote well and fast – and, as I mentioned earlier, he also typed extremely fast, with two fingers. I also type fast, with one or two more fingers than Berger, but not only do I write slowly in the first place, I also spend much time in rewriting what I have written. I think that Berger generally did more of the actual writing than I did, also in the writing of *The Social Construction of Reality*. As for the thinking, I should say that with the exception of the first two chapters, we contributed equally to the development of the main propositions of the book. It would be difficult, if not impossible, to disentangle one individual's contributions from those of the other in what was an ongoing dialogue, a dialogue that had started many years before we sat down to write the book. In any case, few of the ideas were ours to begin with. They were Weber's, Schutz's, Marx's, Durkheim's, Halbwachs's, Gehlen's and so on. If, standing on the shoulders of giants, we succeeded in remoulding and synthesizing their ideas, Berger and I thought in such synchrony and harmony that it would be impossible to attribute solo arias to one or the other.[3] There was one exception, jokes. They were all Berger's.

And so to the mechanics. We met once a week on a fairly regular basis, discussed the next step, sketched the argument to be presented, occasionally found a formulation that seemed good enough to be taken down (they did not always stand the test of time), and decided on the next step. Berger wrote out the results of the meeting, gave me a copy when we met at the university or sent it to me by mail. If I had any pertinent suggestions, amendments, objections or second thoughts, I passed them on to him if there was time or raised them at the next meeting. The first part of our meetings was regularly devoted to what by then had become part of the slowly agglomerating text. If that sounds as if two ex-ex-Austro-Hungarians had forgotten their heritage and embraced the spirit of Prussian order, the sound is misleading. In the background was to be heard the light, although often enough profoundly philosophical, music of the mostly Jewish jokes which Berger had heard since we had last met. In our smallish apartment on Washington Square my wife and two young daughters were neither invisible nor inaudible. Writing books is work; I am not fond of work. That particular book was an exception to the implied syllogism: it did not feel like work and I have fond memories of the gestation of that book.

As I mentioned earlier, the treatment of the first two chapters was somewhat different from the way we wrote the rest of the book. The chapter giving an overview of the formation of the sociology of knowledge and the history of its problems is mainly Berger's. His acquaintance with Marx, Mannheim, Scheler and others was closer than mine. The chapter on the foundations of knowledge in everyday life is a summary formulation by Berger of the first chapters of *The Structures of the Life-World* (Schutz and Luckmann, 1973) which had already been completed by me at that time although they were published much later. Their phenomenological, Schutzian character is unmistakable.[4] In spite of the different – one could perhaps say less dialogical – way in which these two chapters came about, they were discussed in much the same manner as the main chapters of *The Social Construction of Reality.*

For more than a quarter of a century Berger and I did not work together again. We saw each other frequently but not regularly both in the United States and in Europe; we corresponded; I was supplied with the newest (and some old) jokes. But even when I returned to the United States for longer periods we never lived near one another again. When I was in Massachusetts, he was still in New York; when he was in Boston, I was in California.

Retirement was not yet close in those years, and Berger and I did not enter the planning stage for a half-serious retirement project about which we occasionally talked at that time. We never took the first step to start work on a 'definitive' volume on the role of (nationalistic and other) intellectuals in the dissolution of the Austro-Hungarian Empire, to serve as a case study for a treatise on the folly of self-designated prophets. The project was to start after we had retired to Meran in the South Tyrol, and had chosen one of its *cafés* as our centre of studies. Now it seems that we are both getting too old to retire, be it to Meran or elsewhere.[5]

None the less, collaboration between us had not yet ended. In the early 1990s, after participating in a symposium on the so-called crisis of meaning, I was asked by the people responsible for the *Cultural Orientations* section of the Bertelsmann Foundation to write what they called an expertise on modernity and pluralism. I immediately suggested that Berger – whose province these topics were as much or more than mine – join me in the project. They were enthusiastic, and so another, late, instance of joint authorship came about. In spite of the fact that an ocean lay between us, our collaboration was remarkably similar in its intellectual features to the earlier instances of thinking and working together. This time we did not write anything particularly new. Our task was to formulate our views on the matter for a readership without sociological inclinations. Furthermore, the ocean could be crossed. After meetings in Europe, and some correspondence, I spent a week or so in Boston. There was a division of labour with regard to the language of publication. The original 'expertise' was written in German, and the final writing was to be my responsibility. An English translation by J. Adam Tooze was to be looked at by Berger. (This has been published as *Modernity, Pluralism and the Crisis of*

Meaning, Berger and Luckmann, 1995.) Almost thirty years after the writing of *The Social Construction of Reality* our collaboration was marked by the old 'synchrony and harmony'.

Scattered reflections on the results of collaboration

The following remarks deal only with a minor aspect of the results of our collaboration. It would be inappropriate to add my thoughts about the papers and books Berger and I wrote together – even if I had any such belated postscripts to add to them. (I do not.) It would be equally inappropriate to engage in a review of reviews, or in a meditation on the less ephemeral influences at least one of our books may have exerted in sociology and other human sciences. *Habent sua fata libelli*: one aspect of the fate of *The Social Construction of Reality* was to be widely misinterpreted. Who in heaven or hell, more likely hell, invented (social) 'constructivism'?

One question of passing interest it is appropriate to ask is whether books written in joint authorship are read and remembered differently from books by single authors. The answer is that I do not know. None the less, I will add a few sentences of speculation on this matter.

The reception among fellow scholars of publications that are the result of research involving teamwork is probably indistinguishable from the one they would have had had they been the work of a single investigator. In fact, I have the impression that, rightly or wrongly, such joint publications tend to be remembered as if they had been the outcome of the labours of a single author – unless they were written by two authors, for example, Vidich and Bensman, and especially if they are a married couple as in the case of the Lynds. In such cases one does think of the book as the result of dialogue between the authors as intellectual equals and as the outcome of some sort of division of labour, both in the research phase of the work and in the writing. But who remembers the contributors to the *American Soldier* or the *Yankee City Series*? And, more blatantly, how is it possible that the *Authoritarian Personality* is associated almost exclusively with the name of Adorno? It seems that, in general, multiple authorship of empirical studies in the social sciences is taken for granted as normal, certainly for studies of larger scope, but that – with certain exceptions – authors tend to be conflated in memory into one single dominant figure.

It seems to me that theoretical treatises represent a different case. The great philosophers can be visualized with their Xantippes but not easily imagined with co-authors. It is not the builders of the medieval cathedral who serve as the model of theoretical production in the social sciences, but the philosopher or perhaps the poet or composer of the Romantic period. (Painting, with its schools and workshops and the problems of attribution, is different again.) The towering figures of the sociological tradition were unpaired. Durkheim and Duroche, Weber and Weber, Simmel and Schuster?

Ridiculous. (Well, Marx and Engels ...) And later, and not quite as towering perhaps: Sorokin and Sorokin, Parsons and Parsons, Mannheim and Mannheim? No!

In more recent generations things may have changed. But if they have, I cannot even now think of many instances of a theoretical treaty in the social sciences which has more than one author. Berger and Luckmann set no example. We did write individual books and we did publish empirical studies in co-authorship with others. Perhaps we will be forgiven for an episode or two of thinking together by ourselves.

Notes

1   In the middle 1950s Mayer directed a project on religion and the churches in postwar Germany which was sponsored by the Rockefeller Foundation. Berger, one of whose particular interests at that time was the sociology of religion, was one of Mayer's assistants on that project. When he was drafted into the army, I replaced him, less because of my doubtful competence in the sociology of religion than because I spoke German and because, as father of two children, I was less likely to be drafted than my single contemporaries, despite the exigencies of the Korean War. Although I continued on the project where Berger left off, I hardly think that this qualifies as an early form of sequential collaboration.

2   The reasons were neither intellectual nor was there any personal animosity between us. Natanson remained a life-long friend. Kellner, Berger's brother-in-law, collaborated with Berger on several projects and publications. He became my assistant at the universities of Frankfurt and Constance after I had gone to Germany and became an angling companion and family friend. Berger and Pullberg wrote a paper together.

3   In this regard my collaboration with Berger differs significantly from my other experiences of this kind. It differs most radically from what was nominally a joint authorship (Schutz and Luckmann) of The Structures of the Life-World (1973). I may quote what I wrote in the preface to that book: 'The completion of the Strukturen der Lebenswelt combined the difficulties of the posthumous editing of the manuscript of a great teacher by his student with the problems of collaboration between two unequal authors (one dead, the other living), one looking back at the results of many years of singularly concentrated efforts devoted to the resolution of problems that were to be dealt with in the book, the other the beneficiary of these efforts; one a master, always ready to revise his analyses but now incapable of doing so, the other a pupil, hesitant to revise what the master had written' (1973, p. xvii ff.)

The other instances of collaboration were less dramatically dissimilar to the dialogue of equals. In the case of joint authorship with my wife, the intellectual affinities and the dialogical relationship was the most similar to the main features of my collaboration with Berger, except that – as married couples are wont to do – we did argue with one another quite a bit, even heatedly, on some occasions. Some other instances of collaboration were concerned with writing prefaces and introductions to volumes of readings or editions of collected papers. Some of these cases involved former assistants of mine; to the best of my recollection, there was in all cases a fairly clear division of labour as to who was to do what.

The most frequent instances of joint authorship in my experience during the last decades involved publication of empirical investigations. Collaboration on these investigations evidently preceded the writing. My colleagues and research assistants frequently argued with one another and with me about the proper interpretation of our data which consisted of different kinds and sequences of (recorded and transcribed) communicative interaction 'in the field'. These arguments took place within a generally pre-established theoretical frame, a theory of communicative genres developed by myself with some of these colleagues on the basis of Berger's and my approach to the sociology of knowledge and language. There was a clear choice of 'qualitative' methods, ethnographical and conversational, more generally, sequential analysis of texts. In the latter respect, especially, I had much to learn from my collaborators, especially Jörg Bergmann, Susanne Günthner, Angela Keppler-Seel and Hubert Knoblauch, but also from some 'junior' assistants.

If I were to sum up these varied experiences of joint authorship for a typology of scholarly collaboration I would insist, first, on the difference between essentially theoretical and primarily empirical enterprises; second, on the difference between master and pupil (and mutatis mutandis between chief investigators and assistants) relationships, on the one hand, and intellectual-generational equals; third, on the difference between fast and slow writers (is there something of a hedgehog and fox difference here? There certainly is a difference between those afflicted – or blessed – with a certain amount of pedantry and those who survey the intellectual terrain with speed and shrewdness); and, to mention the most obvious and profound difference last, collaboration in living dialogue as against the imaginary dialogue between the living and the dead. Whereas one could still speak of thinking together in this last case, too, working together presupposes an incarnation of the mind in bodies that can tire from long sessions, souls that can become irritated by schedules.

4 My own 'technical instruction' in phenomenology, incidentally, did not come primarily from Schutz but from Dorion Cairns who had joined the Graduate Faculty at the urging of Schutz.

5 However, a correspondence – materialists would say imaginary, a realist of our stripe would prefer to think of it as belonging to 'another' reality – ensued in the early 1920s between Berger, a former district governor of Kaschau/Kosice in the Hungarian part of the empire, retired to Meran, and General Luckmann, also retired. Their friendship dated back to an era before the end of the nineteenth century. Occasional letters from other friends, a Countess Harsanyi, in particular; a book review by a Harvard historian of the memoirs of General Luckmann, etc. were quoted in this correspondence.

3 Berger: theology and sociology

Gary Dorrien

Introduction

The quintessential Berger-moment had arrived, one paragraph before the end of the lecture. Peter Berger had built up to this moment with a variation on Max Weber's argument that an ethic of responsibility makes better politics than a moralistic ethic of absolute ends. The Weber argument had yielded a tapestry of essential Berger-themes: intellectual objectivity is a worthy ideal; there is such a thing as 'value-free' social science; moral protest has its appropriate place; liberation theology is empirically false; capitalist modernization is empirically superior to its real-world alternatives; the 'New Class' of social engineers and academics is self-promoting and self-flattering; practical consequences are usually more important than convictional morality; everyone has a right to be indifferent to politics; most social science has a fatal utopian streak (Berger, 1988, pp. 4–7, 15–18).

The last of these themes brought the lecture to its quintessential Berger-moment. There is something wrong with any social science that speaks the language of hope and progress, Berger contended. Sociology is supposed to be a debunking discipline. It is supposed to make sense of the world by unmasking the façades of social life. In his view, the social sciences were at their best when they focused on the complexes of interest and will-to-power that fuel all social behaviour. Good sociology is always sceptical and anti-Utopian. This was a basic Berger-theme, though Berger is a different kind of debunker from the variable host of academic socialists, liberals and deconstructionists who cite *The Social Construction of Reality* (1966a) as sociological scripture. His closing words expounded the difference.

As a rule, Berger judged, American social scientists are appropriately hard to impress when they analyse the world as it is. Sociologists are masters of suspicion. They expose the interested wellsprings of moral speech. Wielding the tools of a worldly-wise academic discipline, they unmask the struggle for power in present-day politics and everyday life. Berger admonished that the problem with social scientists is that they lose their critical edge as soon as they turn their gaze to the promise of their favoured ideology. The debunking spirit of sociology simply vanishes when academics prescribe solutions for the future. Berger implied without saying that the favoured ideology is usually some kind of democratic socialism or left-liberal communitarianism; he noted explicitly that the favoured ideology is nearly always fuelled by the myth of progress or revolution.

This meant that real sociology is nearly always cheated. It also meant that American politics is cheated of the services of good social science. Berger exhorted that the future needs as much sociological scepticism as the present. It is not only the status quo that needs to be debunked. The same chastening suspicion has to be applied to any political agenda that purports to replace the status quo. 'I have repeatedly used words that some of you, especially if you are still young, may find chilling – "caution", "soberness", "carefulness,"' he concluded. 'Are these not words that portend paralysis? With all this scepticism and all this cautiousness, will one not inevitably end up doing nothing at all?' Did the Weberian debunking of moral politics deliver the political arena to crooks and creeps who had no moral principles? Berger assured that he believed otherwise, though he had only two sentences of argument to support his belief. There was no reason why his cautious, chastened, essentially conservative approach to politics should breed political indifference, he went on: 'If that were true, none of us would ever trust ourselves into the hands of a surgeon' (1988, pp. 17–18). The vocation of politics requires the same ethic of responsibility as the medical vocation. This is not what is normally called 'neo-conservatism', but it is the heart of Peter Berger's neo-conservatism.

Unlike nearly everyone with whom he became politically aligned in the 1970s, Berger has never been a leftist of any kind and has no story of ideological conversion to tell. He was born in Vienna in 1929 and lived in Austria until mid-adolescence. His early conservatism was a familial Lutheran inheritance; it was also deeply Austrian. He once recalled that his youthful political imagination was inspired by stories of the vanished glories of Habsburg Austria. This vision left a lasting imprint on his political consciousness. 'Perhaps the last *really* worthwhile political enterprise in the twentieth century would have been to try and preserve the Austro-Hungarian monarchy', he mused in 1972. 'The cause, alas, is lost, and in any case I was born a quarter-century too late for joining its banners' (Berger, 1977a, p. 115). More recently the memory of the Austro-Hungarian downfall helped to inoculate Berger from the crusading 'world democracy' rhetoric of his neo-conservative friends. It was Woodrow Wilson's imperial democratism that dismembered the empire after the First World War and made the world safe for democracy.

Except for occasional asides to illustrate a point, Berger does not discuss his childhood; in 1946 his family moved to New York, where he enrolled at Wagner College. He gave one year to the possibility of a ministerial career, studying at the Lutheran Theological Seminary in Philadelphia. Berger's theological conservatism and ministerial prospects did not survive his introduction to modern theological scholarship. The historical-critical approach to scripture and theology was interesting to him, but it was not what he expected to learn in the seminary, and it undermined the structure of religious certainties that brought him there. Repeatedly Berger asked himself, 'Could I preach that?' The question finally answered itself. He resolved that he would not seek ordination if he could not espouse the traditional creedal affirmations of the church; neither could he imagine himself preaching theological liberalism (Berger, 1980, p. 44). To his mind, the old orthodoxy was discredited, but the prevailing liberal theologies seemed like poor substitutes for the faith he had lost. It took him nearly fifteen years to assimilate the experience.

Sociology offered an attractive methodological respite from the problems of theology. Berger enrolled at the New School for Social Research, where he studied under Carl Mayer, Albert Salomon, and Alfred Schutz. He completed his doctorate in 1954, a year after he joined the US Army, having become an American citizen in 1952. While serving in the Army he taught at the University of Georgia and later taught at the Evangelical Academy in Bad Boll, Germany, where he became friends with the father of the German academies, Eberhard Müller. In 1958, before the term 'New Class' acquired its present connotation, he gained entrance to the New Class world of institutes, foundations, and consulting by accepting the directorship of the Institute of Church and Community at the Hartford Seminary Foundation. Berger organized conferences on medical ethics, worked with the University of Connecticut to teach professional sociologists how to become church consultants, and wrote his early books.

Experiments in Barthian sociology of religion

The *Noise of Solemn Assemblies* and *The Precarious Vision* were both published in 1961. The former was a semi-Kierkegaardian attack on the triumph of the therapeutic in the churches. 'When I started writing, I was interested in criticizing the church from within, as an avowed Christian', he later recalled (author's interview, 1990). *The Noise of Solemn Assemblies* argued that America's mainline Protestant churches were preaching a therapeutic form of culture-religion, not the transcendent gospel of Christ. Instead of saving souls, the churches had raised their sights to the more respectable mission of socializing middle-class individuals into what Berger called 'the OK world'. From a sociological standpoint, this was an American middle-class variant of the Durkheimian bargain. Mainline religion reinforced its own standing in society by endorsing the existing social order and absorbing its members. Berger allowed that this strategy was working from a sociological standpoint. Mainline American religion was booming; the 'baby boomers' seemed to be well-churched; the churches purveyed and benefited from the message that American society was in good shape.

From a serious theological standpoint, however, mainline religion was a spiritual travesty. Berger's idea of serious theology in 1961 was a vaguely Barthian neo-orthodoxy. He charged that, from the standpoint of a Christian theology that upheld Christian truth in its transcendent character, the churches were guilty of selling bad faith. Mainline religion engendered and reinforced inauthenticity, he explained; it shielded individuals from the truth about themselves and their world. The mainline churches obtained their functionality in society by refusing to adopt a critical or even an independent perspective towards the dominant culture. They reduced religious truth to spiritual nurture, the 'religious needs' of the self, and related consumer goods. 'There occurs a process of religious inoculation, by which small doses of Christianoid concepts and terminology are injected into consciousness', Berger observed. 'By the time the process is completed, the individual is effectively immunized against any real encounter with the Christian message' (Berger, 1961b, p. 116).

By his neo-orthodox lights, it was no part of the church's mission to provide a basis for morality, social order, respectability, or even a good way of life. *The Precarious Vision* (1961a) drew on Dietrich Bonhoeffer's call for a secularized or 'religionless' Christianity to describe how the churches might recover their biblical heritage. Following Bonhoeffer and Karl Barth, Berger argued that genuine biblical faith is profoundly secularizing. 'By denuding the cosmos of its divinity and placing God totally beyond its confines, the biblical tradition prepared the way for the process we now call secularization', he explained. 'It was Protestantism even more than Renaissance humanism which inaugurated the great process which Weber called "disenchantment"' (1961a, p. 177). Not for the last time, he called on Americans to face up to modernity. The challenge of the modern age was to face up to the desacralizing logic of modernity, which brought the secularizing thrust of the Bible to its ultimate conclusion. Taking refuge in 'religion' was a loser. Any church that based its existence on ministering to 'spiritual needs' was doomed to extinction as the secularizing process continued.

Berger did not develop the theological implications of this point of departure. 'Secular Christianity' was a slippery concept; Bonhoeffer's statements on this theme were cryptic and unsystematic; Berger's attempts to amplify Bonhoeffer's remarks were short on theological grounding and substance. In the mid-1960s, after 'religionless Christianity' came into vogue, the idea was taken up by Bonhoeffer-quoting theologians considerably to Berger's left. Harvey Cox's *The Secular City* (1965) epitomized the genre. Not for the last time, Berger's initiative was advanced by academics who did not share his politics. Like several of his later neo-conservative friends, however, he spent the early 1960s tweaking America's religious and political establishments for their conformism. Berger's sarcastic barbs against the churches were read in college chapels across the country and struck a responsive chord among students. His academic bestselling *Invitation to Sociology. A Humanistic Perspective* (1963a), written during this period, similarly invited students to see that what society called 'maturity' was a rationalizing control mechanism. By the time he returned to the subject of normative theology at the end of the decade, Berger had discarded the theological position on which his early books were based. What remained from his early writings was his emphasis on freedom as a personal and social good and his concern with the problem of bad faith.

Constructing the sacred canopy

Invitation to Sociology (1963a) corrected the oversocialized determinism of traditional sociology with an emphasis on the existential notions of freedom and bad faith. Traditional sociology explained a great deal about the human predicament, Berger judged; correctly used, it was even an aid to freedom. The problem with traditional sociology was the problem with mainline religion: it reinforced bad faith. By viewing the human subject as a product of his or her social environment, sociology validated the human tendency to evade personal responsibility. It reinforced the 'bad faith' pretension that something voluntarily chosen was necessary. Berger countered that people are able to choose bad faith only because they are, in fact, free not to accept their freedom. Human subjects are prisoners of society only to the extent that they fail or refuse to recognize the influence of society upon the self, as well as the choices that each situation presents. Sociology reinforces bad faith whenever it reconciles people to fatalistic attitudes about their personal or public choices; on the other hand, social science is liberating in its capacity to inform and empower one's growth in freedom.

This dialectic of 'man in society' and 'society in man' was developed in Berger's major theoretical works, *The Social Construction of Reality* (1966a), co-authored with Thomas Luckmann, and *The Sacred Canopy* (1967). Having joined the Graduate Faculty of the New School in 1963, he teamed with Luckmann to elaborate Alfred Schutz's pioneering phenomenological investigations into the notion of society as a subjective reality. The reigning theoretical models in social science were functionalism and structuralism, they observed, but what was needed was a sociological account of the 'total social fact' that avoided the 'theoretical legerdemain' of functionalism and the 'distortive reifications' of structuralism (Berger and Luckmann, 1966a, pp. 186–8). Berger and Luckmann argued for an understanding of human reality itself as a social construction and urged that the principal subject matter of the sociology of knowledge should be everyday commonsense knowledge. They proposed that sociological inquiry should be the kind of descriptive, empirical, synthetic, non-ideological science described by Weber, in which the single value embraced by the sociologist is that of scientific integrity.

Theoretically this was an argument for a dialectical perspective in the social sciences. Instead of committing sociology to a particular methodology immune from empirical falsification, Berger and Luckmann wanted sociologists to assimilate from various disciplines all of the relevant facts that comprise the total social fact. The dialectic of humanity and society was constitutive of the entire process. Society is entirely a human product, yet society also profoundly influences and shapes its own producer. Berger developed the implications of this dialectic for religion in *The Sacred Canopy* (1967). There is no contradiction in the assertion that society is the product of human subjects and that human subjects are the products of society, he contended. These combined assertions reflect 'the inherently dialectic character of the social phenomenon' (1967, p. 3). No social reality is empirically comprehensible apart from the dialectic of subject and society, including the phenomenon of religion.

The Sacred Canopy described the dialectic of the social world as a three-step process called externalization, objectivation, and internalization. Externalization is the outpouring of human physical and mental energies into the world. Objectivation occurs when the products of human physical and mental efforts attain a reality that confronts its creators as a 'facticity' outside themselves. Internalization occurs when this objectivized reality is subjectively reappropriated by human agents. In this scheme, society is created through externalization, it becomes an apprehended reality through objectivation, and the producing human subject becomes a product of society through internalization. Berger defined socialization as the process by which society transmits its objectivized customs and ideas from one generation to the next. Through socialization, he observed, individuals are taught the objectivized cultural meanings of a society *and* brought to identify with these meanings. The self that internalizes the meanings of a society does not merely possess these meanings, but represents and expresses them.

The socialization process is natural, necessary, and, by implication, worthy of respect and protection. Berger's shifting theology showed through his objectivistic social science prose. His early books were fuelled by the theological claim that normal human socialization reconciles a sinful individual to a corrupt social order. Since normal human development is defective, he reasoned, the proper business of Christianity is not to sacralize the prevailing process of socialization, but to challenge it. Normal socialization reinforces humanity's inheritance of original sin. The Christian church is called to proclaim salvation from this process and the conditions that produce it. The early Berger thus spoke of 'socialization' only with a sarcastic edge.

But now the edge was gone. Berger no longer derided the socializing role of religion. The ostensible difference was that *The Sacred Canopy* was objective social science, but the difference cut deeper than Berger's new-found resolve to pursue the sociology of religion from an objective standpoint. His theology was changing; moreover, his adopted country was in turmoil. *The Sacred Canopy* was written out of Berger's reawakened awareness that order is the first need of all. He observed that the chief cultural meanings of a society can be sustained only if they are internalized by most of that society's members. Though he protested against the Vietnam War in the 1960s, Berger was repulsed by most of the anti-war movement and virtually all of the counterculture. He worried that the social fabric of American life was being ripped apart. *The Sacred Canopy* did not speak to this crisis directly, but implicitly, the book was pervaded by it.

If order was the first need of all, the crucial function of religion was its ordering or 'nomizing' capacity. The socially constructed world was most importantly an 'ordering of experience' in which a meaningful order (or *nomos*) was imposed upon the experiences and meanings of human subjects. From a sociological standpoint, Berger reflected, the purpose of religion is to construct a sacred cosmos. Religion offers a protective canopy of transcendent legitimacy, meaning, and order to the precarious constructions that society calls 'reality'. The fate of any social order is therefore inevitably bound up with the fate of religion. Berger's closing chapters struggled to be objective about the future of religion under modernity. He identified the sociological processes of secularization and pluralization as closely related historical phenomena that undermine the credibility of traditional Western religions. In the concluding chapter, he reviewed the attempts of modern theology to cope with this inheritance and made a social-scientific pitch for the liberal-religious survival strategy he had previously ridiculed.

The pertinent theologians in this account were Friedrich Schleiermacher, Karl Barth, Rudolf Bultmann, and Paul Tillich. Berger gave short shrift to current 'death of God' theologies, which were self-defeating. In his account, Schleiermacher epitomized the liberal-experiential approach to theology; Barthian neo-orthodoxy was the major wholesale alternative to theological liberalism; Bultmann and Tillich were neo-liberals who shared a few themes with Barth. Speaking as a sociologist, Berger judged that it was time for Protestant theology to go back to Schleiermacher. Schleiermacher's strategy was at least grounded in something real – religious experience – while the alternatives seemed increasingly unreal to an increasingly secular culture. Berger dismissed his previous refuge, Barthian neo-orthodoxy, as a 'more or less "accidental" interruption of the over-all process of secularization' (1967, p. 165). The accident was the First World War, which destroyed the liberal belief in progress on which Progressive-era liberal Protestantism had based its apologetics. Barth had given theology a temporary transfusion with his concept of a non-objective Word of God; the neo-liberal theologies of Bultmann and Tillich had taken up where the earlier liberalism left off; now the next generation of theologians was going beyond even Tillich's revisionism.

The Sacred Canopy (1967) ended with a 'value-free' sociological plug for Schleiermacher, but not a very strong one, even as a utilitarian argument. The book gave the appearance of a requiem for Western religion. For that reason, its closing argument seemed a weak recommendation at best. Berger knew it. He felt obliged as a sociologist to deliver the grim truth about the prospects of religion, but his perspective on religion was not exhausted by his sociological vocation. He was also a Christian, and as a Christian he was offended by the arrogance of secularizing relativizers who proclaimed the death of the supernatural. Thus he wrote *A Rumour of Angels* (1969a), which pressed the claim that relativism is self-refuting. Those who dismiss religious claims as relative constructions rarely treat their own world-views as similarly relative, he noted, but modern secular reason is merely one relative possibility among others. Like all belief systems, modern secularism is loaded with unproven assumptions, provincial axioms, and unavoidable socio-historical limitations. Berger granted that, as a religion, Christianity is relative and socially constructed. On this account he relinquished the (supposed) neo-orthodox notion that Christianity is a divinely revealed faith immune from the outside scrutiny applied to mere religions. If Christianity is to be defended, he argued, it has to be open to criticism and defended like any other belief system. To make the best defence of Christianity, he continued, theologians should return to Schleiermacher's inductive experientialism.

A Rumour of Angels (1969a) proposed that a theology liberated from the tyranny of the present might begin to look for 'signals of transcendence' within, but pointing beyond, the natural world. To begin with religious experience is not to focus on the mystical experiences of a saint-figure, but rather to explicate the religious implications of ordinary human experiences of loving, caring, ordering, playing, laughing, encountering evil, and finding hope. Christian experience has no privileges or immunity claims on this common ground, Berger admonished. The Christian Bible is the record of 'a specific complex of human experience'. As such it has no special status compared with the scriptures of other religions. The same questions need to be brought to the Bible as to any such account: 'What is being said here? What is the human experience out of which these statements come? And then, to what extent, and in what way, may we see here genuine discoveries of transcendent truth?' (1969a, p. 84).

This was the crucial turn in Berger's religious thought. All of his subsequent religious thinking flows from his late-1960s turn to the experiencing religious subject. To face up to modernity in the field of religion, he argues, is to face the implications of historical and cultural relativism. All religious world-views are the products of historically conditioned and constructed human experience, whether they posit a divine Revealer or not. A reformulated Christian theology that proceeds inductively will undoubtedly reaffirm certain aspects of classical Christianity over against modern secular consciousness, he contends; at the same time, other aspects of traditional Christianity must be discarded or reinterpreted. The first of the latter aspects is the notion that Christianity is a religion based on infallible, external authority. In 1979 Berger's book, *The Heretical Imperative* (1979a), put this 'heretical' project of retrieval and reformulation at the centre of the modern theological enterprise. To face up to the relativity of theological knowledge requires that one affirm certain elements of the tradition and reject others, he argued. That is the 'heretical imperative'.

Berger did not begin to write seriously about politics until the early 1970s. He was drawn into politics by a confluence of associations and events, most notably his friendship with Richard John Neuhaus, his conflicting feelings about the Vietnam War and the anti-war movement, and his experiences in Mexico. In the early 1970s, prompted by Ivan Illich, he began to apply his expertise in the sociology of knowledge to the problems of Third World modernization and economic development. At the same time he identified with an assortment of formerly leftist friends who moved to the political right mainly as a reaction against what they called the 'McGovernization' of the Democratic Party. The movement phase of American neo-conservatism began as an attempt to take back the Democratic Party from peace activists, feminists, and assorted left-liberals. Neo-conservatism took root as an intellectual movement that promoted militant anti-communism, capitalist economics, a minimal welfare state, the rule of traditional elites, and a return to traditional cultural values. Berger is a fully-fledged neo-conservative by this definition, but against the grain of the neo-conservative movement, he has long represented the possibility of a neo-conservatism that eschews ideological crusades, culture wars, and foreign policy imperialism. His approach to religion makes him odder company yet at neo-conservative conferences. Had his career unfolded in a less politicized time, Berger might have pursued intellectual affinities that were cut off principally by politics (Dorrien, 1993).

Taking Schleiermacher seriously

There is, for example, the fact that Berger has spent the past thirty years defending theological liberalism while declaring that he has no home in the liberal Protestant churches. He blames the 'New Class', especially Christian feminists, for driving him into religious exile. The face of mainline Protestantism in the days of the old middle-class establishment was genial and tolerant, he explains. Mainline Protestantism sacralized the values of its control group, naturally, but because its control group was the old middle-class establishment of white Anglo-Saxon physicians and businessmen, it was characterized by a spirit of 'ingenuous niceness'. Today the churches are dominated by New Class feminists and liberals, in his telling, and the mood has changed 'to a set and sour mien, an expression of permanent outrage'. Berger blames the turn primarily on the rise of feminism:

'Feminism more than anything else has set this tone in recent years. This grimly humorless ideology has established itself as an unquestioned orthodoxy throughout the mainline churches' (Berger, 1990, p. 964).

In the churches, as in the academy, he complains, feminists have ideologized the dominant discourse and punished dissenters. In the academy, 'this campaign for multiculturalism in the curriculum is appalling. It's making a mockery of education. If you want to assign Shakespeare under the new rules, you have to find a black lesbian writer to match up with him' (author's interview, 1990). In both cases, he charges, feminists and multiculturalists have used their power as the ideologues of a new orthodoxy to stigmatize dissenters and exclude them from professional advancement. He counts himself among the exiles, not willing to bear the anger or politics of a 'femspeaking' New Class: 'I don't relish this condition; [but] I can live with it' (Berger, 1990, p. 964). The world of mainline Protestantism, he reflects, 'is a world completely foreign to me at this point, a world that, despite its continuing importance in my own society, barely attracts my attention and is nearly irrelevant to my ongoing concerns' (ibid., p. 969). The world of neo-conservative conferences and think-tanks has had to fill in for the central interests of his early career.

Despite his claims to this effect, however, Berger does not give a convincing impression of a person who has left organized religion behind, even in its liberal Protestant forms. Every ten years, more or less, he gets an itch to revisit the theological issues that absorbed his early career. *A Rumour of Angels* was published in 1969; *The Heretical Imperative* appeared in 1979; his edited volume on inter-religious dialogue, *The Other Side of God*, appeared in 1981; *A Far Glory* was published in 1992. Each of these books repeats his case for an inductive Schleiermacherian approach to theology and inter-religious dialogue; each of them brims with Berger's distinctive wit and insight; each of them evokes and reflects upon the promise of his approach to religion without moving much beyond the state of the argument that he first outlined over thirty years ago. Berger has gained little from the theologians of his generation. Undoubtedly his writing has retained a certain freshness and directness on this account; his theological works are private musings, not interrogations with modern or postmodern academic theology. Without disputing that this lack of engagement with academic theology has some benefits, I believe, however, that it has a down-side. It has diminished his capacity to explore certain intellectual affinities and develop his theological position.

His polemic against theologians Langdon Gilkey, Schubert Ogden and David Tracy in the aftermath of the Hartford Appeal controversy illustrates what I mean. In 1974 Berger and Richard John Neuhaus (see Berger and Neuhaus, 1976) organized a seventeen-member conference at the Hartford Seminary Foundation that blasted certain 'pervasive, false, and debilitating notions undermining contemporary Christianity and its influence in society'. The following January the Hartford group published a manifesto that charged various unnamed theologians and church leaders with promoting heresy. Most of the Hartford accusers were conservatives; Berger and William Sloane Coffin were the group's token theological liberals. The Hartford Appeal accused modern theologians of purveying humanistic and reductionist views about God, Christ, salvation, and the church. Among the 'false and debilitating' beliefs it censured were the claims that 'modern thought is superior to all past forms of understanding reality', that religious language 'refers to human experience and nothing else', that Jesus is to be understood only 'in terms of contemporary models of humanity', that the world's religions 'are equally valid', and that liberation from 'oppressive' institutions and historical traditions 'is required for authentic existence and authentic religion' (Berger and Neuhaus, 1976, pp. 1–7).

The Hartford Appeal ignited a brief controversy and was widely viewed as a rather crude and mean-spirited polemic. Challenged to name the people they were attacking, Berger obliged with a strident article that singled out Southern Methodist University theologian Schubert Ogden and University of Chicago theologians Langdon Gilkey and David Tracy for selling out Christianity. To his mind, Berger was taking the high road; instead of going after the purveyors of 'intellectual vulgarity' who dominated contemporary theology, he went after three of the field's most 'impeccably academic' thinkers. Ogden, Gilkey and Tracy were sophisticated in their reductionism, he allowed, but the fact that they were high-powered scholars made their heresies especially pitiable and alarming. These influential theologians symbolized the pathos of modern theology to Berger because they renounced the supernatural theism of genuine Christianity. Berger made a special target of Gilkey, charging that Gilkey's theology represented a 'cognitive surrender' to secular reason in which the secular mood was not only the starting point, but the criterion of religious belief. Gilkey's ruling maxim was 'no other realm', in Berger's rendering; his most dogmatic conviction was that every form of supernaturalism must be expunged from Christianity (Berger, 1977c, pp. 45–6).

This episode was loaded with irony. Theologically, both Gilkey and Berger were refugees from neo-orthodoxy, but Gilkey's thinking retained more neo-orthodox content than Berger's (see Dorrien, 1997, pp. 128–86). Moreover, the most important example of a recent theological work that developed the kind of approach outlined by Berger was Gilkey's *Naming the Whirlwind: The Renewal of God-Language* (1969). But Berger sharply denied his affinity to Gilkey's work. He insisted that any Christian theology worthy of the name must have as its ultimate referent 'a reality that lies outside the human condition' (1977c). Transcendence was the crucial either/or. Berger allowed that Christianity had often imposed supernaturalist theism upon people in an authoritarian manner in the past, but what matters today, he admonished, is that the oppressive power of our time is secularism. This was the truism that modern theologians failed to grasp. Anti-religious dogmatism has become a respectable form of fundamentalism, Berger noted; it is the single form of prejudice for which no one feels compelled to apologize. He lamented that theologians were responding to this situation by making Christianity as palatable as possible to the modern secular consciousness. He admonished that theologians should stop cowering before the presumed superiority of the secular mind. What was needed was a theological critique of the dominant secular mood. This was Gilkey's project, supposedly, but Berger judged that Gilkey's rejection of supernaturalist theism made his theology not only unworthy of its Christian claim, but a pitiable waste of time (Berger, 1977c, pp. 53–5).

This broadside was unfortunate and mistaken. Gilkey was not a humanistic secularizer. He had declined to join the Hartford group because he believed that modern theologians have no business issuing anathemas against each other. The Hartford Appeal confirmed his expectation; in his view, it was 'inept, heavy-handed and unsubtle'. If taken seriously, he observed, the statement would have excommunicated not only Gilkey and Tracy, but Irenaeus, Augustine, the Reformers, Kierkegaard, Barth, Niebuhr and Tillich. That was the problem with 'anathemas written by eager, not to say nervous, humans in committee' (Gilkey, 1977, p. 1029). Instead of wielding a sharp blade, the accusers find themselves with a blunt instrument that destroys their own theological heroes, their friends and even themselves.

That was the case with Berger, who offended Gilkey deeply. Gilkey judged that Berger's argument was 'theologically unmusical', 'dreamlike and unreal', and conceptually deaf. It revealed mainly that Berger was 'most at home among simple arguments' (Gilkey, 1978, pp. 486–97). Unfortunately neither thinker acknowledged the essential similarity between their theological projects. Both of them were committed to a critique of secular humanism and a reformulation of Schleiermacher's method that disclosed 'signals of transcendence' (Berger) or 'traces of ultimacy' (Gilkey) in ordinary experiences of human creativity, thought, desire and fear. Gilkey noted that Berger failed to comprehend that *Naming the Whirlwind* was a prolegomenon to normative theology, not a work of constructive theology, and that Schleiermacher was not a good person to invoke in support of his own confused supernaturalism.

The latter issue was the heart of the matter. Berger claimed that Schleiermacher conceptualized God as a supernatural being 'outside any conceivable realm of natural existence'. In Berger's rendering, though Schleiermacher's method was grounded in human experience, Schleiermacher regarded Christian experience as experience of a supernatural being belonging to 'another realm' (1977c, pp. 52–4). This made nonsense of Schleiermacher's persistent rejection of hypostatized God-concepts. To Schleiermacher, God was the power of Being and 'Spirit of the whole' known as the 'Whence' of religious dependence, not a hypostatized being known to speculative imagination. Schleiermacher was adamant that any attempt to speak truthfully about God or God's self-disclosure 'can only express God in his relation to us'. It followed for him that any attributes that theology may ascribe to God 'are to be taken as denoting not something special in God, but only something special in the manner in which the feeling of absolute dependence is to be related to him' (Schleiermacher, [orig. 1830] 1928, p. 194). Gilkey aptly remarked, 'It was precisely to "strip off" from theology speculative statements about "that other realm" that Schleiermacher introduced his rigid confinement of theological propositions to "descriptions of religious consciousness"' (Gilkey, 1978, p. 487). Schleiermacher believed that religious language about divine transcendence can be meaningful only if transcendence is conceived as relational to human existence. Tillich, Niebuhr, and Gilkey followed him in this argument. Berger's mistake was that he interpreted this argument, in Gilkey's work, as a denial of transcendence.

There *is* an either/or pertaining to divine transcendence that bears the kind of significance that Berger sought to explicate, but it is not a question of 'realms' or distance. No modern theologian thinks of divine transcendence as God's remoteness or spatial distance from the world. The crucial either/or is whether or not God has transcendent power over non-being. The affinity between Berger's theological purpose and Gilkey's theological work shows through at this point, among others, for Gilkey is an important example of a theologian who conceptualizes and affirms transcendence as God's creative power to overcome the threat of non-being. Much of modern theology is immanentalist in the sense that Berger opposes. Whiteheadian process theology, for example, conceptualizes divine transcendence as inexhaustibility, not as personal power over non-being. For process theology God is not an exception to becoming, but rather, the inexhaustible society of events within becoming that lures its subjects to make life-affirming choices.

Though I believe that Berger misconstrued the problem of transcendence and misunderstood Schleiermacher and wrongly denounced modern theologians, he was right to emphasize the determinative significance of how transcendence is conceived. Though I reject the accusative or polemical-tournament model of theology in this case as well, there is a fundamental either/or with respect to the issue of transcendence that bears immense implications for theology as a whole. Either there is more in becoming than in that which becomes or there is not. If there is more in becoming, then process is the last word and the Schleiermacher/ Tillich/Gilkey model of conceiving divine transcendence is wrong. But if there is more in that which becomes, then this 'more' must derive its being from that which does not become. If God is not free from us in some way that makes God's power transcend the world, God cannot be free for us in our suffering and mortality. God cannot sustain life beyond death if God's transcendence does not include power over non-being.

Therefore it makes an enormous difference whether transcendence is conceived as God's unfailing inexhaustibility or as God's power over non-being. Put differently, it makes an immense difference for everything that Christianity affirms, or seeks to affirm, whether God's transcendence is interpreted as an utimate exemplification of the categories of immanence or as the ultimate ground of all categories. Berger remarks that 'the choice is finally between a closed world or a world with windows on transcendence' (1992, p. 142). The concepts of 'closed world' and 'transcendence' that he invokes require more conceptual precision than he provides, but the sentiment is exactly right.

Part II
Religion, spirituality and the discontents of modernity

4 Homeless minds today?

Paul Heelas and Linda Woodhead

How does it feel, to be without a home, like a complete unknown
with no direction home, just like a rolling stone?

Bob Dylan (1965)

Many people start out walking ... as if they were alone, but discover fellow
travellers along the way.

'Sara', a Baby Boomer returned to the Anglican church,
quoted in Roof (1999, p. 29)

Introduction

The argument in this chapter derives from reflection on the 'homeless mind
thesis' as formulated by Peter Berger, Brigitte Berger and Hansfried Kellner
in *The Homeless Mind: Modernization and Consciousness* (1974, orig.
1973). The thesis concerns the turn to the 'subjectivities' of the self, a turn
which results from loss of confidence in primary institutions, and is seen to
result in a situation of homelessness. A crucial contribution to the sociology
of modernity, this thesis offers not only a key for explaining the
countercultural homelessness of the 1960s, but continuing insights into
subsequent developments. Contrary to what the thesis might have led one
to expect, however, the counterculture and accompanying homelessness
appear to have diminished rather than expanded since the 1960s. Our
argument here is that this can be explained in terms of (a) the development
of what Berger *et al.* (1974) term 'secondary institutions' which increasingly
offer a 'middle way' between primary institutions and the fragile resources
of the homeless self drawing upon itself and (b) the broadening of the turn
to the interior self or life into a more inclusive 'turn to life' – whereby life
is understood not only as subjective and 'self-focused', but as relational,
humanitarian, ecological or cosmic. As will be explained in what follows,
we believe that these two developments are intimately related, with
proliferating secondary institutions *supporting* the turn to life, and the turn
to life *enhancing* secondary institutions.

In short, the argument is that there has indeed been a turn to the individual self, and for the kinds of reasons argued in *The Homeless Mind*. But instead of reproducing the homelessness which Berger *et al.* found in the '1960s', the turn has been catered for by those secondary institutions which have proliferated during the past few decades. Such institutions offer a middle way between the failures of primary institutions on the one hand and the vacuous, 'lost' homelessness of the self left to itself on the other. Crucially, they contribute to that 'broadening of life' which takes the self away from its 'mere' self.

Two images of modern times

Max Weber and Karl Marx offered two of the most arresting and enduring images of modern times. For Weber (1985, orig. 1904–5) modernity was an 'iron cage': a world once charged with religious significance had been 'disenchanted' by 'the tremendous cosmos of the modern economic order' which 'is now bound to the technical and economic conditions of machine production which today determine the lives of all the individuals who are born into this mechanism, not only those directly concerned with economic acquisition, with irresistible force' (p. 181). By contrast Marx's image (1977, orig. 1848) was of 'all that is solid melt[ing] into air':

> Constant revolutionizing of production, uninterrupted disturbance of all social conditions, everlasting uncertainty and agitation distinguish the bourgeois epoch from all earlier ones. All fixed, fast-frozen relations, with their train of ancient and venerable prejudices and options, are swept away, all new-formed ones become antiquated before they can ossify. All that is solid melts into air, all that is holy is profaned ...
>
> (p. 224)

Two powerful images, and at first sight two contradictory images. For how can modernity at one and the same time lock people into the dismal routines of an iron cage if indeed there is nothing solid to get locked into? One of the great strengths of Berger and his co-authors' 'homeless mind' thesis is that it reconciles the 'iron' and 'melting/crumbling' portrayals.

The 'homeless mind' thesis

The Homeless Mind is wide-ranging in scope: not only does it deal with the impact of modernization and its institutions on 'modern consciousness', it also analyses the significance of modernization in the 'third world'. However, there is a strong focus on 'youth culture', the 'counterculture', and the '1960s' developments associated with 'the campus'. Indeed, the homeless mind thesis is most clearly developed in connection with the development of the counterculture – no coincidence, perhaps, given the volume's date of publication (1973). It is in the counterculture that Berger, Berger and Kellner find the developments they believe to be constitutive of modernity standing out in starkest relief.

One set of developments falls within the category of the 'iron cage'. It is associated with technology, bureaucracy and rationalization. Thus we read that the 'rationality that is intrinsic to modern technology imposes itself upon both the activity and the consciousness of the individual as control, limitation, and, by the same token, frustration' (p. 163); that 'modern technological production brings about an anonymity in the area of social relations' (p. 163); and that 'the result' [of bureaucratization] is tension, frustration and, in the extreme case, a feeling of being alienated from others' (p. 164). The argument here is that modern men and women who find themselves frustrated, emotionally deprived, constrained and unable to be themselves inevitably begin to show 'unrestrained enthusiasm for total liberation of the self from the "repression" of institutions' (p. 88). The counterculture in particular can be explained as an attempt at liberation from 'straight' society.

The second set of developments analysed in the volume is associated with Marx's image of all that is solid melting into air. Here our attention is drawn to processes which dissolve the great meaning-systems of modernity as well as those inherited from pre-modern worlds. We read that:

> The institutional fabric, whose basic function has always been to provide meaning and stability for the individual, has become incohesive, fragmented and thus progressively deprived of plausibility. Institutions then confront the individual as fluid and unreliable, in the extreme case as unreal.
>
> (1974, p. 85)

Pluralization in particular is held to undermine the great traditional source of meaning, religion:

> The 'homelessness' of modern social life has found its most devastating expression in the area of religion. The general uncertainty, both cognitive and normative, brought about by the pluralization of everyday life and of biography in modern society, has brought religion into a serious crisis of plausibility. The age-old function of religion – to provide ultimate certainty amid the exigencies of the human condition – has been severely shaken. Because of the religious crisis in modern society, social 'homelessness' has become metaphysical – that is, it has become 'homeless' in the cosmos.
>
> (1974, pp. 165–6)

For Berger and his co-authors the counterculturalists (with their widespread rejection of traditional religion) exemplify this kind of homelessness. They are exiles not only from religion, but also from politics. Religion has become implausible while 'political life has become anonymous, incomprehensible and anomic' (p. 165).

In sum, iron cage characteristics of modernity, together with loss of plausibility of 'the institutional fabric', mean that mainstream institutions 'cease to be the "home" of the self' (p. 86). Rebelling against the mainstream (in particular its iron cage properties) and disillusioned with the meanings which the mainstream has to offer, people (in particular counterculturalists) have to look elsewhere for what can be called *source/s of significance*. So where do they turn?

Homeless minds are *forced* to turn to the only remaining source of meaning and significance: their own subjectivities. As Berger *et al.* put it, '*Inevitably*, the individual is thrown back upon himself, on his own subjectivity, from which he must dredge up the meaning and stability that he requires to exist' (p. 85; our emphasis). Or again, the individual has to seek 'to find his "foothold" in reality in himself rather than outside himself' (p. 74). 'An inevitable consequence is that the individual's subjective reality or "psychology" becomes increasingly differentiated, complex – and "interesting" to himself' (ibid.). Thus the climax of the argument is that 'The concept of the naked self, beyond institutions and roles, as the *ens realissimum* of human being, is at the very heart of modernity' (p. 190; see also p. 182).[1]

The 'homeless mind' in its radical form is the individual left alone. It is the 'rolling stone', the hippie, stoned out of her/his head, exploring experiences while adrift in India, with no one to rely on and quite literally no home. And, as Berger *et al.* argue, such radically deinstitutionalized selves, with only their own 'naked selves' to rely on, inevitably find life difficult: 'Social life abhors a vacuum, probably for profound anthropological reasons. Human beings are not capable of tolerating the continuous uncertainty (or, if you will, freedom) of existing without institutional supports' (1974, p. 168). The way is thus paved for 'homeless minds' to seek out what Berger *et al.* (following Gehlen, 1957) call 'secondary institutions' (ibid.). These are less strongly institutionalized than the primary institutions which are experienced as iron cage meaninglessness and rigidity. At the same time, they are sufficiently institutionalized to provide some guidance, and thus to serve as a refuge and support for homeless minds. Secondary institutions may cater for those who seek liberation from the iron cage, who want to find identity and growth by way of what lies within, but who feel the need for guidance with regard to what their 'subjective reality' has to offer. In Berger's view the secondary institutions which catered for the homeless minds of the 1960s counterculture included not only psychoanalysis and psychotherapy, but 'occultism, magic and mystical religion', together with 'Pentecostalism ...

and the Jesus People'. All these movements are, in part, 'efforts to cope with the discontents of modernity' (p. 183).

The homeless mind thesis is even able to go some way to explaining the *timing* of the counterculture. The argument here centres around the so-called 'gentle revolution' (p. 173). Those who became 'homeless' during the 1960s were predominantly the 'baby boomers' born during the years shortly after the Second World War who were raised according to those 'Dr Spockian' values which came to revolutionize childcare and education. And this, it is argued, helps explain why they rebelled against the primary institutions of the mainstream when they were coming of age and going to university or college:

> The 'gentle revolution' has been conducive to the socialization of individuals used to being treated as uniquely valuable persons, accustomed to having their opinions respected by all significant persons around them, and generally unaccustomed to harshness, suffering or, for that matter, any kind of intense frustration. Without intending the adjective to be pejorative, we may say that individuals produced by these socialization processes tend to be peculiarly 'soft'. It is precisely these individuals who, at a later stage in their biographies, confront the anonymous, impersonal 'abstract' structures of the modern technological and bureaucratic world. Their reaction, predictably, is one of rage.
>
> (p. 173)

Hence the relative explosion of rebellion and the associated turn to 'subjectivity' so characteristic of the countercultural 1960s.

The thesis and the counterculture

The arguments of *The Homeless Mind* are bold and compelling. A more finely textured analysis might have paid more attention to the fact that most of those living in the conditions of the early 1970s were still striving to achieve the good life *within* mainstream, primary institutions. More attention might also have been paid to the role of specific historical factors noted by theorists of the counterculture such as Steven Tipton (1982) – not least the Vietnam War and disillusionment with American foreign policy. Yet the thesis is the more powerful for stripping away all but the most essential elements in its account of modernity. It provides a highly illuminating explanation of the counterculture, and seems congruent with the experiences of many of those who drifted towards countercultural homelessness. Counterculturalists did indeed experience mainstream institutions as repressive and rebel against what they found; they did lose faith in the (dissolved) meanings and values offered by mainstream institutions; and the argument about the 'gentle revolution' helps to explain the timing of these developments. Furthermore, the homeless mind thesis ingeniously marries aspects of the two (apparently contradictory) images with which we began: iron cage and melting/crumbling cage. On the one hand, counterculturalists judged mainstream institutions to be coercive and 'straight'; on the other, they judged them to be 'fluid and unreliable, in the extreme case ... unreal'. What Berger *et al.* show is that the (coercive) iron cage continues to operate at the level of practical necessity in the conditions of modernity, though its significance as a source of meaning and value has faded.[2]

The thesis today

But how does the thesis fare today? Although Berger, Berger and Kellner do not indulge in explicit futurology, it is interesting to reflect on what the thesis seems to predict about the decades which followed its publication. Other things being equal, the forecast would appear to be of increasing homelessness due to increasing pluralization (through globalization), accelerating bureaucratization and technologization, and the spread of the 'gentle revolution' through the population as a whole. Much bears this out. To give just one example: business after business and educational establishment after educational establishment have seen the growth of new disciplines (accountability systems, the audit, job descriptions, targets, mentoring, the training and so on) which might have considerable functional power but which often appear to have little to do with deeper 'meaning' and significance. However, the result does *not* appear to have been a growth in countercultural homelessness. On the contrary, the counterculture has largely faded away.

We believe that the homeless mind thesis can be developed to take account of this apparent anomaly, that the kinds of processes that Berger *et al.* identified as generating homelessness are still as active today as they ever were in the 1960s, and that they continue to fuel the turn to 'subjectivity'. But we would expand the thesis to take account also of a broader turn to life, and we would suggest that disillusionment with primary institutions has not resulted in (much) countercultural homelessness *because those concerned have found new homes for their lives in all those secondary institutions which have proliferated since the 1960s*. This development of the thesis picks up a suggestion from Berger and his co-authors where they insist on the *self-limiting* nature of the homeless condition. Their argument is that the self left to itself and thrown back on its own subjectivity is insufficiently substantial, plausible or meaningful to provide the basis of a good life. The broader turn to life, the fading away of the counterculture, and the proliferation of secondary institutions may be viewed as proof of – as well as response to – this insufficiency.

Loss of faith in primary institutions

The loss of faith in primary institutions to which Berger and his co-authors drew attention has not been stemmed since the time when they were writing. If we take the churches in Europe as an example, in Sweden today a mere 2 per cent of the population are regular church attenders, while in the UK Anglican and Roman Catholic attendance has dropped by between 40 per cent and 50 per cent in the past two decades, with the total now standing at just 7.5 per cent (Brierley, 2000). Research such as that carried out for the World Values Survey also reveals declining support for other primary institutions, including political parties and 'traditional' work cultures (Inglehart, 1990, 1997; Nevitte, 1996). Instead of being dedicated to an employer, a business, the value of work itself, or even simple material gain, recent research suggests that in many cases workers' commitment has shifted towards 'self-realization' (Zanders, 1993). Similarly, in the political realm support has shifted from party politics and governmental institutions to less conventional forms of political action and protest (Dalton and Kuechler, 1990).

The turn to life

One effect of this loss of faith in primary institutions has undoubtedly been the turn to the self and subjectivity to which Berger draws attention. Yet in our view the decades following the publication of *The Homeless Mind* have witnessed not so much the intensification of this turn, but its broadening into a more general 'turn to life'. The hypervisibility of values such as equality, freedom and self-expression in theoretical reflection on modern culture may have served to deflect attention from the emergence of this new value of 'life'.

The turn to the 'inner' self may still have a primary importance in the sense that it has become the 'starting point' in much modern life. Few people are now willing to subordinate self to *any* 'higher authority' – whether God, nation, employer or any so-called 'superior' – and few people now recognize any value to be higher or more sacred than self. The self has become the primary point of reference for life and lifestyle decisions (no longer, for example, do people subordinate self to the *institution* of marriage – instead, the satisfaction of the self has become the *raison d'être* of marriage). But, rather than trapping the individual in self and self-concern, the primacy of the self has gradually become the starting point for a wider concern with the lives of self *and* others. If *my* own life has sacred value, then does it not follow that other lives have the same value? And if *I* object to being dictated to by so-called higher authorities, then should I not recognize, respect and protect the autonomy of others? (It can be argued that capitalism, by opening up the possibility that I can and may occupy *any* space in the social order – rather than being tied to one particular role and status by birth – has accelerated this empathetic tendency.) Thus it is not just the life of the self which is of concern, but the lives of other human beings, and even of non-humans. Life plays itself out in different ways in modern cultures. Like ripples in a pool, it has spread out in a series of concentric circles. '*Self-life*' may still be the centre from which the ripples emanate, but it is often recognized – in practice as well as in theory – as opening up into '*relational life*', '*humanitarian life*', '*eco-life*' and '*cosmic life*'.

1 *Self-life* or *psychic life* is the 'subjectivity' of which Berger *et al*. speak in *The Homeless Mind*. It was such 'psychic life' that Georg Simmel had in mind in pioneering the notion of a turn to life. Writing in 1918, Simmel claimed that 'this emotional reality – which we can only call *life* – makes itself increasingly felt in its formless strength as the true meaning or value of our existence' (1997, orig. 1918, p. 24).   For Simmel, 'life' is ultimately the 'inner' realm of one's experiences, one's consciousness, one's psychology, one's personal ethicality, the health/vitality of one's nature, the importance of being authentic, the imperative of being true to oneself, the importance of finding out what one truly is and is capable of becoming, one's sense of being alive in the here-and-now, drawing on memories and expectations to enhance the present while neither diminishing the quality of life – now – for the sake of obeying the past or investing too much in the future. This understanding of life as psychic life has been transmitted through Simmel, Arnold Gehlen (1980, orig. 1949), Peter Berger *et al*. (1974) and Thomas Luckmann (1967), to name only the most important theorists.

2 *Relational life*. At first glance the continuing proliferation of the 'self-help' genre might seem to indicate merely a preoccupation with self-life. If we look more closely at these books, however, it becomes apparent that many have to do with the enhancement not simply of self-life, but of life in relationship with others. This is the concern of a number of the most successful recent offerings, including John Gray's *Men are from Mars, Women are from Venus*, Daniel Coleman's *Emotional Intelligence* and M. Scott Peck's *The Road Less Travelled*. 'Relational life' is primarily the life lived in *intimate, face to face* relation with others. Romantic life and family life are obviously included, but (as we argue below), the development of spheres of intimacy outside the family (within the context of new or transformed secondary institutions) is a striking feature of recent times. Such intimate affective relationships are now possible in work (particularly those new workplaces described below), in the 'new social movements' which are the preferred context for the institutional expression of political energies that might once have taken shape within party-political and governmental frameworks, and in the small group movement (also discussed below). Relational life is closely linked to self-life to the extent that it has to do with the emotions,

drives, needs, and satisfactions of the self rather than with the more traditional (self-negating) virtues of duty, honour, sacrifice and loyalty.

3 *Humanitarian life* embraces the more formal, judicial, legislative dimensions of the turn to life. The discourses and conceptualities of 'human rights', 'humanitarianism' and an 'ethic of humanity' have expanded massively and on a global scale since the Second World War. They leave their imprint on international relations and law, in the rapidly expanding realm of human rights legislation, equal opportunities programmes, harassment procedures and so on. These developments are premised not only on the value ascribed to freedom and equality, but also and perhaps even more fundamentally on the now almost unquestioned value of 'human life'. This value is mediated through film, fiction and popular music – all of which are perfectly adapted to 'showcase' concrete, unique and irreplaceable human lives in all cultures. Nothing better illustrates the outward seepage of the value of self-life to embrace the whole of humanity in the uniquely modern universalism of humanitarian ethics and legislation.

4 *Eco-life.* The value ascribed to life has expanded outwards from the self and the human to encompass the whole of nature. It is now increasingly common to hear of the 'rights of animals' and the sanctity of 'nature'. Like the self, nature is often understood to have an inherent value; to 'meddle' with it is analogous to violating the autonomy and dignity of the self. The different forms of ecological consciousness and organization which are such a striking feature of the contemporary scene all bear witness to the power of this way of thinking. In many of them – certainly those of a more metaphysical bent – the 'life' which they strive to honour and protect is explicitly understood as something common to both the self and the environment which sustains it. There is a conscious attempt to break down dualisms which would divide life up, and to emphasize the unity and interconnectedness of the whole planet.

5 *Cosmic life.* The last of the spreading ripples of life is that of cosmic life. The monistic idea that there is a cosmic life force which runs through all things and forms the deep ground of reality has often been expressed in modern philosophy, theology, spirituality and literature of a mystical bent. This is the 'Life' celebrated by such as Emerson, Bergson, Albert Schweitzer and Rabindranath Tagore. Such ideas often found more popular expression in the counterculture, frequently in spiritual guise. Today they live on not only in some forms of deep ecology, but in the widespread fascination with the truth 'out there' (to use the slogan of *The X Files*). In their different ways, much science fiction and a general fascination with UFOs, lost civilizations founded by aliens, the occult, unexplained phenomena and the 'mysteries of life' all witness to some sense of – or longing for – a cosmic life which undergirds and gives

meaning and stability to this life. The large number attesting to belief in a 'life force' in many recent polls suggests that belief in some sort of cosmic life is widespread.

All these different dimensions of life and the turn to life can take a more or less religious or spiritual form. At its most spiritual the turn to self-life, for example, conceives of the true self as a 'god within' and of self-realization as the ultimate spiritual journey; at the other end of the spectrum, in its most secular form, the turn to self-life is manifest as utilitarian individualism. In the same way cosmic life can be conceived (in spiritual mode) as a spirit force which can be contacted only through meditation or other spiritual exercises, or (in more secular mode) as a final frontier for scientific discovery – or both. It is noticeable that in relation to life the spiritual/scientific boundaries often begin to blur. The current fascination with life associated with the human genome project is an exemplary illustration. Even the most sober newspapers carried headlines about 'unlocking the secrets of life', 'probing the mysteries of life', and nearing an end to the 'quest for the holy grail' when it was announced that the mapping project was complete. It is also interesting to note the massive investment in scientific research which is now directed not just at preserving life, but also at manipulating, improving and even 'creating' it – and to note how the 'alternative' and 'complementary' medicines and methods of healing are increasingly accepted as part of the same project. Such activities may centre round the interests of self-life, or may broaden out to include humanitarian aims and/or to engage with some of the ideals surrounding cosmic life. Equally, they may be articulated in spiritual and quasi-spiritual or more secular terms.

In all its forms, the turn to life is at the same time a turn away from 'life as' – life as a parent, a wife, an employee, a manual labourer, a Republican. The turn to life is a turn away from life '*as*' constituted and regulated by the roles, duties and obligations of the institutional order. Berger *et al.* are surely right that the turn to life has come into prominence precisely because 'life as' a citizen, a Christian, a family member, a cog in the bureaucratic machine has proved ultimately unsatisfactory. Our argument is that the response since *The Homeless Mind* has turned into *more* than simply a turn to self-life and psychic life. In significant sectors of the population today (primarily among Inglehart's (1990; 1997) 'postmaterialists') 'life as ...' is eclipsed in significance by 'life itself': the ultimacy of 'feeling alive', of participating in the on-rushing life of the universe, of getting in touch with as much as possible of what life has to offer, of truly relating to other human lives; of experiencing 'the quality of life' and helping others to do the same, or respecting and protecting the sanctity of all life.[3]

Secondary institutions as a 'middle way'

Many today value '*life*'. Given that life 'alone' is homeless, with all the problems that go with that, people seek ways of *catering* for their lives. At the same time, many have little faith in what primary institutions have to offer with regard to their lives. Accordingly, people seek out a 'middle way', between the homelessness of countercultural tendencies and the homelessness experienced in relation to the primary mainstream.

In our view the turn to life goes hand in hand with the growth of secondary institutions. Indeed the proliferation of secondary institutions can be viewed as the institutional dimension of the turn to life, while the turn to life can be viewed as the cultural dimension of the proliferation of secondary institutions. Both counter the homelessness Berger and his collaborators rightly identify as the fate of the wholly unencumbered self. Secondary institutions are not just a response to the turn to life, but contribute to it – and vice versa. They provide a 'middle way' in late modern times for individuals who would otherwise be caught in a world of 'hard' and 'meaningless' primary institutions on the one hand, and existential homelessness on the other.

Compared with primary institutions, secondary ones are relatively detraditionalized. Whether by being grounded in a faith-inspired past or in rules and regulations worked out by the exercise of reason, the traditionalized primary institution provides *an order of thing*s to be obeyed. True, the traditionalized institution might not be impervious to revision and reform. But the essential thrust has to do with obedience or deference to what is given and authoritative. Such institutions are *life-denying* in the sense that they require some element of deferral of one's own interests in favour of the institution and its ways; some 'giving up' of one's personal life in favour of living life as determined by the institution. By contrast, secondary institutions are considerably less regulative and authoritative and therefore provide much greater freedom for people to exercise autonomy. Much greater value is accorded to the experiential rather than the deferential, with participants encouraged to express themselves, explore their feelings, grow individually and in relation to one another. In this sense secondary institutions are *life-affirming* and *life-expanding*. They are 'soft' rather than 'hard'; autonomous rather than heteronomous. Although structures and procedures are in evidence (they are, after all, institutions), they are kept to a minimum and are (relatively) 'open ended', non-judgemental, democratic and intra-personal: not 'work from 9.00 to 5.00' but 'let us discuss the best way we can organize our time'. The language is of 'advice', 'guidance', 'facilitation'; of being provided with 'opportunities', 'possibilities' or 'challenges'; of 'sharing' and 'supporting'. The individual is not subordinated to the institution, but '*is*' the institution and is encouraged to identify with it. The comfortable sofa might be a better defining image than the iron cage.

It is useful to distinguish within the category of secondary institutions between (a) those that are fairly independent of primary institutions (such as the 'new spiritual outlets' which will be discussed below), and (b) those that operate within – while transforming – primary institutions. The latter will also be discussed in the case studies which follow and will be seen to include the institutions of 'soft capitalism', relatively detraditionalized new forms of church, and 'small groups'. While the former more clearly belong to the counterculture and seem to be more what Berger *et al.* have in mind in their discussion in *The Homeless Mind*, we suggest that the latter represent a more recent development whose significance is only beginning to be appreciated.

The case studies which follow have been chosen to illustrate and ground the argument that secondary institutions have come to play an important role in ameliorating the homeless thrust of modernity. While studies from other realms – such as politics, law, medicine – could have been chosen, we have concentrated on those which are most central to the work of Peter Berger, including *The Homeless Mind*: religion and economics/the workplace. Our first case study shows how those who have lost faith in the traditional workplace and its ethic can turn to various forms of 'soft capitalism' which offer significance-laden alternatives by construing work as a way of/to life rather than a duty or necessity.[4] The second concerns religion/spirituality and suggests that (a) those who have lost faith in traditional religion, or who have never had such faith, can turn to the rapidly proliferating 'new spiritual outlets' which offer experiential guidance for life and some form of partnership on the life/spiritual journey – and so offer an alternative to dredging up meaning from their own subjectivities alone, while (b) those who retain some allegiance to tradition but want to explore their own lives rather than being content with what religious authority dictates can turn to new, less traditionalized forms of Christianity (particularly what we term 'experiential religions of difference') as well as to small groups.

The case studies thus illustrate some of the ways in which secondary institutions can provide *homes for life*, life-enhancing ways of feeling at home with life while (apparently) avoiding problems with primary institutions and that homelessness generated by reliance on self 'alone' as a source of significance.

Case study 1: 'soft capitalism' as a secondary institution

The characteristics of 'soft capitalism'

The term 'soft capitalism' has become current only recently, while the strongly culturalized form of economic organization which it describes has (largely) evolved over the past fifty or so years. The basic idea, as Larry Ray and Andrew Sayer (1999) put it, is that economic success lies with '"soft" characteristics rather than straightforward technological or cost advantages', and that these 'soft' characteristics include 'culture, knowledge and creativity' (p. 17).

What is new about this form of capitalism is the *degree* to which culture is called upon; the *degree* to which outside experts (management consultants, training organizations and so on) exercise an influence; the *degree* to which human creativity is brought into play; the *degree* to which expressive values are encouraged. Rather than thinking in terms of imposing a particular work culture (according to a particular tradition or corporate vision), facilitation experts draw on globalized culture to try out cultural items to find what works best for the particular enterprises they address. Consider the use of Shakespeare as a cultural input in the workplace, as described by Matthew Campbell (2000):

> American business and government have found an unlikely guru in William Shakespeare, whose plays are being used as a tool for teaching modern management techniques ... In one session recently, executives from Northrop Grumman's electronic sensors and systems sector watched in bewilderment as their boss was invited to put on a cardboard, ruby-studded crown and utter the famous lines delivered by Henry V to rally his men on the eve of the battle of Agincourt: 'Follow your spirit; and, upon this charge/Cry "God for Harry! England and Saint George!"' The message, Adelman tells clients, is that 'successful corporate leaders dig deep within themselves which makes that critical difference between victory and defeat'.
>
> (p. 25)

At the heart of soft capitalism are narratives, discourses and practices which are designed to enhance personal commitment and motivation; to identify and unblock barriers to success; to establish new identities (what it is to *become/be* a good manager or call-centre operative, for example); to enable team 'bonding' and co-operation; to open up and address emotions and relationships in the workplace. As Arlie Hochschild's (1997) study of a blue-collar company in middle America shows, these characteristics of soft capitalism affect not merely white-collar workers and the 'new economy', although they perhaps have most obvious application in the service sectors, 'knowledge industries' and small-scale new technology companies.

Equally central to soft capitalism is a new work ethic. This 'self-work ethic' views work as a means to *self* and *life* development, as much as, although together with, financial profit. The 'bottom line' no longer refers exclusively to the annual accounts, but to the personal rewards which my work brings *me* – rewards which are personal, psychological, even spiritual as much as material; as much of the soul as the body. The World Values Survey conducted by Inglehart and others provides compelling evidence for this shift (Inglehart, 1977, 1990, 1997; Nevitte, 1996). While the utilitarian aspect of work does not disappear, discourses and practices which teach that one works on oneself and one's productivity through one's work have become increasingly prominent and popular. And the workplace comes to seem no longer an iron cage, but a source of significance precisely as it provides opportunities for identity exploration, cultivation and expression. Call-centre work might be strongly utilitarian and instrumentalized, for example, but the training manuals are replete with psychological rules and assumptions to do with overcoming personal negativities. Likewise, salespersons are no longer working simply for the sale or the company, but to be/become *themselves* at work. Similarly, while management trainings retain an instrumental dimension, they place equally strong emphasis on the *psychological* growth of participants.[5]

Soft capitalism in practice

Towards the beginning of her study of 'Amerco', the Fortune 500 company located in the Midwest of the United States, Arlie Hochschild (1997) writes:

> In *Haven in a Heartless World*, the social historian Christopher Lasch drew a picture of the family as a 'haven' where workers sought out refuge from the cruel world of work. Painted in broad strokes, we might imagine a picture like this: At the end of a long day, a weary worker opens his front door and calls out, 'Hi, Honey! I'm home!' He takes off his uniform, puts on a bathrobe, opens a beer, picks up the paper, and exhales. Whatever its strains, home is where he's relaxed, most himself. At home, he feels that people know him, understand him, and appreciate him for who he really is. At home, he is safe.
>
> (p. 36)

Haven in a Heartless World was published in 1977 when many academics (including Berger (1964)) were worried that what Lasch describes as 'the cruel world of work' had led to a situation in which people no longer put their lives into their work. Twenty years later, Hochschild offers a very different picture. For as the sub-title of her book – *When Work Becomes Home and Home Becomes Work* – indicates, she charts a massive reversal whereby the haven in the heartless world becomes not the family but the workplace. As she puts it, 'The emotional magnets beneath home and workplace are in the process of being reversed ... Overall, this "reversal" was a predominant pattern in about a fifth of Amerco families, and an important theme in over half of them' (pp. 44–5). And to illustrate the phenomenon she writes:

> In its engineered corporate cultures, capitalism has rediscovered communal ties and is using them to build its new version of capitalism.

Many Amerco employees spoke warmly, happily, and seriously of 'belonging to the Amerco family', and everywhere there were visible symbols of this belonging. While some married people have dispensed with their wedding rings, people proudly wore their 'Total Quality' pins or 'High Performance Team' tee-shirts, symbols of their loyalty to the company and of its loyalty to them. In my interviews, I heard little about festive reunions of extended families, whilst throughout the year, employees flocked to the many company-sponsored ritual gatherings.

(p. 44)

In her rich ethnographic material Hochschild goes on to describe the ways in which the 'self managed production teams' at Amerco shape the emotional culture of the workplace and strive to foster an environment of trust and cooperation in order to bring out the best in everyone. At the middle and top levels of the company, employees were invited to periodic 'career development seminars' on personal relations at work. The centrepiece of Amerco's personal relations culture was a 'vision' speech that the CEO had given called 'Valuing the Individual', a message repeated in speeches, memorialized in company brochures, and discussed with great seriousness throughout the upper reaches of the company. In essence, the message was a parental reminder to respect others. Similarly, in a new-age recasting of an old business slogan ('the customer is always right'), Amerco proposed that its workers 'value the internal customer'. This meant: Be polite and considerate to your co-workers as you would be to Amerco customers. 'Value the internal customer' extended to co-workers the slogan 'Delight the customer'. Don't just work with your co-workers, delight them. 'Employee empowerment', 'valuing diversity' and 'work–family balance' – these catchphrases, too, spoke of a moral aspect of work life. Though ultimately tied to financial gain, such exhortations – and the policies that follow from them – made workers feel the company was concerned with people, not just with money. In many ways, the workplace appeared to be a site of 'benign social engineering where workers came to feel appreciated, honored, and liked' (p. 43).

Work ethicality at Amerco, it would appear, is a sophisticated blend of organizational and self-work. The organizational is in evidence in that employees typically take great pride in living in terms of company visions and missions, seeking to become yet more professional by following corporate pathways. At the same time, the professional, organizational collectivity is brought alive by the operation of self-work ethicality. There is a strongly 'exploratory' aspect to much of what is going on, and it is clearly working. Whatever 'problems of work' the company might have experienced in the past, the 'meaning' now found at work surely goes a long way towards explaining why the workforce is so committed, so enthusiastic, so much at home and *alive* at work. Indeed, it explains why it is by no means uncommon for people to arrive at work early and leave late – without extra pay.

Many other examples of soft capitalism in operation could be given. Following in the footsteps of the 1960s pioneers – Douglas McGregor with his *The Human Side of Enterprise* (1960), Frederick Herzberg and his *Work and the Nature of Man* (1968) and Abraham Maslow with his *Eupsychian Management* (1965) – management consultants, advisors, trainers, personnel officers and others have blazed a trail with messages concerning 'the humanization of the workplace', the importance of 'self-development for productivity', the value of being 'yourself' at work, the 'unlocking of human potential'. To illustrate by reference to just a handful of publications, one can cite Roger Harrison's *Organization Culture and Quality of Service: A Strategy for Releasing Love in the Workplace* ('to balance the powers of intellect and human will in organisations with the powers of intuition and will' (1987, p. 3)); Mike Pedler and others' 'Learning Company Project' ('how can we create organizations which are opportunity structures enabling people to grow and develop ...' (1988, p. 9)); and Craig Hickman and Michael Silva's *Creating Excellence* ('By applying the art of meditation to organizational introspection, you gain a deeper understanding of a business and its environment' (1985, p. 32)). Or, to give an example from India, V. S. Mahesh's *Thresholds of Motivation*, has as its sub-title 'The corporation as a nursery for human growth', and its introduction begins with a section on 'Corporate excellence through human self-actualization' (1993, p. xv). Equally one may cite the innumerable New Age-inspired management trainings and consultancies which have proliferated since the 1960s and which take the exploratory message of soft capitalism to what one can only assume is something approaching its limit by drawing out the spiritual dimension of the self-work ethic. Here one is not simply working on self through work activities, but working to realize the spirituality which is integral to one's very nature, essence or *life*. The workplace is valued, that is to say, as a vehicle to the end of self- or life-sacralization.[6]

'Bringing life back to work'

One of the great slogans of soft capitalism is 'bringing life back to work'. The slogan suggests the close connection between the development of soft capitalism and the turn to life. It is not merely *self*-realization which workers now seek, but the enhancement of life as a whole – including relationships with others. In some cases work even takes over from family as the place where intimate and creative relationships are forged and developed (Hochschild, 1997), and the image of the family is mobilized to describe the company or corporation. Thus the management experts and trainers interviewed by Hansfried Kellner and Frank Heuberger (1992) in their study of the 'hidden technocrats' of the 'new class' of the 'new capitalism' stressed that industry should take into account 'the prerogatives of the subjective life, emotional well-being and intimacy against the demands of rationalized industry, with its controlling pressures, coldness, and abstractness'. What is more, they insisted that work should cater for 'the individual's search for "meaning" in a world that is held to be devoid of meaningful symbols, plausibility, and credibility' (p. 57).

The workplace, in other words, is now increasingly seen as the primary arena in which employees should *live* out a full *life*. Work is necessary; but there is more to life than 'mechanical' productivity. Soft capitalism, especially in its exploratory mode, feeds off and doubles back on the cultural turn to life. This is not life as disciplined for God, or life subordinated to instrumental or corporate goals, but life explored and expressed at work. It seems somewhat ironic that loss of faith in work as a primary institution has contributed to the turn to life – which in turn has contributed to the life-enrichment of the workplace by way of the development of soft capitalism. Certainly much less is heard these days about 'the problem of work' as it was diagnosed by Berger (1964) and others throughout the 1960s and 1970s. Problems, of course, remain. One thinks of the perils of the short-term or part-time contract, for example. But Berger's (1964) claim – 'they do not live where they work' (p. 217) – has been severely undermined by the dynamics of 'bringing life back to work'. One might say that the secondary institution of soft capitalism, with its 'life-values' and 'life-ethic', has stepped in to handle the failures of the primary institution of 'raw'/'hard' capitalism. And in the process, those concerned who might once have felt homeless find a home.

Case study 2: religion/spirituality and secondary institutions

The observations of Berger and his co-authors about the decline in faith in primary religious institutions have been amply confirmed by the figures showing rapid decline in religious observance in the West, particularly in Europe. The result does not, however, appear to have been a rise in secularity. The number of those identifying themselves as atheist or agnostic has not risen significantly, while the number who identify as 'spiritual' and who believe in a 'higher force', 'life force' or 'soul' has risen – 70 per cent of the adult population in Britain now believe they have a soul. Have these people who have lost faith in primary institutions but not in the spiritual realm been rendered homeless? Are they lonely seekers of their own salvation, dredging the depths of their own selfhood in search of meaning and significance? While these questions are still pertinent, we suggest that the spiritual scene which has unfolded in recent decades is one in which homelessness is *not* as salient a feature as it looked set to become from the perspective of the 1960s. This is not to deny that religion has become more a matter of personal concern than ever before. But it should not be concluded from this that it has become a purely private and subjective matter, wholly centred on psychic life.

Three developments which appear to have countered the spread of homelessness in the religious/spiritual thesis will be discussed below. First, at the level of cultural expression, religion and spirituality in recent times has been characterized by the turn to life in its broader as well as its narrower senses. Indeed, it may not be an exaggeration to say that spirituality today is characterized by concern with relationship and the life of the planet as much as with self-life. The institutional counterparts of this turn have been, secondly, the proliferation of secondary institutions to cater for religion and spirituality, institutions which range from 'new spiritual outlets' to the small group movement, and, thirdly, the detraditionalization of primary religious institutions as they shed their 'iron cage/melting cage' characteristics and become 'homes for life'. These institutional developments form a continuum from the more individualized (new spiritual outlets) through to the more communal (detraditionalized forms of church).

The turn to life in the religious and spiritual realm

The turn to life in religion reverses the priorities of traditional forms of Christianity (and Judaism) in which the self is subordinated to the higher authority of a transcendent God and the mediating authorities of (for example) priesthood, church or scriptures. Instead *this* life becomes the focus of spiritual concern. In its spiritual form, life (whether self-life, relational life, eco-life or cosmic life) is understood as ultimately mysterious and 'more' than the human mind can grasp. Against scientific materialism, the spiritual turn to life insists that there is 'more to life than is dreamt of in your philosophy'. This 'more' is a source of unity and a *mysterium fascinans* which can and should draw all individuals out of themselves. The turn to life postulates realms of hidden possibilities, a transcendent depth to experience, a 'beyond' which draws us ever onwards. Religion/spirituality ceases to be a matter of obedience to given natural or scriptural laws, and becomes a never-ending *journey* in which the believer explores the mysterious depths of what life has to offer.

The mysterious life which draws the spiritual quester onwards encompasses the individual's own life. It may be true that the self retains some primary significance in the spiritual turn to life. But it does *not* follow that it is the sole focus of concern. For every 'seeker' who is trying to get in touch with his or her true self or discover the God within, there is another who is equally or more concerned with relationship, with other lives both human or animal, and with the life of the planet as a whole.

Examples of a strongly *relational* form of the contemporary spiritual quest are not hard to find. In many cases they relate to women. One of the most famous emerged from Robert Bellah and others' *Habits of the*

Heart (1985) – Sheila Larson. Because of her self-proclaimed religion of 'Sheilaism', Sheila was pilloried by many commentators as an example of the socially destructive individualism which was infecting the United States and destroying its primary and intermediate institutions. Yet this reaction overlooked the strongly relational aspect of Sheila's religiosity. She was, after all, a nurse caring for the sick and dying, and her religion was 'try to love yourself and be gentle with yourself. You know, I guess, *take care of each other. I think He [God] would want us to take care of each other'* (p. 221, our italics). An interesting comparison can be drawn between Sheila Larson and Princess Diana, who also developed a spirituality of her own which had important Christian influences and New Age borrowings, but which was fundamentally *relational.* Woodhead (1999) calls it a 'religion of the heart' and describes it as a 'warm, emotive, tender-hearted humanitarianism' which blurs 'the line between the supernatural and the natural, the human and divine' and represents a significant departure from a more ascetic, self-denying Christian conception of love or *agape* (p. 131). The nature and scale of the mourning after Diana's death suggest that such a religiosity was widely shared: love and the heart were the main motifs in the thousands of tributes left to Diana (pp. 134–6). Recent research on the spirituality of young people in the United Kingdom suggests that relationality holds the key to understanding the nature of their deepest ethical and spiritual values and behaviours as well (Collins, 1997).

Princess Diana also serves as an interesting example and reminder of the way in which the *humanitarian* turn to life may take a spiritual form, and link closely to the turn to relational life. In speaking of the public role which she wished to carve out for herself she often used the language of humanitarianism ('an ambassador to humanity'), but clearly grounded such discourse in the sacred value of human life and affective face-to-face relation. As she said in the BBC documentary filmed in Angola in 1997, for example: 'I am not a political figure, nor do I want to be one. But I come with my heart, and I want to bring awareness to people in distress ... The fact is, I'm a humanitarian figure. I always have been and always will be' (quoted in Woodhead, 1999, p. 130). In this context one could mention, too, the powerful strand in (liberal) Christianity which has also developed a religious form of humanitarian discourse and emphasis, a good recent example being Hans Küng's 'Global Ethic' based on belief in the sacred *'humanum'.* Other world religions have followed suit: the Dalai Lama's relational and humanitarian rendering of Tibetan Buddhism being one of the most celebrated examples of recent times. (These and other examples can be found in Woodhead and Heelas, 2000.)

Spiritual renderings of the turn to *eco-life* and *cosmic life* are also plentiful. The most striking examples of the former are furnished by the many active ecological movements and networks which invariably have a spiritual dimension. This dimension is usually more, rather than less, apparent – in the 'deep ecology' movement, in eco-feminism, and in Prince

Charles's naturalism, for example. The distinction between new social movements and new spiritual movements is often an artificial one – no coincidence that Anthony Giddens has coined the apt term 'life-politics' which can encompass both. Equally, as has already been noted, the spiritual dimension of the turn to cosmic life is evident in the vast popular literature on the mysteries of the universe, as well as in numerous forms of contemporary spirituality (such as New Age) which believe that all reality is indwelt by a unifying spiritual life force. And survey research indicates that beliefs in a 'higher power' or a 'life force' are widely held in Britain, and no longer the preserve of esoteric or alternative groups.

What all these examples show is that the disillusionment with primary religious institutions which Berger, Berger and Kellner observed has not led to a homelessness in which the individual is thrown back on his or her (inadequate) subjective resources. Certainly in much contemporary spirituality the individual has now become the final arbiter of spiritual truth, and a shift has taken place 'from a world in which beliefs held believers to a world in which believers hold beliefs' (Susan Harding, quoted in Roof, 1999, p. 42). But contemporary spirituality takes many forms besides those that dwell on the self and its inner potential – forms which naturally lead the pilgrim on a journey beyond self and in relation with others. This cultural turn is being reinforced, activated and embodied by the proliferation of secondary institutions, and the transformation of primary ones.

Secondary spiritual institutions

The growth of secondary spiritual institutions has been one of the most striking (though least explored) features of the late twentieth- and early twenty-first-century religious scene. Some of these secondary institutions are independent of primary religious institutions, while others are more closely related to them.

Some of the most independent and least institutionalized secondary spiritual institutions are the plethora of outlets catering for spiritual seekers who are pursuing their quest outside traditional religious frameworks – what Heelas (2000, p. 61) refers to as 'new spiritual outlets' or 'NSOs'. Even a small town such as Kendal in Cumbria in the north of England (population 27,000 and currently the subject of a locality study of religion and spirituality being carried out by Heelas, Seel, Szerszynski, Tusting and Woodhead) has over forty NSOs. Such outlets cater for those who are not satisfied with the fixed menus of spiritual fare on offer in primary religious institutions but want to pursue a more individual spiritual quest in which they assemble a mix of spiritual nourishment designed to fit to their own lives and lifestyles. The parallel with shopping is obvious and may be helpful – so long, that is, as it is recognized that some consumer choices (and certainly many of those in this area) can be serious and substantial.

Some NSOs actually take the form of high street (or back street) shops. Seekers can wander in off the street, browse among the goods and services on offer, and make their choices. Their commitment to the institution may be no more than one's commitment to the convenience store – certainly the authority of self is not surrendered in any way.

The loose network of such secondary institutions is currently being rapidly extended through the virtual communities and electronic highways and hubs of the Internet and a rapidly expanding multi-media, interactive entertainment and information industry. 'e-spirituality' is already a reality. There are virtual communities for almost every traditional and alternative form of religion and spirituality. 'Home pages' allow individuals to articulate, share and advertise their own spiritual quests and any spiritual services they might offer. The possibility of linking up by e-mail with others who share your particular spiritual 'niche' is vastly enhanced. New ideas and techniques can quickly circulate, cut loose from the inhibiting factors of time and geography. What emerges is a democratic 'free for all' in which no voice (or 'site') is more able to be heard than any other, and in which even the authority of the Vatican home page (www.vatican.va/) has to compete on more or less equal terms with those of eastern gurus and women healers. Equally significant, what emerges is a world of information and entertainment in which spirituality is just as likely to be channelled through music or art or film as through primary religious institutions, personnel, and 'experts'. Here individuals are free to give or take just as much spiritual nourishment as suits them, and in whatever combination they think best – though in communication with others (however 'virtual') rather than in lonely isolation.

Yet the possibility of greater commitment and face-to-face community in NSOs and other loose spiritual networks remains. In many cases new spiritual outlets physically cluster together – in centres which offer health foods, alternative remedies, and various forms of healing and spiritual practice. Neal's Yard in London's Covent Garden was an early example in Britain; most cities and towns now have their own variants. Communities often arise in such settings – communities of those who live and/or work in the outlets, as well as loose communities of clients and consumers. Such centres become hubs in the loosely spreading network of alternative spirituality, and gateways to other branches of the network. Information in the form of advertisements and newsletters is on offer and directs seekers in other directions – towards other centres, groups, meetings, spiritual groups, alternative communities, virtual communities and networks. These may appear to be skeletal social forms, but they draw individuals together and make possible considerable cross-fertilization of ideas, as well as face-to-face meetings and exchanges at weekends, workshops, conferences, festivals, and so on. As such, they undoubtedly serve to counteract homelessness.[7]

While new spiritual outlets exist (relatively) independently of primary religious institutions, in many cases they cater not only for those who have no faith in such institutions, but for those who (at the same or different times in their lives) belong to churches, chapels, temples and synagogues. The latter often supplement their spiritual diet with an offering or two from the alternative fringe – and do not appear to feel any contradiction in doing so (one of our research students even found that the bulk of those active in feminist spirituality groups also attended traditional churches (Pryce, 1999)). Research by Roof (1999) confirms this picture of constant to-ing and fro-ing between the two spheres on the part of 'baby boomers' in the United States. Increasingly there are also virtual communities and churches which make it almost optional to attend a 'real' church.

But the most significant development in the sphere of secondary spiritual institutions as these relate to primary religious institutions may be the widespread growth of small groups.[8] While such groups are extremely diverse in what they cater for, and run the whole gamut from Weight Watchers to Bible study groups, the majority have a religious aspect (Wuthnow, 1994). Indeed, most appear to exist within the ambit of churches or similar bodies, often with their approval, sponsorship or patronage. Wuthnow and his team found that four out of every ten Americans surveyed currently belong to an organized support group that meets regularly, and that 39 per cent of the other 60 per cent had been involved in such a group in the past (pp. 4; 48). Of those four out of ten currently involved, 61 per cent say that their 'faith or spirituality' has been influenced by being in the group, and between half and two-thirds of all small-group members have connections of one kind or another with religious organizations or teachings and practices (pp. 55; 92).

At first sight small groups may seem the antithesis of primary religious institutions. They reject received wisdom in any form – creeds, dogmas, theological tradition, the special authority of the clergy. In its place they rely on the experience and hard-won insights of their members, insights which can be articulated and owned within the intimate and safe space such groups provide. Likewise, these groups reject hierarchical authority and organization. They may have convenors and group facilitators who exercise the limited leadership any group needs in order to function and survive, but a defining characteristic is to insist on the right of equal participation by all members. They are face-to-face, open, tolerant, inclusive, non-judgemental and democratic – and in all these respects small groups might seem to cut across the implicit and explicit values of mainline churches. In Troeltschian terms, they contradict the social structure and teachings of both 'church' and 'sect' types of Christianity, while having most in common with the somewhat amorphous and organizationally weak 'mystical' type. Yet major studies of small groups and their relation to the churches find the relationship between the two to be generally mutually supportive and constructive. On the one hand, churches are often the originators of small groups, which meet under their auspices (and often on their premises) and whose members are largely drawn from their congregations. On the other hand, small groups help to nurture spiritual growth, sustain existing members in the faith and (in some cases) bring new members to the church.

The apparently complementary nature of the relationship between church and small group is partly explicable in terms of the turn to life. By their very nature small groups tend to be oriented towards 'life': 'the life of the soul' as Wuthnow puts it (1994, p. 5). As Wuthnow also writes, 'What happened [in the groups] took place so incrementally that it could seldom be seen at all. It was, like most profound reorientations *in life,* so gradual that those involved saw it less as a revolution than as a journey. The change was concerned with daily life, emotions, and understandings of one's identity. It was personal rather than public, moral rather than political' (p. 3; our emphasis). Small groups are ideally suited to discussion of life. The individual life of their members is their starting point, and they are valued precisely as a space in which this life can be explored in a safe and intimate space, and face to face. Practically oriented, small groups also help people to grow and develop in their life paths, albeit by drawing on tradition (Bible reading in particular). Thus small groups complement congregations by allowing the latter, as it were, to open up to life, while the congregations are at the same time moving towards small groups by themselves becoming more oriented to life and increasingly detraditionalized.

Detraditionalization of primary religious institutions

The comments in *The Homeless Mind* about the way in which primary religious institutions are experienced as 'iron cages' devoid of significance and too rigid to allow individuals to find their own meaning within them, while at the same time becoming 'crumbling cages' whose plausibility is undermined by pluralization, still retain enormous explanatory value. Far more modern men and women now accept the designation 'spiritual' than 'religious', and in doing so distance themselves from what they perceived to be external, oppressive, inflexible, ritualized, 'dead' and 'second-hand' (Roof, 1999, p. 81). Thus 64 per cent of the 'baby boomers' interviewed by Roof (1999) call themselves 'spiritual', 30 per cent 'religious', and 6 per cent 'secularists' (p. 321) – remarkably similar figures have been confirmed by a surprising number of recent surveys in both the United Kingdom and the United States. Yet the capacity of primary institutions to reinvent themselves – and the capacity of spiritual 'consumers' to use them as they will – can too easily be underestimated. As well as fostering the growth of small groups, many primary religious institutions are currently 'detraditionalizing': downplaying the 'hard' authoritative, hierarchical, patriarchal, heteronomous nature of traditional religious communities in favour of 'softer' characteristics and forms of belonging which allow individuals to find homes, exercise autonomy and resource their lives. The emphasis, in other words, increasingly shifts from without to within, from God to self, from church to community and from after-life to this life.

In very few churches these days does a newcomer have to undergo the uncomfortable and drawn-out process of learning how to belong: when to bow, when to kneel, which book to use, what vocabulary to adopt, which theology to ascribe to. The process was a vivid illustration of the initiation of an individual into a tradition which was greater and more important than he or she: their task was to *conform*. Today, by contrast, most churches have become much more 'user friendly'. They avoid language, liturgy and rituals which are 'hard' to grasp. They accommodate themselves to the needs of congregations, and even shape their language and practices to fit. Tradition is now made for self, rather than self for tradition. A clear example is furnished by the 'seeker churches' in the United States which deliberately avoid imposing *any* 'dogma' or teaching at all, and try instead to guide all comers gently into Christian ways, whatever belief (if any) they come with (Hunter, 1996).

It is not only the more liberal churches which illustrate this transformation. James Davison Hunter (1987) has traced what he views as the 'subjectivization' of evangelicalism in the United States, whereby it loosens its 'orthodox' boundaries, relaxes its exclusivism, becomes open to 'interpretation' of the scriptures, uncertain about some doctrines such as hell and damnation – and generally displays a turn to the self whereby the individual and his or her needs become the focus and locus of attention and authority in place of an 'external' God and tradition. Equally we may cite the new evangelical-charismatic churches in California which are the subject of a study by Donald Miller (1997). Miller sees such churches as a 'new paradigm': 'they are restructuring the organizational character of institutional religion; they are democratizing access to the sacred by radicalizing the Protestant principle of the priesthood of all believers' (p. 1). Such churches, Miller believes, cater to the needs of those who are disenchanted with 'church religion' and distrustful of primary institutions, yet equally dissatisfied with narcissistic countercultural individualism. Thus they abandon the 'traditional' characteristics of Christianity such as clerical authority and its symbols (vestments and liturgies), unquestionable and 'authoritative' preaching, stiff and formal ritual, dull hymnody and bureaucratic procedures. However, they retain an emphasis on the authority of the Bible, the transcendence of God, the importance of 'Christian living', and the sovereignty of Jesus. All, however, are directed at 'transforming people's lives by addressing their deepest personal needs' (p. 183).

Much of this detraditionalization is achieved through charismatic Christianity's characteristic emphasis on the Holy Spirit – the *'giver of life'*. By invoking the Spirit, such churches maintain authority, albeit an authority which is cut loose from traditional 'containers' and which is available for the empowerment of each individual. In many ways the 'Holy Spirit' and the 'Higher Self' of alternative spirituality are closely related. As Steven

Tipton notes in his study of an evangelical fellowship (1982), both the counterculture's drug ideology and charismatic churches value experience and self-surrender, but the latter 'insist more strongly on the related need for commitment to the object and practice of one's surrender, and from this experience they construct some form of cosmic and social authority' (p. 55). Not only is the Holy Spirit the perfect mediator between God and man, it also turns out to be the perfect mediator between tradition and individualism in many partly detraditionalized forms of Christianity – what we have elsewhere referred to as 'experiential religions of difference' (Woodhead and Heelas, 2000, pp. 148–68).

Primary religious institutions detraditionalize not only 'internally', but also 'externally'. That is to say, power shifts from tradition to individual not only through conscious institutional reform but through individual members of a church 'using' that tradition in new ways and performing the role of 'congregant' in a new fashion. Instead of treating a church community as something into which one is born and to which one must thereafter remain loyal, for example, modern men and women are now much more likely to elect which church they will join. They may move from church to church within a lifetime – or even in and out of church altogether. One of the most striking of the findings of Wade Clark Roof and his team about the religion of American 'baby boomers' is that one-third of those who when sampled in the late 1980s were 'dropouts' from religious services are now 'returnees', while one-third of those who were then 'returnees' are now 'dropouts' (Roof, 1999, pp. 115–20). Roof concludes that: 'What is striking is *the dynamic, fluid character* of Boomer religiosity, which is almost like a game of musical chairs: loyalists and returnees drop out in sizeable numbers while dropouts, some of them inactive for twenty or thirty years, find their way back to churches, synagogues and temples' (p. 120).

Do these new patterns of detraditionalized affiliation suggest an underlying homelessness and imply a lack of commitment on the part of those who 'chose to belong'? Quite the contrary says Roof (1999), while Nancy Ammerman (1997) reaches the same conclusion in her recent study of American congregations. Borrowing a phrase from Stephen Warner, Ammerman finds that 'elective parochialism' characterizes most contemporary Christian belonging. In her view the new primacy of self and of choice in religion does not, however, imply a lack of commitment or sociality. Churches and small groups are 'spaces of sociability where real commitments are made', and both are:

> Communal gatherings, collectivities, that afford their members an opportunity for connections with persons, groups, divine powers, and social structures beyond their own individuality. The substance and depth of these commitments is no less real because an individual is

committed to other institutions, or because this commitment may not last a lifetime.

(p. 352)

One effect of Ammerman's comments in *Congregation and Community* (1997) is to break down a hard and fast distinction between primary and secondary institutions, and to deny the relative weakness of the latter. In her view the former are now rarely characterized by non-ascriptive forms of belonging and identity, and few religious communities are now based round such 'givens' as physical proximity, economic interdependence or biological relation. Neither primary nor secondary institutions now demand life-long commitment of their members, and both tend to be purposive, intentional and voluntaristic. Equally – one might add – both are now oriented to life. Perhaps the homes they offer are somewhat less stable as a result – just like the domestic unit – but they are homes none the less. The breakdown of the nuclear family does not necessarily signal the end of patterns of intimate and committed relation any more than the breakdown of traditional religious communities signals the end of spiritual community. Such developments may simply require us to be more sensitive in discerning the shapes that new patterns of commitment and belonging are taking.

Conclusion

In *The Homeless Mind*, Berger, Berger and Kellner painted a vivid and compelling picture of a modern world in which men and women are alienated from rigid and 'meaningless' primary institutions, thrown back on subjectivities of the self, and ultimately left 'homeless'. Without disagreeing with this powerful analysis, we have drawn attention to aspects of late modern society which have become more visible since that book was written, and which help to explain why homelessness did *not* become as widespread as many feared. In particular we have drawn attention to two interlocking cultural and social processes: the broadening of a turn to life from a concern with self-focused self-life to encompass concern with relational, humanitarian, eco- and cosmic life, and the proliferation of secondary institutions which offer homes for such life by providing a middle way between the homeless tendencies of both the under-institutionalized realm of the countercultural and the over-institutionalized realm of primary institutions.

Clearly, there is much more to be said about why homelessness has not become as widespread as might have been expected when Berger and his co-authors wrote *The Homeless Mind*. Without going into detail, the key to the matter would appear to lie with the fact that key values – the freedom to live one's own life to the full (the liberation and expression of life), the importance of respecting the lives of others (the democratization of life) – have meant that the hierarchical, traditionalized, regulated, patterned 'hard' institutions of 'high' ('1950s') modernity have increasingly given way to the more egalitarian, detraditionalized, de-authoritized, expressive, fluid, voluntaristic and relational. We have referred only to the spheres of religion and work. One can also cite, for example, the wide popularity of alternative healing and complementary medicine; the increasingly important hospice movement; new politics, based around the quality and reciprocity of relationships; the detraditionalized family or classroom; youth culture, in particular clubbing ('live your life' being a great slogan), life-informing television and magazines, the music industry; that form of secondary institution constituted by a network of regular contact by telephone and text message; travel (and not just overseas) with associated life-expanding experiences; consumer culture and activities focusing on quality of life matters; 'intimate ethicality', with people working out or through life-issues with those most closely involved; and much else besides, including the secondary institutions of soft capitalism, small groups, experiential religions of difference, and new spiritual outlets. And all these secondary institutions serve to provide home after home – *for* life.

Such developments suggest that secondary institutions have proved more resilient, adaptable and capable of sustaining life and providing homes than seemed likely from the perspective of the 1970s, not least because they cater for such highly valued values. With the benefit of hindsight we can say that Berger, Berger and Kellner (1974) may have underestimated their potential when they wrote in the following terms:

> the underinstitutionalization of the private sphere has produced new institutional formulations. These have been called 'secondary institutions' ... They are meant to fill the gap left by the underinstitutionalization of the private sphere. There is, however, a built-in paradox in the way in which they function. If they retain the optional, and therefore artificial, quality of private life, they are not able to meet the demand for stability and reliability which brought them about in the first place. If, on the other hand, they are so constructed as to meet these demands, they take on the character of the larger [primary] institutions of modern society ... the cold winds of 'homelessness' threaten these fragile constructions. It would be an overstatement to say that the 'solution' of the private sphere is a failure; there are too many individual successes. But it is always very precarious.
>
> (p. 168)

As well as suggesting the greater resilience of secondary institutions, our analysis suggests that the hard and fast distinction between primary and secondary institutions may be breaking down. Within obvious structural constraints, *both* now have to cater for the individual and individual freedom, and *both* have to cater for *life*. Detraditionalized churches and new workplaces provide examples. Ammerman (1997) argued that modern society should now be understood 'as containing anonymous relationships and bureaucratic structures *alongside* overlapping pockets of communal solidarity' (p. 363). We would go further and suggest that modern society now contains anonymous and traditional relationships *within* pockets of communal society – and vice versa. Men and women in the workplace and the religious sphere negotiate and move between traditional, ascribed roles and newly forged and chosen ascriptive ones. Sometimes the two exist in tension, sometimes in harmony; sometimes in destructive conflict, sometimes in creative connection.

The examples we have offered suggest that the image of dwelling in many homes may now be more appropriate than that of homelessness. Berger and his co-authors were certainly correct that the 'home' of the mind or the self *per se* would prove inadequate. Proof may lie in the fact that so many have indeed sought more secure and encompassing homes since the 1960s. As Roof (1999) observes, 'What had begun in the 1960s as a quest for the "ideal self", an excessively individualistic quest, had by the early 1990s become more contained, opening the way for people in the presence of other people to share aspects of their lives, even their very intimate lives, in ways that were potentially nurturing and transforming' (p. 40). As we have tried to suggest, the 'turn within' became the wider turn to life, and the imperative of self-development transformed into the desire to preserve and enhance life – understood in its fullest sense. The growth of secondary institutions and the transformation of primary ones goes hand in hand with this development. In the face of a *flight from deference* seen in an increasing unwillingness to defer to rules, tradition or authority and to defer the gratification and cultivation of life, institutions have begun to be reshaped in order to draw on and enhance life, and to harness its energies. Increasingly, they provide homes for life.

It may not be an exaggeration to say that the cultural and institutional turn to life constitutes a revolution. In the religious sphere in particular (simply because this is our area of greatest expertise) we feel justified in claiming that what has occurred over the past few decades amounts to a 'spiritual revolution' – with a significance comparable to that of the industrial revolution in the material realm. As yet this revolution has hardly begun to be systematically mapped.[9] The existing categories of the sociology of religion are probably inadequate to the task, which demands nothing less than a new vocabulary and conceptuality. We believe that when this does emerge it will be characterized not only by a new sensitivity to what is happening on the ground, but by a new sensitivity to its own institutional affiliations, biases, and interests. This claim is based on our observation that most of the pioneering studies in this area (some of which we have cited) are of precisely this kind: ethnographically sensitive and methodologically self-aware. We also believe it is no coincidence that many of these studies are either written by women, and/or have a clear gender awareness – a remark which can be clarifed in relation to the debate discussed in this chapter.

This thought prompts a concluding comment on an issue which merits further investigation than we have been able to give it here. At first glance the notion of 'primary' and 'secondary' institutions may appear neutral and descriptive, as may the closely related distinction between 'public' and 'private' spheres. Looked at from a gendered perspective, however, it appears loaded and value-laden. Feminist critiques of the private/public distinction have long pointed out its persuasive nature: by relegating women's work and women's spheres of activity to the 'private' realm, it renders them less visible and justifies lack of economic reward and inferior cultural standing. The primary/secondary distinction *can* work in the same way – i.e. the institutions in which men are most active, such as the church, law, business and politics, are defined as the strongest, 'hardest', most important, and most essential for social cohesion. By contrast, secondary institutions (often those in which women are more prominent) are viewed as relatively fragile and insignificant.

One benefit of problematizing such loaded dualisms is to be able to see behind them to the more complex realities of social life which they may disguise (Ammerman's work furnishes an excellent example). Another is that it is then easier to see that the fear articulated and generated within much social and cultural debate since the 1960s about the breakdown of primary institutions may not have been wholly divorced from institutional and gendered interests: those who had most to lose from the breakdown of 'primary' institutions (men) were perhaps the most vocal and alarmed. To a large extent the image of the iron cage and the crumbling cage may have served to *disguise* these interests, generating the picture of impersonal forces at work rather than very personal power interests in conflict. To put it bluntly, the reason why so many rejected the 'traditional' 'primary' institutions may not simply have been that the 'hard' world of the iron cage no longer suited their 'soft' 'baby boomer' natures, but that they were rebelling against a white, male, middle-aged (and older) 'establishment' which had been in power for too long. From this point of view, the iron cage did not just crumble or melt, it was pulled down. So what from some perspectives looks like loss, from others looks like gain; what from some standpoints looks like decline, from others looks like growth; and what from some angles looks like homelessness, from others looks more like a homecoming.

Notes

1 A number of theorists have argued in similar fashion to Berger *et al.* (1974), drawing attention to the discontents of modernity and the subsequent turn to the self. This is how Philip Rieff (1979; orig. 1959), for example, explores 'the emergence of psychological man': 'What has caused this tyranny of psychology,

legitimating self-concern as the highest science? In part, no doubt, it is the individual's failure to find anything else to affirm except the self' (p. 355).

2 For further discussion of the homeless mind thesis and the development of countercultural spirituality, see Heelas (1996, chapter 5).

3 Cupitt (1999) provides evidence of the turn to life's cultural importance by demonstrating just how many life-idioms (such as 'get a life') have entered everyday discourse.

4 This case study draws on material to be found in Heelas (2001).

5 As far as we know, Hansfried Kellner and Frank Heuberger (1992) were the first to use the term 'soft' in connection with capitalism. As they write of 'modern' as opposed to 'classical' (Taylorian 'scientific management'), it 'has very much to do with the cultural, behavioural, and psychic aspects of people and events of an organization. From this "soft" side, it "organizes the organization" just as systematically as classical consulting does from its more technical side' (1992, p. 51). Nigel Thrift (1997) has developed usage of the term. Kellner and Heuberger, together with Thrift, provide good illustrative material of soft capitalism. See Art Kleiner (1996) for a listing of the subject literature of some of the wilder reaches of this development.

6 Heelas (1996) discusses New Age management trainings and their contribution to 'life' in greater detail. See also Huczynski (1993).

7 It can also be argued against the homeless mind thesis that in the religious realm the turn to life's strongly holistic emphasis leads to a very important emphasis not just on the mind or the psyche, but on the unity of 'mind, body and spirit'. As such, the turn to life is as much to do with developing the body as it is with developing the soul or the psyche, and the 'subjectivities of the self' are only a part of its concern.

8 The growth of the small-group movement may be widespread throughout the West, but research has so far been concentrated on the United States. The argument which follows is based on this evidence.

9 Roof (1999) is one of the few attempts.

5 A New Age theodicy for a new age

Colin Campbell

Introduction

Max Weber's scheme for the classification and analysis of the world's religions was based on his extensive research on Christianity, Ancient Judaism, Hinduism, Buddhism and Chinese religion (Weber, 1951; 1952; 1958; 1965). He assumed that the world-views contained in these religions had a certain inner logic that determined their development, a 'directional logic' in Guenther Roth's terms (1987, p. 87), and that the engine that drives this logic is the tension between the world-view itself and reality, that is between the expectations that world-views create in people and the experiences they actually undergo. This discrepancy, and hence the tension arising from it, is not only inevitable but, the more systematized and logically coherent the world-view, the greater it is likely to be. The meaning puzzle presented by this discrepancy Weber referred to as 'the problem of theodicy'. Consequently this term, although originating in natural theology, has come to have a special significance within the sociology of religion, such that it is this 'problem', together with the various solutions offered by the world religions, which, as Bryan Turner (1981) suggests, 'is central to Weber's sociology of religion' (p. 148).[1]

One of the more surprising omissions in Weber's otherwise subtle and revealing discussion is his failure to bring his analysis up to modern times, preferring to stop with the Calvinist theodicy that he seems to have regarded as the culmination of the process of theodical rationalization in the West. There are several possible reasons why Weber omitted to investigate post-Calvinist solutions to the problem of meaning, including his preoccupation with the role that religion played in the emergence of modern capitalism and his presumption that people would have little time to reflect on such matters when trapped in the iron cage of secular rationality. However, it is not clear that there are good grounds for assuming that the problem of theodicy will be any less acutely experienced by men and women in the modern era than was the case in former times.

Rather, it seems more realistic to treat the need for meaning, as indeed does Weber himself in his general discussion of the nature and function of religion, as a constant of human experience. Here he comments on the 'metaphysical needs of the human mind as it is driven to reflect on ethical and religious questions, driven not by material need but by an inner compulsion to understand the world as a meaningful cosmos and to take up a position toward it' (1965, p. 117). In the light of this presumption it simply does not seem reasonable to assume that such a need will disappear with the emergence of modernity. Rather it seems more reasonable to assume, as Weber implies, that this is a universal need, experienced by all peoples in all societies. Indeed he also refers to 'the natural rationalistic need to conceive of the world as a meaningful cosmos' (p. 124). This is also the position adopted by Peter Berger, who similarly treats the need for a theodicy to address the problem of meaning as a universal feature of human existence. However, he elaborates on the nature of this need, and, rejecting Weber's more psychological treatment of the problem, stresses its basis in certain crucial characteristics of human sociation as such (1973, p. 63). Indeed, Berger's analysis – echoing Durkheim's treatment of religious phenomenon as much as Weber's – stresses how theodicies serve to enable individuals to transcend themselves, and in so doing deny the individual self and its needs in the interests of social order. This transcendence, Berger (1973) suggests, embodies a fundamental masochism in the sense that 'Not being able to stand aloneness, man denies his separateness, and not being able to stand meaninglessness, he finds a paradoxical meaning in self-annihilation' (p. 64). However, whether one stresses the personal or the social functions fulfilled by theodicies it is clear that they are as necessary in the contemporary as in the pre-modern world.

For, as Roland Robertson (1978, p. 70) has observed, we actually know very little about the theodicies that people adopt in the modern world. Indeed, as he notes, we tend to know more about the minority or sectarian meaning-systems or world-views than about the mainstream theodicies adopted by the majority of people in contemporary society. Consequently, this chapter will attempt to make a small contribution towards redressing this imbalance by examining one of the more common of contemporary 'theodicies' (if arguably not necessarily that which constitutes the 'mainstream'), namely that contained in the New Age world-view. Before tackling this question, however, it is necessary to attempt some further clarification of the precise nature and function of theodical systems of meaning.

The nature and function of theodicies

Theodicies can be regarded as those cultural systems that specifically serve to meet the universal human need for meaning at the highest level. That there is such a need arises from the fact that life itself contains no inherent or intrinsic meaning, or message, such that people's experiences only become meaningful when set within a frame that culture supplies. Although the emphasis is often placed by sociologists and anthropologists on the role played by culture in enabling individuals to act out a coherent and ordered way of life on an everyday basis, it is important to recognize that it also serves to provide meaning at a more fundamental level. That is to say, in attempting to provide answers to such questions as the meaning of 'life, the universe and everything'. It is that part of a society's cultural system that addresses these ultimate questions that constitutes its theodicy.

Now there has been a tendency historically, in keeping with the origin of the word, to restrict the term 'theodicy' to religious systems of meaning, and even then to apply it simply to those attempts to provide an answer to the problem of reconciling the existence of evil with an omnipotent and good god. However, there seems to be no very good reason for restricting the usage of the term in this way since the need to have answers to the fundamental questions of existence would appear to be a cultural universal, as apparent among the non-religious as among the religious, while among the latter it is as apparent among non-theists as among theists. It is also important to recognize that theodical systems do not simply deal with issues of justice or morality – even though this may be their focus – but necessarily also deal with meaning-puzzles more generally.

In fact, one can distinguish three analytically distinct dimensions to the 'meaningfulness' that such systems are required to supply. The first, and in many ways the most obvious, is that of cognitive meaning. Theodical systems, whether truly religious, or merely secular and quasi-religious in character, are all required to give a descriptive account of the reality that human beings experience. In simple terms they are required to explain why things are as they are. Such accounts normally include a cosmology – or an account of the nature, origin and possibly the destiny of the cosmos in general – as well as, more especially, of this particular world. A creation story, or creation myth, is thus often central to this aspect of theodicies. In addition, there is also usually an account of the nature of human beings and of their relationship to the divine (or whatever serves the same function in secular systems).

But then secondly, there is, in addition, a dimension that is concerned with emotional meaning. For it is not enough to know 'what is'. It is also important, if human experiences are indeed to be rendered meaningful, that people should know exactly what they are meant to feel about the picture of life and the universe that has been presented to them. Should they perhaps be awestruck, amazed and fearful, or perhaps hopeful, joyous and welcoming? Or perhaps, quite simply indifferent, and resigned? But then, in addition to indicating what general attitude or emotional tone individuals should take towards life and the universe, theodicies also usually offer more specific guidance on what individuals should feel, and under what circumstances. In this respect the beliefs and values contained in a theodical system assist individuals to handle their emotions. Crucial to this process is the fact that theodicies typically offer a framework of meaning that enables individuals both to experience catharsis and, more specifically, to translate such negative feelings as fear, anxiety, or despair into the positive ones of calm, confidence, optimism and contentment.

Finally, the third dimension of theodical systems, and the one that normally receives most attention, is that concerned with moral meaning. This concerns the need that people have to understand why things are as they are when judged not simply from a disinterested scientific standpoint but from the very interested and partial perspective of human desires, hopes and expectations. Consequently the need here is for an account of experience which is meaningful morally rather than simply intellectually and emotionally. That is to say, the interpretation provided must explain not only why human life is characterized by such universals as pain, suffering, failure and disappointment (not to mention the universal fact of death itself), but more importantly why these negative experiences should be differentially distributed in a manner that appears unfair if not unjust. In providing meaning of this kind, therefore, a theodicy must not simply explain why these are features of human existence but also provide some justification for their unequal distribution. In addition, we may note that in providing guidance on how people should understand themselves, their experiences, and the world around them, theodical systems also necessarily provide guidance on how individuals should act in the world. For, clearly, it is not really possible to influence how people think and feel about life without also affecting the way in which they act. Furthermore, the solution offered to the problem of moral meaning – even in the absence of the belief that one should obey the commandments of a personal god – also leads directly to suggestions concerning how individuals should conduct themselves in the world.

Hence we may briefly summarize the meaning provided by theodicies by saying that when functioning as successful and comprehensive meaning-systems they should tell people what to think and feel about the world and about themselves, on what basis their own experience of life – and indeed existence in general – is 'fair' or 'deserved', and if predominantly undesirable, can be, or will be, 'compensated for' in due course, while also indicating what actions they themselves ought to perform in order to ensure this outcome.

Now it is clearly important, in considering theodicies in this way, to escape from the overly theistic formulations that, following Weber, have tended to predominate in sociological discussions of the issue. The tendency, following on from eighteenth- and nineteenth-century discussions of this topic, to presume that 'the problem of theodicy' concerns the nature and intentions of a personal, creator God, is clearly unhelpful when considering the issue in the context of the largely non-theistic (if not actually atheistic) cultures of modernity.

Fortunately, a more pertinent description of the nature of 'the problem of theodicy' as experienced by individuals in modern societies than the rather overly theistic version favoured by Weber can be found in the work of William James. James's view was that all religions seek to provide 'deliverance'; something that is consummated in the transition from 'an uneasiness' to its 'solution'. This uneasiness, when reduced to its simplest terms, 'is a sense that there is something wrong about us as we naturally stand', and 'the solution is a sense that we are saved from the wrongness by making proper connection with the higher powers'.[2] This formulation of 'the problem of theodicy' is a good deal more vague than that favoured by Weber, eschewing as it does not merely any reference to God (or gods), but also to suffering, injustice or death.[3] None the less, it still corresponds to Weber's general formulation of a discrepancy between peoples' hopes and expectations on the one hand and their experience of reality on the other. Here then we have that minimum formulation of 'the problem of theodicy' as understood by modern mankind: a simple specification that there is 'something wrong' with individuals and their lives, but that this can be put right through 'identification with higher powers'.

The New Age theodicy

Identifying and describing the New Age world-view is not an easy task. As those scholars who have studied the New Age movement have observed, this phenomenon is difficult to define and hence to delimit (Hanegraaff, 1996; Heelas, 1996; York, 1995). The New Age tends to be something that one knows when one sees it, but otherwise finds difficult to describe. However, if there is a single New Age world-view discernible in the eclectic diversity that comprises this movement, it is the belief that ultimate reality is spiritual – if not actually divine – in form; the basic assumption being that there is such a power present throughout the universe. This power is envisaged as contained in all things, inanimate as well as animate, such that there is a portion of spirit, or spirit being, present in everything that exists. Therefore it is not merely assumed that there is a spirit present in every person, or even in all plants and animals (symbolized by the elves, fairies, gnomes, fauns and so on of folklore), but also in the elements, such as earth, wind, fire and water, as well as the planets and the stars. This is generally presumed to be one single, unified, power, or force, one that does, however, manifest itself in myriad unique and differentiated forms.

Consequently, considered as a divine, rather than as merely a spiritual force, this approximates to an immanent, rather than a transcendent conception, one in which 'god' is envisaged as present 'within' all creation, indeed as equal to all creation, rather than as separate from and above a world that 'He' (or 'She') has created. In fact, of course, this single universal immanent divine presence is not usually conceived of in personal terms at all, although it is often envisaged as a form of consciousness, mind or intelligence. More usually it is thought of as a form of 'energy'. Critically, reality is therefore assumed to be fundamentally monistic rather than dualistic, or pluralistic, in nature; thus the divine and humankind are one, as too are human beings and all of nature, together with the spiritual, mental and physical, and mind and body. A central and recurring New Age theme is indeed one that stresses this fundamental holism and the basic inter-connectedness of all things.

The New Age world-view also assumes that the extent to which spirit is 'manifest' in matter can and does vary significantly, with the result that some objects and entities (including people) are judged to be more spiritual than others. There is thus a scale, or 'ladder', of spirituality upon which all things, including all people, can be placed. However, because of the basic assumption of the superiority, or primacy, of spirit, it is assumed that there must be a law that states that everything in the universe will evolve spiritually. That is to say, there is a presumption that spirit will become more and more manifest over time, with objects and entities, including people, therefore moving 'up' this ladder; a process that, spanning all eternity, presupposes re-incarnation or rebirth. It is this presumption of the reality of spiritual evolution that led originally to the proclaiming of a 'New Age', and also explains the prevalence of the belief that eventually all apparently separate entities in the universe will be united in the One that is All Spirit (York, 1995, p. 148). Given this emphasis upon the essentially spiritual nature of reality, therefore, together with the importance attached to the rejection of dualism, the basic ontological New Age position is probably best described as metaphysical monism.

The New Age world-view is one that involves a condemnation of contemporary, materialist, scientific and Christian-dominated Western civilization as inimical to true spiritual awareness, and hence as being the central obstacle to enlightenment and real spiritual progress. In this respect, the usual view of the history of 'The West' as one of 'progressive' historical development is rejected. Indeed, New Age thought frequently contains the presumption that there was a time in the distant past, often in the early pre-history of mankind, when a greater level of spirituality existed than in the recent past; an assumption that favours the strong esoteric and occult tendencies found in the movement as individuals strive to recapture this lost 'gnosis' or spiritual insight. Despite this, the New Age world-view is an optimistic one. For, as the term itself implies, it centres around the belief that the present age – the Aquarian Age – is a time of spiritual awakening and renewal; a time when, after a long period of at least stagnation if not 'backsliding', a major advance in spiritual enlightenment is occurring.

It follows that, within the New Age world-view, and in accordance with the fundamental law of spiritual evolution, it is the purpose or goal of all forms of existence to seek to give full expression to their true spirituality; that is to seek to 'manifest' this spirituality as far as they are able, and thereby, it is hoped, to move to a 'higher level' of spiritual awareness. For human beings, this translates into a process of seeking out the person they 'really are'; that is, finding that 'true inner being' or 'spiritual essence' that it is assumed exists within each and every person.

Assessing the New Age theodicy

The first thing to be said about this theodicy is that, when considered as a cognitive belief system, one that seeks to answer basic questions concerning the nature of reality, it is more easily integrated into contemporary Western culture than the traditional world-views supplied by religions such as Christianity or Judaism. Fundamentally this is because it does not rest on a basis of historical fact and hence cannot come into conflict with Western science and scholarship. At the same time, the metaphysical assumptions made concerning an unseen spiritual order are sufficiently vague in formulation, and make so much of the concept of 'energy', that they can easily be presented as not merely compatible with, but actually endorsed by, modern or 'new' science (essentially this means relativity theory and quantum physics). Secondly, one can note that the optimism, which until it was overtaken recently by postmodern angst, was such a characteristic of the Western world-view, is preserved. Once again this is achieved by abandoning the realm of history and transposing hope for the future into the spiritual or metaphysical realm. However, the real strength of the New Age theodicy lies less in its success in providing answers to the cognitive and emotive dimensions of meaning than in its ability to combine these with plausible *solutions* to the central moral aspect of 'the problem of theodicy'.

New Age theodicy and primitive religion

In one intriguing respect the New Age theodicy (and more especially the neo-Pagan variant) is reminiscent of that implicit theodicy that is found in most primitive religion. This is the suggestion that 'the life of man is not sharply separated from the life that extends throughout the universe' (Berger, 1973, p. 69). This feature derives from the notion of a universal spiritual immanence and interconnectedness that is such a feature of the New Age world-view and is expressed in more particular forms in such beliefs as astrology, neo-paganism, and shamanism. However, there is a fundamental difference between the modern New Age pantheism and that of traditional, tribal peoples. This is that in the latter case it is generally the collectivity – typically the tribe – that is seen as the basic human unit that is fundamentally interconnected to nature and the physical world (as in totemism), whereas, despite attempts within the New Age movement to stress collectivities and communities – even humanity in general – the individual tends to remain the basic unit. In this respect there is little self-transcendence through identification with the collectivity, as stressed by Peter Berger (except possibly at the invisible spiritual level). Rather, the attempt is made by individuals to engage in transcendence by identification directly with nature and the cosmos.

This feature of the New Age theodicy does mean that it is able to address the problem of natural disasters. For these can be accounted for by blaming mankind's ignorance, stupidity, and general arrogance and insensitivity in the face of nature. Thus the occurrence of floods, storms and droughts can be blamed on the ignorance and foolishness of unenlightened humans themselves, who by inducing climate change through global warming have brought these natural disasters on themselves. In a similar way human sickness and disease, such as asthma and CJD, can also be blamed on human foolishness since they are caused by the pollution of the air and by 'unnatural' interference with the food chain. In this respect the New Age theodicy, although in some ways reminiscent of traditional Christian notions of God's punishment for sin, has the advantage that responsibility is placed firmly and directly on the shoulders of mankind: thereby avoiding any suggestion of a vengeful divinity.

New Age and messianic theodicies

At first sight the New Age theodicy would appear to have little in common with traditional salvation religions such as Christianity or Islam, rejecting, as it does, the idea of transcendental monotheism, the fall, sin, heaven and hell, the opposition of spirit and flesh, together with an historically based revelation. However, there is at least one respect in which the New Age theodicy does indeed carry echoes of a messianic-millenarian form of theodicy (whether formulated in the traditional religious or the modern secular forms). This is in postulating a golden future in which all present inadequacy and suffering will be overcome, the very term 'New Age' embodying the hope, and indeed the anticipation, that such an era – marked by a generally higher level of manifest spirituality – is currently dawning.

This belief derives from the assumed superiority, or primacy, of spirit over matter, and the consequent 'law' governing the evolution or development of the universe. This law is, however, qualified in a significant fashion since humans can assist or obstruct it depending on their own degree of spiritual awareness and understanding, and hence 'right action'. This is true most obviously in relation to their own spiritual development but it is also true in relation to the spiritual development of other forms of life and matter (for example, humans can either help or obstruct the spiritual evolution of the planet). Such obstruction can indeed push spiritual development into reverse, although the ultimate triumph of this process is also usually assumed. This assumption is embodied in the widespread belief in a 'golden age' in the pre-history of mankind when a greater level of spirituality existed than at present, and from which mankind has 'fallen' into a lesser state of spirituality. Like the traditional messianic models, therefore, the New Age theodicy tends to assume a former 'Eden' as well as a future 'Kingdom of God on Earth', while there is also a similar ambiguity over the extent to which the coming of the promised golden age is actually dependent on human action.

Progressivist theodicies

Unlike progressivist secular theodicies such as Communism or Socialism, the New Age theodicy does not appear to address the critical issues of social injustice and the legitimacy of the social order. Indeed, it appears to endorse a remarkably individualist, a-social ethic. None the less it has been suggested that the New Age world-view can (on occasion) serve to legitimate modern capitalism (Heelas, 1991; 1994). Certainly it could be said that the considerable emphasis placed on the ethic of individual responsibility, in conjunction with the pursuit of secular this-worldly goals such as wealth and success, suggests that this philosophy can indeed serve to justify both existing inequalities and capitalism in general: a conclusion that seems to be supported by the enthusiasm with which the corporate sector has taken up New Age ideas and techniques of self-development.

At the same time the New Age movement has its origins in the counterculture of the 1960s, and still today contains echoes – in the New Age travellers, for example, or the simple living movement (Elgin, 1981; Shi, 1985; 1986) – of this move to reject modernity and consumerism. In this respect, the New Age theodicy can be seen to possess that vital ingredient which is needed if it is to become truly successful and widely adopted: the ability to be adapted to serve both legitimatory and compensatory functions.

An even more obvious point of comparison with modern progressivist theodicies is that both presume both the reality and the desirability of progress, even if this is conceived of in more 'spiritual' terms in the New Age world-view than is true of modern collectivist theodicies. However, unlike these 'scientistic' philosophies, in the New Age context this emphasis on personal progress and achievement – usually defined in terms of 'fulfilment' – can be seen as pushing the New Age theodicy in the direction of providing pragmatic guidance, and hence towards an emphasis on 'magic' at the expense of a fully rationalized system of meaning.

New Age and mysticism

In so far as processes of rationalization are at work within this theodicy, one obvious issue concerns the status of mysticism. Given that the New Age perspective emphasizes the ubiquity of the spiritual and its controlling function within all life – indeed within the universe in general – it follows that one of the key logical issues subject to rationalization within this world-view is likely to be whether the apparent world is real or simply an illusion. Once the assumption is made that pure spirit can exist, it is hard to escape the conclusion that it is a higher form of reality, a conclusion that in turn implies that matter is in some sense less real, if not actually unreal. On the other hand, to assume that spirit and matter are equally real aspects of one overall reality is to imply a denial of the superior role accorded to spirit as well as the suggestion that spirit can exist independently of matter.

However, if spirit cannot exist independently of matter, problems arise in explaining the fundamental postulated interconnectedness of everything, both in space and over time. Consequently, grappling with this problem tends to push a New Age world-view in the direction of full-blown mysticism. One factor that is inclined to keep this tendency in check is the central focus accorded to the self, together with the above-noted stress on this-worldly ends. Consequently, the emphasis tends to be on becoming a god – and hence enjoying the pleasures that life can offer – rather than on losing one's identity within God. At the same time, there is a tendency within the New Age paradigm to draw upon the new physics, and by identifying spirit with energy to succeed in escaping from the ontological problem by claiming that science itself has demonstrated that matter is not in fact 'real' (Davies and Gribbin, 1992).

New Age and karma-samsara

The theodicy with which the New Age perspective most obviously invites comparison is the classic karma-samsara teaching that underpins Hinduism (and in somewhat different fashion, Buddhism), the two endorsing the notion of both divine immanence and rebirth, if not of reincarnation. However, there is a critical feature that separates the manner in which reincarnation is treated in the two theodicies.

Thus in the New Age theodicy it is the individual's experiences in a previous existence (or existences), rather than his or her actions, which are considered crucial in determining the nature of the person's present life or character. In this critical respect it cannot be said that the individual's actions in a previous life justify his or her fate in this one. On the contrary, since an individual cannot really be held responsible for experiences in the same way as for actions, past lives are invoked to excuse rather than justify present failure or inadequacy. In this respect reference to past lives is really no more than an extension of the therapeutic outlook that is such a dominant feature of the New Age perspective in general, with past-life therapy being a logical, if metaphysical, next step backwards from primal therapy. The assumption, as in most therapy, is that the 'recovery' of traumatic events that occurred in previous existences will serve to eliminate or nullify their unfortunate effects in the present (there appears to be little interest in establishing how good experiences in previous lives account for happiness and success in the present). This perspective thus enables failure, or 'bad' experiences, in the present to be explained away in terms of previous life events that are, by definition, not the responsibility of the person concerned.

However, it should be noted that in some versions of the New Age philosophy such experiences are deemed to have been 'chosen' by the individual (or the individual's divine self) in order to facilitate a 'learning process'. In this respect there could not possibly be a starker contrast with the original Hindu doctrine of karma. The idea that one can, in effect, travel back in time and correct the original event or events that determine one's current spiritual state being directly contrary to the notion of an inescapable fate. Of course, the most basic difference, from the perspective of the overall cosmic viewpoint adopted in the two theodicies, is that the ultimate aim in the Hindu scheme is to escape from the cycle of death and rebirth altogether, while in the New Age scheme there appears to be a greater concern with continuing the cycle indefinitely, and thereby enjoying the pleasures that an endless series of lives can bring.

The individual, time and history

To what extent, then, can the New Age theodicy be said to involve the individual in a fundamental process of self-transcendence? One that, as Peter Berger suggests, embodies a fundamental attitude of masochism in the sense of the paradox that meaning is found in self-annihilation? On the face it, the very opposite would appear to be the case, as the self is the very centre and hub of the New Age world-view. Indeed, what the central emphasis on rebirth, or reincarnation, achieves is to render both history and community somewhat irrelevant. The idea of historical progress necessarily becomes meaningless, as the concept of a purely spiritual form of progress occurring in a cosmic dimension takes its place. This, in turn, leads to a disregard for institutions and a disinterest in any conventional form of politics. What is more, the stress on an immortal self that survives innumerable actual lives means that the individual's cosmic destiny no longer has any connection, let alone any continuity, with real previous generations. Consequently, the bond between an individual and his or her historic human community is completely severed, and with it any possibility of believing that one can attain a form of immortality through generational continuity.

Hence it would seem that this theodicy, unlike those described by Berger (or indeed Weber), would not appear to be based in either history or society. It is not, in the strict sense, a social theodicy, that is one that links individuals and generations in common rituals or through common institutions. This is an acutely individualistic theodicy, one that in linking the self directly with the cosmos, tends to bypass both society and history. Hence it seems unlikely that a New Ager could really be said to ' "lose himself" in the meaning-giving nomos of society' as Berger (1973, p. 63) puts it, since the meaning-giving system in question, although stemming from the society's culture, is essentially one of his own making; in effect, a personal myth. Self-transcendence is most certainly involved, but through a scheme that links directly with a spiritual universe. However, the individual does not so much 'lose' himself or herself in this larger system of meaning, as become inflated by it, since in general the cosmic scenario is employed purely as a backcloth or setting for the personal drama of the self. Consequently, it could be said that the basic psycho-pathological disposition underlying the New Age theodicy is less masochism than theomania.

Notes

1   Indeed Turner (1981) goes further than this, for, after observing that Marianne Weber's testimony suggests that Weber himself identified closely with certain Old Testament prophets, Turner comments that 'The problem of theodicy is not, therefore, merely a technical problem in Weber's sociology of religion, but a major component of his metasociological and personal outlook on society, which is dominated by the demon of godless rationality' (p. 166).
2   William James, cited by Schneider and Dornbusch (1958, p. 48).
3   Weber was acquainted with James's work and cites *The Varieties of Religious Experience (1960)* in a footnote in *The Protestant Ethic and the Spirit of Capitalism* (1985). However, as one might expect, he takes issue with James over the relative importance of religious ideas compared with that of religious experience.

Part III
Secularization and Sacralization

6 The curious case of the unnecessary recantation: Berger and secularization

Steve Bruce

Introduction

Until the 1980s, most social scientists supposed that the modern world was becoming increasingly Godless. Peter Berger was influential in developing the secularization thesis (though 'paradigm' might better describe what is a complex and at times only loosely articulated body of descriptions and explanations). He is also the most eminent of those who now challenge the thesis. In 1974 he began to question his own conclusions: 'In the last few years I have come to believe that many observers of the religious scene (I among them) have over-estimated both the degree and irreversibility of secularization' (1974b, p. 16). Two decades later his reservations had hardened into repudiation: 'The big mistake, which I shared with everyone who worked in this area in the 1950s and '60s, was to believe that modernity necessarily leads to a decline in religion' (1998, p. 782).

Whether trying to save an intellectual hero from himself is treacherous, I am not sure. But it is certainly arrogant. I wish to argue, despite what Berger now says, that his original contributions to the secularization approach remain valid, that he is confessing to sins he did not commit, and that his arguments against his own views are unpersuasive.

Berger's contributions to secularization

Berger's early work already contains two very different voices: the sociologist and the Lutheran. It could well be that his changing assessment of secularization is a product of the changing balance within his own character of the social scientist and the Christian. However, why someone believes something and whether it is true are two separate questions. I will confine myself to assessing the case he now makes against secularization and say no more about why he might now wish to find persuasive what did not convince him forty years ago.

Berger made two important contributions to the secularization approach. First, he strengthened Max Weber's stress on the increased rationalization of the world. Berger's early essay (1963c) on the Israelite prophets was important in locating the seeds of rationality in the monotheism of the Old Testament, thereby contributing to the argument of Weber, Ernst Troeltsch, Robert Merton, and David Martin that Judaism, Christianity, and Protestantism inadvertently and ironically incubated and nurtured the seeds of their own decline. By simplifying the supernatural, by permitting what pleased God to become codified, routinized and rationalized, and by making the operations of the divine predictable, this strand permitted the growth of science and technology and aided the rise of capitalism. The connections are complicated but we can find in Berger's early work the argument that one type of religion was centrally implicated in modernization and helped to create the conditions in which large numbers of people could come to live without much or any religion.

Berger's other contribution came as part of promoting the phenomenology of Alfred Schutz. In particular, he drew our attention to the impact of the 'pluralization of life-worlds' on the 'plausibility' of religious belief-systems:

> Our situation is characterized by a market of world views, simultaneously in competition with each other. In this situation the maintenance of certitudes that go much beyond the empirical necessities of the society and the individual to function is very difficult indeed. Inasmuch as religion essentially rests upon supernatural certitudes, the pluralistic situation is a secularizing one and, ipso facto, plunges religion into a crisis of credibility.
>
> (1979b, p. 213)

Although Berger spends most of his time on the social-psychological consequences of cultural diversity, he is fully aware of the political and social consequences. If it has to encompass diversity, the modernizing state – unless it is prepared to accept high levels of social conflict (and none were) – has to become increasingly religiously neutral. The public square is gradually evacuated. This not only removes formal state support for a particular religion. More importantly, and this is where Berger's focus on 'taken-for grantedness' is vital, it removes a whole range of opportunities for the religious tradition to be reinforced in day-to-day interaction. Where a community shares a common religion, big events such as births, deaths and marriages can be glossed by the church and thereby reinforce its beliefs. The passing of the seasons can be similarly treated. And everyday conversation can reinforce the shared beliefs as people gloss even mundane matters such as the weather in religious terms. The fragmentation of the religious culture into a range of competing alternatives drastically curtails the social reinforcement of belief.

Recantation

Since 1974 Berger has offered a number of reasons for doubting his initial confidence that modernity undermined religion. Before considering them, we might note that his recent writings on religion take the form of lectures or articles written for popular journals (a lot of them religious). Hence his comments are brief, popular in style, and lack the detailed qualifications that he would doubtless have added had he been writing a book-length treatment or an academic journal article. It may well be that his views have been revised less than would appear from one or two brief statements.

With varying degrees of commitment to them, Berger has offered the following as reasons to revise his confidence in the secularization thesis: (a) the growth of conservative and evangelical churches in the United States; (b) the decline of liberal churches; (c) the persistence of interest in religion (if not church-going) in other Western societies; and (d) the vitality of religion in other parts of the world.

Religious revival in the United States

Berger has made far less of this than others and he rightly expresses some doubt about the extent of evangelical growth in the United States. But he none the less refers to it in the context of discussing liberal failure (of which more below). I am even less persuaded by the claims for revival in the heartland of modernity. Much church growth has been the result not of increased popularity but of population increase and increased longevity.

There is also a crucial issue of time-frames. I will return to this, but the crucial test for any theory of social change is not what happens in a range of societies in the same year but what happens when the changes that purportedly cause secularization occur. Thus if we believe that urbanization is a key consideration (either as an autonomous cause or as a surrogate for some more nebulous change with which it coincides), we should compare levels of religious vitality in societies A and B when they are equally urban. The United States did not reach until the 1920s the degree of urbanization of Britain in the 1850s. I do not want to pursue the point here, but there is a case to be made that because the onset of modernization was much later in the United States and in some European countries, its impact will be felt proportionately later. There is certainly considerable evidence that church membership and attendance is now declining in the United States (Hadaway, Marler and Chaves, 1993).

Equally importantly, as Wilson (1968) argued thirty years ago, much of American religion has become what, for the sake of brevity, we might call 'secular'. From the fundamentalist breakaway until the 1970s, American evangelicals prided themselves on having avoided the 'easy-believism', secularity, and self-interest of Norman Vincent Peale's 'power of positive thinking'. But many evangelicals now embrace the very liberal and permissive lifestyle their parents and grandparents so vehemently opposed. Asceticism is largely dead and as evangelicals have become more like everyone else in behaviour, so they have lost ideological distinctiveness. Sacrifice has gone. Heaven remains but hell is barely mentioned. Believers now feel free to select. Most significantly, there is a clear change in attitudes to the reach of religion. James Davidson Hunter's (1987) work on young evangelicals in the early 1980s shows that many accepted the requirements of the gospel for themselves but were no longer sure that they were binding on others. Unless this germ of relativism is killed off, it is hard to see what will prevent the conservative wing of American Protestantism following the mainstream churches. To his credit, Berger refers to Hunter's work and thus uses the apparent strength of American religion in a much more nuanced way than does, for example, Jeffrey Hadden (1987).

Rather than cite a wide range of sources for the various elements of this description, I will offer a general observation of Wade Clark Roof's as support for the general assertion that the general direction of change in American religion is that predicted by Berger: 'the religious stance today is more internal than external, more individual than institutional, more experiential than cerebral, more private than public' (Roof, 1996, p. 153).

Liberal failure

As well as offering conservative 'growth' as evidence of the general (and unexpected) vitality of religion, Berger has presented liberal decline as evidence that the secularization thesis is mistaken. 'If we really lived in a highly secularised world, then religious institutions could be expected to survive to the degree that they manage to adapt to secularism' (1997b, p. 33). This is a curious argument because it is not at all clear why adapting to secularism should mean imitating it and there is nothing about Berger's original arguments for secularization that requires such a link. Although committed to the same core ideas as Berger, I have been arguing since 1982 that liberal religion has been precarious because the tolerance and individualism at the heart of its ideology undermined the cohesion that is required for a large variety of organizational tasks that are vital to the survival of any shared belief system (Bruce, 1982, 1999). Some aspects of liberal religion (such as the unfortunate fondness for claiming aspects of secular culture as being more Christian than Christian ideas) are conscious attempts to regain relevance by aping the secular world and are doomed to failure. But the roots of its problems are not specific innovations; it is the diffuseness that permits such innovations and diffuseness is a result of secularization, not a deliberate attempt to 'adapt' to it.

Religion in 'secular' Europe

Berger is much impressed by Grace Davie's (1994) thesis that the decline in participation in religious institutions should not be taken as a decline in religious interest *per se*. He summarizes her work thus:

> What she found is that, despite the dramatic decline in church participation and expressed orthodox beliefs, a lively religious scene exists. Much of it is very loosely organized (for instance, in private gatherings of people) and has odd do-it-yourself characteristics ... the presence of these phenomena casts doubt on any flat assertion to the effect that Western Europe is secular territory.
>
> (1998, p. 796)

That depends. First, I am less impressed by the claims for 'private gatherings' than is Berger. Attitudinal survey data show a steady fall in orthodox Christian beliefs and even for such nebulous claims as a self-description as 'religious' (Gill, Hadaway and Marler, 1998). Second, the numbers involved in such organized religious innovations as there have been (the rise of the 'new churches', for example) are of a different order of magnitude than the losses to the mainstream churches: in thousands rather than in the millions that would be required to offset the losses. Third, for reasons I will pursue below, there are very good grounds for supposing that the 'odd do-it-yourself characteristics' will make it hard for such innovations to be sustained, reproduced or transmitted.

Religion in the Second and Third Worlds

Berger would probably not dissent much from the above; he makes relatively little of signs of religious resurgence in western Europe. What most causes him to doubt the inevitability of secularization is the evidence that 'Most of the world today is as religious as ever it was, and in a good many locales, more religious than ever' (1998, p. 782). Although I am a committed proponent of the secularization thesis, I would have no trouble at all in endorsing the first half of that sentence. Indeed I have long argued that religion, when combined with ethnicity, remains a far more potent force than social class. One only has to consider the wars in the former Yugoslavia, Afghanistan or the Caucasus, or the rise of Islamic fundamentalism to recognize that religion is very important. Without considering the religious element, we cannot explain why some of the former Warsaw Pact countries better resisted Soviet communism than others (Bruce, 1999). However, I have some difficulty with the second half of Berger's proposition. We need to be very careful in how we describe religious change. In many parts of Latin America, a taken-for-granted Catholic culture, heavily informed by pre-Christian spirit cults, has been replaced by an increasingly secular society with very large numbers of highly committed Protestant Christians. It would seem a particularly Protestant view to describe the latter as more religious than the former. While we would describe the spread of Orthodoxy to former Russian Communist Party cadres as 'more religion', would we use the same description for an increase in frequency of church attendance by elderly peasants who had never given up their faith? I can think of many places where religious people are 'reforming', and I can think of places where the end of secularist repression has led to more and more open religious observance. But I cannot think of any major reversals in fairly thoroughly secular settings. There is no religious resurgence in Germany, Britain, the Netherlands or Denmark.

But, more importantly, I cannot understand why Berger thinks that religious vitality in the Third World has any bearing on his work on secularization. To return to the point introduced above, the secularization thesis is not a claim that the passage of time undermines religion. Rather, it is a number of related claims about the impact of certain social changes in certain circumstances. Obviously the claim that pluralism requires the state to become increasingly neutral on matters of faith refers only to democracies (or at least to polities informed by the general principle that all people are much-of-a-muchness) and to a very limited range of autocracies that have good reason to wish to avoid religious and ethnic conflict. Otherwise one gets the more common reaction to diversity, which is to murder or expel the deviants. Berger (1969c) knows this: he offers the post-Reformation wars of religion as an example of the extermination response and the 'territorial formula' of the Treaty of Westphalia that ended those wars as an example of the segregation response (pp. 48–9). Creating a climate in which alternatives can peacefully co-exist and compete on equal terms is just one of the possible responses, and it is typical only of modern liberal democracies. Berger has written about the circumstances under which he expects one aspect of modernization to weaken religion; it is hard to see why, thirty years later, he presents as evidence against his original arguments the fate of religion in quite different circumstances.

Similarly, the claim that pluralism undermines the certainty with which any group can hold its beliefs implies a number of things about the *source* of pluralism. Berger offers many observations about the differential plausibility of different sources of knowledge and information. Although I cannot recall one place where he spells this out, I have always assumed that the cognitive threat of pluralism varies in ways that can at least partly be explained by Bergeresque sociological observations about power, plausibility and authority. Berger and Luckmann (1966c) certainly provide the framework for elaborating the challenges of different sources of pluralism in their work on 'machineries of universe-maintenance' (pp. 122–46). While they are not talking specifically about religion, the following comment about the nihilation of deviant views is apposite: 'The threat to the social definitions of reality is neutralized by assigning an inferior ontological status, and thereby a not-to-be-taken seriously cognitive status, to all definitions existing outside the symbolic universe' (1966c, p. 133). When Irish Catholics migrated to Scotland in large numbers in the late nineteenth century, Scots Presbyterians did not immediately lose confidence in their own world-view. Instead, they dismissed the religion of the Irish by creating invidious stereotypes of its carriers: they portrayed the Irish as drunken, illiterate, intemperate, compliant, slothful layabouts.

Berger and Luckmann (1966c) add that nihilation 'involves the more ambitious attempt to account for all deviant definitions of reality in terms of concepts belonging to one's own universe' (p. 133). Again Scottish Presbyterians can provide a fine illustration of people explaining the errors of others in a way that bolstered their own beliefs. They dealt with the fact that, taken globally, Presbyterians were a very small minority by arguing (a) that societies differed in their intellectual maturity and (b) that God in his kindness had revealed himself to various societies in a form which, with their limited intellects, they could comprehend. So child-like Hottentots were animists. God had shown himself to the Arabs, who were more advanced, as Allah. The southern Europeans, who were more advanced yet, had been gifted with Catholic Christianity. And God had shown himself in his full and complete revelation to the most advanced people: Scottish Presbyterians. Muslims perform a similar trick with their view that Islam is the final revelation that encompasses and supersedes the previously flawed versions of Judaism and Christianity.

The early historians who traced their own people back to Adam knew that other peoples claimed similar origins. They also knew that non-Christian civilizations had Adam-like Creation myths and Flood stories. Rather than seeing similar alternatives as casting doubt on the unique truthfulness of their particular version, they took the popularity of such stories as proof that something like them must be true, and then asserted that their version was indeed the true undistorted one. Rather than see the Hindu trinity of Brahma, Vishnu and Shiva as evidence that trinity stories were a commonplace best explained by similarities of human imagination, Christians confronting Hinduism saw it as proof that man had a 'God-given faculty for reason [that] inclined him towards the core tenets of Christian belief [which were] ... of course, buried in heathen culture cladding' (Kidd, 1999, p. 42).

While it is interesting to explore nihilation strategies, they do not explain their own success. It remains a sociological issue why they work at some times and not at others. It would be a mammoth task to pursue this question, and I will make only a few brief suggestions here. One point that is well elaborated in more abstract terms by Berger and Luckmann is that it is much easier to dismiss the culture of foreigners than to dismiss the religious diversity that results from fission within one's own religious tradition. The ignorance of the backward can be tolerated and forgiven. The defiance or deviancy of people 'like us' cannot as readily be neutralized.

A second point is that wealth (or other sources of high status) confers a degree of plausibility on any deviant minority. Some local magnates victimized George Fox, the Quaker founder, but many others took him into their homes and listened to him politely because he was a gentleman. As the Quakers and Methodists rose in social status, so the objections to them fell away. Partly this is a matter of power. The wealthy man has greater resources to sustain or promote his protest. Catholicism survived in parts of the north-east of Scotland because a number of powerful landed figures refused to join the Reformation and were able to protect their servants. But it is also a matter of persuasiveness; many of the invidious stereotypes used to blacken Irish labourers could not be deployed for the Quaker brewer and the Methodist manufacturer. But then wealth and high status are not always a protection; nor do they guarantee that the views of the carriers will be sympathetically heard.

But this sort of detail is secondary to the general point: Berger himself knows that the consequences of various elements of modernization differ according to circumstances. No one who understands the work of Berger (or Weber, Troeltsch, Wilson or Martin) would regard the explanation given there of what has happened in the past of some societies as being a template for the future of very different ones. In the same way that we must regard Weber's Protestant Ethic thesis as being historically specific, so we must regard the secularization thesis as being an account of the past of western Europe (and its settler society offshoots) that is only generalizable to other settings *to the extent that the specific elements are reproduced in those settings*. As Iran is unlike Essex in most regards, I see no reason why the secularization thesis should fall because the religious evolution of these places has differed.

That being said, there is one element of Berger's secularization work that is perhaps vulnerable to the criticisms of the mature Berger. And that is his exploration of the connections between technology and secularization. It has long been a staple of the secularization approach that technology undermines religion because it gives better solutions to specific problems and thus reduces the occasions for a recourse to religious explanations and offices. It also gives us an increased sense of mastery over our own affairs. To those observations about the effects of the *content* of technological advance, Berger, in association with Brigitte Berger and Hansfried Kellner (1974), added an interesting claim about the subtle psychological effects of the method of technology. Technological production assumes that every object can be reduced to a series of infinitely replaceable components: the switch for any 1996 Dimplex Model 3 radiator will fit any 1996 Dimplex Model 3 radiator. Similarly, all actions can be broken down to their essential components and endlessly repeated, each time with the same effect. Technology also supposes constant change and regular reflexive monitoring. If production processes can be improved, then they are improved. Nothing is sacred; nothing is unique. People who use modern technology cannot help but be influenced by the assumption of instrumental rationality.

This does seem to be a universal and predictive claim. If Berger, Berger and Kellner are right, as technological work spreads around the globe so it should create a more secular climate. If the nations of the Middle or Far East are able to adopt modern technology without there being some corresponding decline in religious vitality or change in the religious climate, then this specific element of the secularization approach fails, or, at the very least, requires substantial embellishment. Although the prediction may not have been met in every circumstance, it does seem to have been borne out in the general patterns identified by Ronald Inglehardt (1990; 1997). In almost every society for which data are available, economic growth and industrialization have been accompanied by a decline in commitment to the traditional religion.

If the expectation has not been met in every setting, this may mean not that the general expectation is false but that the effects of one social force are offset by another. It may well be that Berger is right about technological consciousness and hence that scientists and technicians and industrial workers in Iran, for example, were more likely to be subtly secular than village dwellers and agricultural workers. There is some evidence for such a conclusion. But such a difference may well have been overridden by the more powerful and immediate effects of the social unrest and cultural responses that the Shah's rule produced in Iran. The failure of the Shah's strategy to promote economic development by imitating the science and culture of the West combined with his repressive response to dissent to create a powerful resentment among members of the very class that was furthest from traditional Islam. Their faith might have been weakened by technological consciousness. But in their particular situation they were also alienated from what was taken to be the Western model of development by specific attacks on them as the potential carriers of democracy and by the failure of the economic reforms to deliver results. Some at least of that class were then recruited to the radical movement and to the Islamic branch of that movement. All this tells us is that the real world is far more complicated than our models; that sociology cannot be conducted without economics, political science, geography and history.

In summary, the evidence cited by Berger does not lead me to join him in his recantation. First, I do not find the data which he offers as persuasive or compelling as he does. Second, I do not share his view of the status of the secularization approach. I have always thought that it was an historical explanation of specific changes in the religious climate of particular societies. It only has implications for other societies to the extent that the causes implicated in the original basis for the thesis are repeated elsewhere.

Theoretical reservations

In addition to the above evidence-driven doubts, Berger also offers theoretical reasons for doubting his earlier writings, which were mostly of a functionalist nature. Talking of anomie, he wrote:

> Individuals can live in such a condition, unhappy though it is, for a long time. Societies probably cannot (though the phrase 'a long time' means something different for a society and an individual). ... societies afflicted with widespread anomie have either perished or have regenerated themselves through a renascence of their fundamental values. For reasons that are probably rooted in the constitution of man, such renascences have usually had a powerful religious dimension.
>
> (1979b, p. 235)

He makes the same point in condemning alternative sources of meaning:

> I am impressed by the intrinsic inability of secularized world views to answer the deeper questions of the human condition, questions of whence, whether, and why. These seem to be ineradicable and they are answered only in the most banal ways by the ersatz religions of secularism.
>
> (1974b, p. 15)

We may accept that any major pulling together of very large numbers of people is likely to have a religious ideological base. We may accept that any grand cultural solution to the problem of anomie will be religious. However, I am not persuaded that 'needs' must always be met. People need food but die of starvation. We may need cultural consensus and fail to achieve it. Indeed Berger's own observations about the deleterious effects of pluralization would suggest that we can yearn all we like but still be unable to reverse the changes that undermine the plausibility of religious belief systems. When applied to abstractions such as social systems, the functionalist language of needs is even more unconvincing. Functionalist biology works because we know what counts as liver failure: the person turns yellow and dies. System failure allows us to work back to the 'needs' of the organism. It is difficult to reason in the same way from societies. Although Berger uses the term 'perish', this is metaphorical. Societies constantly change. Some changes are more dramatic than others but at what point do we pronounce one incarnation 'dead' and christen the new one? If we cannot translate the metaphor into a technically viable concept, then the functionalist claims become untestable.

Although it does not necessarily lead to the conclusion that severe social problems will inevitably call forth a religious revival, there is a more moderate form of the functionalist claim that is implied in the grander version. We could argue (and hope to demonstrate) that religious societies are 'healthier' than non-religious ones. There is a considerable empirical literature that tries to test such claims and the best that can be said at present is that the case is not proven. It would certainly be hard to assert that the United States, with its higher rates of church adherence, shows fewer marks of social disorganization or lower indices of deviance than the United Kingdom or the Netherlands or Sweden. But, even if there were bodies of convincing evidence that getting right with Jesus would make us as individuals happier and make our societies more pleasant, it does not follow that a religious revival will occur. The obstacles to such a response are obvious. Berger, like the rest of us, recognizes that one of the master features of modern societies is individual autonomy. This could be spelt out in more detail, but I am sure few will dissent from the view that modern societies are unusual not only in the degree of freedom of action they permit their citizens in private, but also in the extent to which they permit freedom of thought.

We long ago accepted that in matters of art and music appreciation, for example, authoritative judgements were impossible (and offensive because they are 'undemocratic'). 'I may not know much about art but I know what I like' used to be a sentiment imputed by the *cognoscenti* to the lower middle and working classes as an insult. Now it is a basic operating procedure. Even in fields of knowledge such as science and medicine, where most thoughtful people would insist that there is truth and there is falsehood, we are reluctant to insist that this or that view is just plain stupid. In matters of religion, personal preference has long dominated the mainstream churches and, as I have suggested above, is now becoming common even in churches that fifty years ago prided themselves on requiring subscription to an orthodoxy. And it is even more the case for those outside and on the fringes of the main religious traditions. A respondent in a study of New Age religion put it bluntly when he said: 'I have a problem with a lot of mainstream religion, because they're fucking with other people's business' (Bloch, 1998, p. 295). Although no wise man says 'never', it is remarkably difficult to see what circumstances will causes Westerners to give up their freedom to differ or agree to narrow the range of areas in which differences of taste are legitimate. Or to put it more practically, politicians and lay people are keen to insist that social evils be eradicated by everyone else getting back to *their* basics; we hear very few voices willing to give up their preferences in order to support someone else's programme. To return to Berger, even if he is right to identify some social problems that could be resolved with a religious renascence, the pluralism which he did so much to bring to our attention prevents the mobilization of a common response to those problems.

The future of liberal religion

I have taken Berger's reservations about the secularization thesis and his revisions at their strongest. Yet it is clear that Berger remains committed to one of his original observations: the role that pluralism plays in undermining certainty. For example, in 1998, he wrote: 'whether we like it or not, if we are honest, religion for us cannot be based on knowledge, only on belief. The question is how we cope with this situation. Can we live with it?' (p. 782).

The crux of the matter can be put either in terms of belief systems or in terms of forms of association. This simplifies, but we can describe some belief systems as 'strong' and others as 'weak' or 'diffuse'. I should stress (because it is misunderstood) that this is a sociological consideration and involves no suggestion that strong beliefs are better than weak ones or that 'true religion' must be 'strong'. The strong–weak characterization was popularized by Dean Kelley in his explanation of *Why the Conservative Churches are Growing* (1972). In Hoge's (1979) summary:

> Strong churches are characterized by a demand for high commitment from their members. They exact discipline over both beliefs and life-style. They have missionary zeal with an eagerness to tell the good news to all persons. They are absolutistic about beliefs. Their beliefs are a total closed system, sufficient for all purposes, needing no revision and permitting none. They require conformity in life-style, often involving certain avoidances of non-members or use of distinctive visible marks or uniforms.
>
> (p. 179)

The behavioural characteristics in the first four sentences and the last sentence follow from the characteristics of the beliefs given in the fifth sentence. In order to be strict and maintain zeal, believers must view their beliefs as authoritative. If one permits that there are a variety of sources of truth and a variety of equally legitimate sources of interpretation, then one inevitably has diversity and a tolerant attitude to those who differ.

Allowing for some slippage, we can describe conservative Catholicism and evangelical or fundamentalist Protestantism as 'strong' and the liberal variants of Christianity as 'weak'. Elsewhere I have explored the problems of strong religion (Bruce, 1999), and will only say here that the sacrifices it requires (primarily of social isolation and the forgoing of individual liberty) seem willingly made by large numbers only in circumstances that are relatively rare in the West: for example, where the believers are geographically isolated or otherwise already excluded from the social mainstream. But we can let that pass because what is at issue in Berger's revision is the future of liberal religion. He believes that it is possible for people to sustain a loose and amorphous faith that accepts uncertainty. I disagree.

My empirical grounds for disagreeing are simply that secularization seems to have had the greatest impact, as Berger notes, on religions that are denominational rather than sectarian. In the United Kingdom, for example, the rare incidents of net growth or stability are to be found among the sects; the mainstream churches have been declining for fifty years and continue to do so. In 1979, about 12 per cent of the English attended church. In 1989 the figure was 10 per cent. In 1999, it was just under 8 per cent (Brierley, 1999).

My theoretical grounds are extensive (see Bruce, 1999). But the basic disagreements can be readily conveyed. First, I believe Berger exaggerates the stability of liberal Christianity because he fails to appreciate the extent to which its cohesion is an historical contingency. The essential diffuseness of liberal religion is a constant: as soon as one permits that the truth can take a variety of forms, the epistemological basis for discipline is removed and proliferation of permissible interpretations is possible. However, the degree of cohesion in liberal religion is variable, and currently mainstream churches retain some coherence from their more orthodox past. All the major denominations began life as churches or sects. This is often repeated in the biographies of individuals. Most of those responsible for the development of liberal Protestantism, either as an intellectual force or in its organizational form in the ecumenical movement, were raised in conservative homes. They found it possible to be undogmatic about their faith because they had been thoroughly socialized in the dogmas. The problem is that this cultural capital, like the invested financial capital that provides a very large part of the funds for the liberal denominations, is a wasting asset. With each generation that passes, commitment to the core beliefs (and even knowledge of them) becomes weaker and weaker.

A further sense in which denominational Christianity is precarious is that much of its appeal rested on a contrast with sectarian Christianity. Many liberals of Berger's generation were attracted to their present faith because it was a liberation from the stifling orthodoxies of their upbringing. So long as sectarian religion was popular the liberal alternative had a pool from which it could recruit. An open prison seems like a welcome release to someone who transfers from a high security prison. But for the ever-increasing number of people who have not been socialized in a sectarian version of the Christian faith, the liberal version has very little appeal.

Finally, I would like to mention reproduction. Crucial to the fate of liberal, diffuse, denominational religion is success in transmitting it to the next generation. Let us put the problem in a contrast of two imaginary couples. The liberal Protestant, because he does not have a hard line between the saved and the unregenerate, marries a non-practising Jew. He continues in his faith but what does that couple transmit to its children? How can they insist that the children go regularly to Sunday school, read their Bibles every night, and have family prayers before meals? If their children develop any interest in religion at all, it is likely to be the autonomous open seeking perspective of those who end up creating their own mixture from a wide variety of religious traditions. Now imagine an evangelical Baptist. He spends a lot of time in church-related activities and marries another evangelical Baptist. They send their children to an independent Christian school, have family prayers and Bible studies, and intensively socialize their children in their faith. Of three children one may fall away, but there is a good chance that at least one of the other two will continue in that faith.

This, then, is the core of my disagreement with Berger's view of liberal religion. He believes that its appeal will allow it to survive the organizational problems inherent in having a diffuse belief-system. I think not. If there is no reversal in membership trends that have been stable for fifty years, British Methodism will disappear entirely around 2030. If we wish to identify a model in our days of what religion beyond the sects will look like in fifty years' time, we should look not at the liberal Christian denominations, which are doomed, but at the world of New Age spirituality: a world in which individuals select from a global cafeteria ideas, rituals and therapies that appeal to them. Precisely because they are so thoroughly individualized, such beliefs will have very little impact even on those who carry them – let alone on their wider societies.

Conclusion

Had I thought that Berger was offering some universal template for social evolution, I would never have been attracted by his arguments. Had I thought that he was arguing that secularization was inevitable, I would not have become a disciple. I take the early Berger to be arguing the following: insofar as anything in this life is certain, it is that secularization of a certain type and extent is *irreversible* because the conditions required to construct, sustain, and reproduce across generations a shared supernatural world-view are destroyed by individualism and pluralism. I see nothing in the First World to make me believe that he needs to recant. Far from getting them wrong, the changes since 1960 have been those Berger predicted: increased individual autonomy; increased compartmentalization, decline of authority, and declining indices of involvement. Whether the societies of the Second and Third Worlds will evolve in the same direction is a fascinating question. Inglehart's massive cross-national surveys (1990; 1997) suggest a strong and almost universal connection between increasing prosperity and a decline in commitment to religious orthodoxies. But in any case what happens in Africa or Asia, though it is important for illuminating the conditions for secularization, does not bear critically on the value of the secularization thesis for explaining what happened in the rise of the first generation of modern industrial societies.

7 The persistence of institutional religion in modern Europe

Grace Davie

Introduction

The idea of European exceptionalism is increasingly, if not universally, accepted by scholars interested in the sociology of religion in the modern world. European patterns of religion are no longer seen as a global prototype, but constitute an unusual case in a world in which vibrant religiosity becomes the norm. Peter Berger is a notable exponent of this idea (Berger, 1992; 1998; 1999). It follows that explanations for European patterns of religion must lie in Europeanness rather than in the connections between religion and modernity *per se*, an argument that I have elaborated in some detail in Davie (2000a) and summarized in Davie (2000b). There is no need to repeat these arguments over again here.

A number of refinements have appeared with respect to the notion of 'European exceptionalism'. Berger (1998), for example, accepts that the institutional churches are very much weaker in Europe than in the United States, but that a diffuse and for the most part a nominally Christian form of religiousness continues to exist – hinting that Europeans may not be quite as irreligious as they seem at first glance. A second point follows on: 'weak' forms of institutional religion are not synonymous with no institutional religion at all. Indeed, religious institutions continue to exist all over Europe, but in forms that are increasingly voluntaristic (as they are in the United States) – with all the advantages and disadvantages that this term implies (Berger, 1998).

In this chapter I will argue that the role of the churches in western Europe has, in fact, been written off far too soon. The material will be approached in two ways. First, the institutional churches will be firmly located in the voluntary sector of modern European societies, in which they do as well as many of their secular counterparts. (The argument will be supported by a wide range of empirical evidence.) In order to understand the role of the churches fully, however, a second factor needs to be taken into account – that of 'vicarious religion'. Vicariousness (a specifically European characteristic) concerns not only the churches themselves but the populations on whose behalf they continue to operate. Sociological analysis has, for the most part, concentrated on the former only, an approach that ignores an important part of the overall equation. Weak churches are less weak if they have the tacit support of considerably wider sections of the population.

European churches as voluntary organizations

The historic churches in most European countries have not been voluntary organizations for the greater part of their history; they have been more or less strongly linked to the state whether as privileged institutions (for example Catholic churches favoured by a concordat arrangement) or as state churches *per se* (the case in most of Protestant Europe). Christianity has been the 'official' religion of Europe for at least a millennium and a half, a situation which had – and up to a point still has – both advantages and disadvantages. No mainstream church in Europe can deny this history, however equivocal its legacy. But there are interesting debates to be had concerning its mutations in recent decades. It is quite possible, for example, that a 'weak' state church has opportunities for representativeness denied to its historic forebears – such a church no longer has the capacity for exclusion and exclusiveness and begins necessarily to operate in a different manner.[1]

This section, however, concentrates on the voluntary sector *per se*, in which the European churches are *de facto* located whatever their constitutional status. Religion is essentially a leisure activity in modern Europe; it takes place in leisure time and competes alongside a whole variety of other possibilities, many of which (including shopping) now take place on a Sunday. Conversely, no public sanctions exist to prevent the European citizen from opting out of the churches' influence either partially or completely. Indeed, the very idea that this might be otherwise is looked upon with extreme distaste in almost every country in western Europe.

How, then, does religion compare when placed alongside some of its competitors in the field? The following data, taken from the European Values Study, are necessarily selective, but are none the less revealing: it is clear that 'religion and church' do as well as many voluntary activities and better than most across fifteen West European societies (see Table 7.1).[2]

The European Values Study is an important source not only of religious data, but of sociological evidence relating to a whole range of economic and social activities in postwar Europe; hence its importance for the kind of argument sustained in this chapter.[3] Such data should, however, be amplified by more detailed information from particular countries and for particular activities, in which church-going or church membership as such becomes a variable quite apart from voluntary (or unpaid) activities associated with religion.

Interesting parallels emerge, for example, if religious activity (including church membership) in both France and Britain is compared with

Table 7.1 Percentage of Europeans engaged in voluntary work by type of
organization, 1990

Type of organization	%	Type of organization	%
Animal rights	1.0	Religion and church	5.8
Conservation, environment	1.5	Social welfare services	4.1
Education, arts, culture	3.8	Sports and recreation	6.8
Health	1.8	Third World, human rights	1.2
Local community action	1.5	Trades unions	2.0
Peace movement	0.6	Women's groups	1.4
Political parties and groups	2.3	Youth work	2.9
Professional associations	1.9		

Source: The European Values Study 1981–90, Summary Report, Barker, Halman and Vloet,
1992:39. The Gordon Cook Foundation, London

membership of and changes in the trades union movement. To take religious
activity first, the statistical basis for decline in church-going in Britain and
France in the postwar decades is well established; such figures are rarely
questioned and are frequently cited in support of the 'secularization thesis'.[4]
(The validity of these assumptions will be put on one side for the moment.)
It is quite clear, in addition, that the rates of church-going in both countries
at the turn of the millennium are some of the lowest in Europe – i.e. around
10 per cent of the adult population (perhaps a little higher in France) with
some dispute at the margins depending on which particular figures are used
and how these were gathered. The decline is uneven and takes place for a
variety of reasons, but no one seriously disputes that a significant drop in
church attendance has occurred in the postwar period.

Turning now to the trades union movement in both countries, the picture
is remarkably similar. In Britain, for example, the number of trades unions
has halved between 1976 and 1995 (from 473 to 238), the number of
members has been reduced by a quarter, a fall which is equally visible in the
proportion of the active workforce which chooses to be unionized (*Social
Trends*, 1994; 1998). In France there is a similar picture. The Confédération
du Travail is the oldest trades union confederation in France and for a large
part of the twentieth century dominated the union movement. In 1948, the
CGT had 4 million members; by the end of the century the number had
dropped to 600,000 (Milner, 1999) – a truly dramatic fall. Aggregating the
figures for trades union membership in France at the turn of the millennium
– the figures are taken once again from Milner (1999) – suggests a total of
between 2 million and 2.5 million activists overall; far fewer, in other
words, than the total number of regular church-goers in France, never mind
the more loosely affiliated.

Of course, the drop in membership in the trades union movement in both
countries is a complex phenomenon which requires careful interpretation.[5]
It is brought about by a significant change in the structure of the economy
as all European societies move from a primarily industrial base to a post-

industrial model dominated more by consumption than by production. One consequence of these profound mutations can be found in the changing nature of the labour market. The sections of this market which were traditionally strongholds of unionism (labour intensive, male-dominated heavy industries) simply cease to exist; so do their unions. The crucial point to make in this connection is that changes in the patterns of church-going require equally sensitive treatment. They too are complex and reflect changes in the structures of society just as much as, or indeed rather more than, shifts in religious belief. Indeed, it is likely (following Gill, 1999) that the decline in church-going in western Europe is the cause rather than the consequence of different patterns of religious belief. People who cease to go to church undoubtedly lose their moorings in institutional Christianity. It should not be assumed, however, that they necessarily adopt secular alternatives – indeed, the evidence points in a very different direction (Davie, 1994; 2000a). This point will have resonance in the second section of this chapter.

A fascinating study that brings religious organizations and the trades union movement together in a particular locality can be found in Chambers (2000). Chambers looks in detail at four churches or church types in Swansea, a rapidly evolving city in south Wales where the shift from an industrial to a post-industrial economy is particularly striking. Two of these churches are declining and two are growing. Chambers' study reveals the complexity of these processes, taking into account the economic, social, demographic and cultural environment of each congregation, in addition to a range of internal factors. The particular point that resonates for this chapter is the following: the factors that account for the decline of the traditional Free Churches on the east side of Swansea – the collapse of the close-knit working-class community centred on the docks – are precisely the same as those which account for the collapse of the trades union movement in the same area. Both the organizations concerned with religion and those concerned with labour have lost their *raison d'être* – i.e. a community the serving of whose common interests (whether religious or work-based) required institutional articulation.

Similar shifts in the nature of society can be detected in other aspects of leisure activity. The huge drop in cinema admissions in postwar Britain is a case in point (see Figure 7.1). This drop is particularly dramatic in the 1950s and 1960s and was undoubtedly brought about by the advent of television and, in due course, of video. It was part and parcel of the privatization of leisure and had little to do with a rise or fall in the appreciation of film-making as such. Films continued to have an important place in British culture but were accessed in the home rather than in the cinema. Much the same is true of sport if the attendances at soccer league matches are taken into account. These were infinitely higher immediately before the Second World War than they have ever been since and – in the lower divisions at least – display a trajectory rather similar to the churches

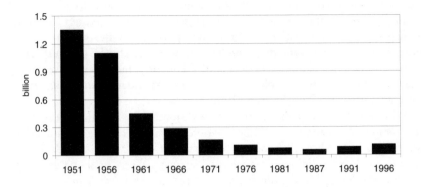

Figure 7.1 Cinema admissions in the UK, 1951–96

Note: 1987 is shown because data collection was suspended in 1986.
Source: *Social Trends* 1998: 222, Office for National Statistics, © Crown Copyright 2000

for much of the postwar period (*Social Trends*, 1995). Once again, the reasons for the change lie in the shifting nature of society and more especially in the break-up of working-class neighbourhoods in the major industrial cities of Britain (these in turn are closely linked to the changes in the trades union movement). Moreover, sport (just like films) is accessed through television; the interest continues even if attendances at the grounds have fallen.

A further point is, however, worth noting with respect to both the cinema and sporting pursuits; that is the noticeable, if relatively small, rise in both activities in the mid- to late 1990s (*Social Trends*, 1995; 1998). It seems that new patterns of consumption are beginning to emerge, possibly in response to careful marketing and considerably improved facilities (small screen cinemas and better equipped stadiums). Some equivalents can, moreover, be found in the religious sector, in for example, the growing number of successful evangelical churches and the marked success of student Christian Unions among a huge range of campus activities.[6] As yet such successes are insufficient to compensate for overall decline. The complexity of the situation must, however, be borne in mind – trend figures based on averages are necessarily misleading and mask considerable internal variations (Jenkins, 1999; Chambers, 2000).

As a conclusion to this section, the following contrast should, perhaps, be borne in mind. Patterns of church-going based on a sense of obligation no longer resonate for the great majority of the population in Britain – and probably for the greater part of western Europe. People no longer go to church because they have to or for the more subtle obligation of social respectability. It follows that congregations that rely on a sense of obligation to bring their members to church on a regular basis are likely to be struggling. In contrast, those congregations which derive their strength from consumption – i.e. this is something that I choose to do (maybe regularly, maybe not, sometimes for long periods and sometimes for short) – display close similarities to the leisure pursuits of the secular world. Indeed, as we have seen, the churches are as successful in this respect as many of their secular equivalents and frequently more so. In terms of aggregate figures, for example, far more people attended church than league football games in 1999 (Brierley, 2000).

What remains an open question, in my view, is the relative size of these sectors in – say – fifty years' time. I would, I think, be more cautious than Steve Bruce (see above, Chapter 6) with respect to the necessary decline of certain forms of religious organization against others, in that there is as much diversity within denominations or sects as between them – not least in terms of the distinction that I have outlined in the previous paragraph. In the meantime, it is equally important to explore further the delicate and complex relations between the great diversity of religious institutions in European society and the wider public, for strength or weakness can quite clearly be derived indirectly as well as directly.

Vicarious religion

In the course of my own writing on the changing nature of European religion, I have become increasingly convinced by the concept of 'vicariousness'. Such thinking derives from my attempts to bring together the active religious minority in modern Europe with the much larger number of nominal believers, who should (in my view) be taken into account even if their relationship with the churches is at best spasmodic and sometimes hardly visible. Vicarious religion is at its clearest in the Lutheran societies of northern Europe – societies in which well-funded state churches operate on behalf of populations which rarely, if ever, attend religious services. It is hard to believe, however, that populations which observe the occasional offices to a far greater extent than the British and who agree to church-funding through the tax system on an exceptionally generous scale are fundamentally disapproving of the institutions they pay for. The role of such institutions in Scandinavian society is widely approved, taking into account that many of the activities undertaken by the churches are cultural rather than religious.[7] Additional evidence from Sweden underlines the importance of church buildings in the lives of many Swedish people; such places should be properly maintained for without them public life would be severely diminished. Attitudes towards the churchyard or burial ground were an important feature in these unexpectedly strong reactions (Bäckström and Bromander, 1995).[8]

In other parts of Europe, vicariousness takes slightly different forms. In Britain, for example, there is in some ways a rather similar willingness on the part of the population to delegate the religious sphere to the professional ministries of the state churches and, as a way of policing this delegation, to be profoundly critical of such elites when things go wrong (in the form of deviant beliefs or inappropriate modes of behaviour). It is for this reason that sections of the tabloid press are so intolerant of 'doubting bishops' or priests who misbehave. What, after all, is the point of a bishop who doubts if his job is 'to believe', and to do this on behalf of those who find it rather more difficult? And why else would the same papers take notice of priestly adultery or financial impropriety, given the fact that most pages of the paper are full of such stories – considered commonplace in the population as a whole. Somehow, a religious professional is expected to behave differently. 'Why?', is the crucial question.

Whether or not the same ideas can be extrapolated to the Catholic countries of Europe remains a difficult question given the confrontational nature of the past in much of Catholic Europe and a rather different attitude to public morality. But a similar resonance lies, perhaps, in the notion of Catholic identity – in that a sense of being Catholic appears to endure even when practice has ceased to be anything except spasmodic (far more so, in fact, than in Protestantism). Residual Catholicism re-emerges, for example, at the time of a death (see below) and in the choice of schooling for the next generation. Whatever the case, I am increasingly convinced that significant numbers of Europeans remain grateful to, rather than resentful of, their churches at the turn of the millennium, recognizing that these churches perform, vicariously, a number of tasks on behalf of the population as a whole. From time to time, for instance, they are asked to articulate the sacred in the life-cycle of individuals or families or at times of national crisis or celebration. It is significant that a refusal to carry out these tasks would violate both individual and collective expectations.

The two most obvious examples of this process in recent years were the very public funerals of President Mitterrand (in 1996) and Princess Diana (in 1997). The latter has been extensively scrutinized (see, for example, Richards, Wilson and Woodhead, 1999; Walter, 1999). The crucial point to grasp amid everything else was the evident need for a public marker of Diana's death in addition to the multiple individual or community gestures that took place in the week following the accident. It was assumed that the ceremony would take place in one of London's major churches; had the Dean refused the request to use Westminster Abbey, there would have been uproar. President Mitterrand's funeral is both similar and different (Hervieu-Léger, 1996). If anyone, surely, merited a secular funeral (albeit a socialist ceremony), at the end of his agnostic (though mystical) and politically committed life, it was François Mitterrand. In the end, however, not one requiem mass but two were arranged – the first amounted to a state funeral in Notre Dame de Paris, the second in Jarnac in south-west France took the form of a private mass for the immediate family. Once again the refusal of the Catholic Church to host either of these ceremonies was unthinkable.

Doing something vicariously, i.e. on behalf of others, implies that the majority as well as the minority have some idea of what is going on; in other words that the wider public are not entirely indifferent to the activities of the religious institutions even if they take no – or very little – part in them on a regular basis. It is this tacit understanding which is both the key to the whole enterprise and an impossibly difficult field to research; it is not amenable to anything but the most subtle of methodologies. Despite such difficulties, I am convinced that the notion of vicariousness offers not only an innovative, but an empirically useful approach to the notion of secularization as it is experienced in European society at the end of the twentieth century. It is a method of working considerably more subtle than those based simply or primarily on the numbers of regular church-goers. Not everyone has to be active in religious institutions for the latter (a) to continue in existence and (b) to have an appreciable effect upon the society in question – provided that certain conditions are met. Such conditions concern the viability as well as legality of the institutional churches, a statement requiring ongoing and careful scrutiny, and at different levels of society.

Three points lead me to a positive conclusion regarding the viability of the European churches at national level at the turn of the millennium. First, the evidence from central and eastern Europe in the early 1990s where the need to reconstitute (rapidly) both the constitutional presence and public acceptability of the churches was immediately apparent (life without such institutions was not an option, though the particular form that they should take was not only much less clear but frequently disputed). It is all too easy to concentrate on the disputes and the difficulties and to ignore the fundamental issue: that populations deprived of legally constituted churches for two to three generations are anxious to restore these institutions – whether or not they attend them in great numbers or with great regularity. In the same societies it was, of course, the museums of atheism that came to an abrupt end.

A second point lies in the attempts to extend the privileges of the historic churches on an equitable basis to the newly arrived religious communities in all parts of Europe. It is clear that the non-historic religious groups (both Christian and other faith) both covet and compete for these privileges in western Europe; they do not despise them. The minorities, just as much as the majorities, appreciate the need for constitutional, legal and financial status, in that religious communities of all kinds require public as well as private recognition if they are to function effectively in a European context.

My final observation is rather different and reflects the attitudes of many Europeans towards religious buildings (Davie, 2000a). Such attitudes are revealed in the disputes that arise in connection with payment for access to churches or cathedrals. Invariably such requests provoke protest. Underlying the vehemence of such reactions lies, I think, a conviction that religious buildings are in some sense public property and belong to everyone, regardless of formal church membership, attendance or even belief. The result can be paradoxical. Those most closely involved in the upkeep of such buildings see the need to restrict access, to protect fabric and to boost income; the less closely attached assert their right of entry – for whatever reason. Unpicking the debates that go on in this area reveals a truly wonderful confusion, within which exists a significant spiritual dimension. Small wonder that people are so 'unreasonable'. It follows that the future of these institutions and the law that surrounds them should, once again, form an aspect of public rather than private debate. It is evidence, following Casanova (1996), of the deprivatization of religion.

The question of buildings provides a link to the place of churches in local rather than national affairs. Here the discussion forms part of the continuing debate about civil society, whether this be in societies previously dominated by communism or in those exposed to the rigours of the free market. What, the civil society advocates ask, are the most effective forms of organization to ensure a functioning democracy at all levels – a situation, that is, in which the state engages with a wide diversity of economic, social, political and cultural organizations in order to create an effective and inclusive social agenda? Clearly, the faith communities of modern Europe are crucial players in this sphere, representing – directly or indirectly – a wide variety of interests, including some of the most disadvantaged sections of the population as a whole.[9] The evidence from the first section of this chapter needs to be taken into account at this point, notably the statistics relating to volunteering.

It is in local communities, moreover, that the values embodied in the confessional parties of western Europe are most likely to gain, or regain, their purchase. Like all political parties in this part of the world, the confessional parties (notably Christian Democracy) have undergone a profound mutation in the closing years of the twentieth century, partially if not totally ceding their place to a multiplicity of pressure groups and social movements (Hanley, 1994; van Kersbergen, 1995). Some of these movements are overtly religious (those, for example, advancing or resisting liturgical change); others have a secular agenda but incorporate substantial sections of the religious constituency (those, for instance, who feel strongly for or against abortion or euthanasia); yet others (the green movement or aspects of the women's movement) can be analysed as if they were religions. Confessional parties as such may or may not cease to exist; the connections between the religious and the political sphere will continue. Working out these relationships at the intermediary level is central to the understanding of civil society.

Such questions are, moreover, directly related to the argument of this chapter in that they provide a further link between its two sections. Political parties, just like the trades unions and the denominational churches, do not fit easily into late modern societies. The lines of cleavage have altered in the latter and, unsurprisingly, the political agendas of parties established in the late nineteenth or early twentieth century no longer resonate (Laborde, 1999). One result of this situation is a widespread disillusionment with politics in general (a feeling that parallels attitudes towards some aspects of institutional religion) – a sentiment which in some parts of Europe lies behind an alarming drop in voting rates, quite similar in many ways to the fall in religious commitment.[10] Once again it is the nature of society which is changing just as much as the religious sector *per se*.

What, then, can be said in conclusion? In many respects the notion of vicarious religion is hardly new, though the proportions of active and nominal members have changed markedly in the postwar period. It is, moreover, legitimate to enquire whether there is a minimum size beyond which the minority must not drop if it is to operate vicariously. Indeed, there are some, Steve Bruce probably among them, who would argue that this limit has been reached already. I disagree. Despite the gradual mutation of all churches in Europe from privileged bodies attached to the state to *de facto* voluntary organizations, it seems that the vicarious role continues.

The most obvious source of evidence for this statement can be found in the occasional offices, remembering first that the relatively large falls in the proportion of the newly born baptized in France, Britain and the Low Countries are not repeated either in Scandinavia or in southern Europe where baptism rates remain high. The question of religious marriage is complex: different parts of Europe display very different patterns (Dittgen, 1994). Within this complexity the proportion of marriages that have a religious element is roughly related to levels of church-going (given a certain time lag – rates of church-going fall first), but the noticeable rise in the proportion of religious marriages in much of Scandinavia (between 1975 and 1990) needs to be taken into account. Above all, however, the persistence of a religious ceremony at death binds the vast majority of Europeans to their churches. There is a noticeable evolution in the nature of these ceremonies – shifts that reflect a more individualized culture – but relatively few take place outside the influence of the churches altogether. In this respect both Princess Diana and President Mitterrand were typical, not exceptional, Europeans.

A final point concerns the future. I have argued that the concept of vicariousness should be given more attention if the present situation of the churches in Europe is to be properly understood. An evident fall both in religious practice and in religious knowledge in the postwar period does not lead to a parallel loss in religious sensitivity (the data quite clearly suggest otherwise) or to the widespread adoption of secular alternatives. On the contrary, religious belief persists, but becomes increasingly personal, detached and heterogeneous. This is a new situation in the religious life of Europe. In my view, it is better served by careful attention to the changing nature of the religious institutions of Europe and their relations to a mostly sympathetic and at times dependent wider public than by an attitude which suggests that such institutions have no future at all.

Notes

1   The Church of England is an obvious example of this process; it has gradually shifted its stance from defending a particular version of the faith, to defending 'faith' in general. The increasing pluralism of modern British society encourages this trend.

2   The term voluntary should, however, be used with caution in that it has two distinct meanings, not always distinguishable in the literature. The first understands 'voluntary' as something that takes place in the non-governmental sector of modern societies; the second understands 'voluntary' as unpaid activity chosen by the volunteer from a wide range of possibilities. It is the latter meaning that this table exemplifies.

3   The European Values Study is a cross-cultural longitudinal study of values in post-war Europe (and, indeed, beyond). It was first undertaken in 1981, repeated in 1990 and again in 1999. The data used in this chapter are taken from the 1990 study (the more recent findings were not available at the time of writing) and can be found in Barker, Halman and Vloet (1992).

4   Data for the British case can be found in Brierley (1997 and 1990); the French case is summarized in Davie (1999).

5   Nor should the analysis be extrapolated to all western European societies; trades unions are differently constituted in different European nations with different implications for membership.

6   Religious organizations hold their own very well on campus, far more so, for example, than political groups – which in some universities fail to attract sufficient members to merit a financial subsidy from the student union.

7   I am aware that the constitutional position of the Swedish Church is changing in response to the demands of a more pluralist society. I do not think that this undermines the basic argument of this chapter.

8   The significance of both religious buildings and religious personnel has had particular resonance in the Nordic countries in the wake of several recent disasters: after the sinking of the Estonia in 1994; after the nightclub fire in Gothenburg in Sweden in 1998; and after the rail crash in Norway at the end of 1999. It is striking that the secular press of the Nordic countries regards the vicarious role of the churches in this kind of situation as entirely normal (information from Pal Repstad).

9   An excellent example of analysis at this level can be found in Smith's work on the multiple faith communities in East London (Smith 1998).

10 It would be unwise to generalize about rates of political participation; different legal arrangements exist in different European societies which result in markedly different patterns of voting behaviour.

8 The twofold limit of the notion of secularization

Danièle Hervieu-Léger

The interminable debate over secularization

Is there anything left to be said about secularization? For more than thirty years the subject has been so much discussed and written about that it would seem to have become distinctly tired, if not played out. Yet the debate remains open. Proper assessment of the changing contours in the modern religious landscape still awaits clarification of a major contradiction, which research inquiry has not so far managed to resolve. On the one hand, there is evidence of the continuing autonomization of the different spheres of social activity and the corresponding, though variable, decline in the social influence exercised by the major religious institutions that claim a monopoly of the symbolic organization of society. On the other hand, one can point to the astonishing vitality of beliefs, the renewal of forms of religiosity and the potency of the different religious traditions, which are invariably capable of nurturing the movements they give rise to.

Secularization has for long been associated with the idea of the loss of religion in modern societies, a loss which followed directly from the disenchantment of the world brought about by the irresistible rise of scientific and technological rationality. The empirical discovery of the significance of forms of belief in societies that were taken to be rationally disenchanted has led to a lessening of the reliance being placed on the assumption of loss. The approach to the phenomena, at once complex and contradictory, that are now subsumed by the term secularization has become more subtle, less cut and dried.

At the same time, the awareness has grown that the concept of modernity takes in more than the advance of scientific thought and of the technical mastery of the world. It encompasses affirmation of the autonomy of the individual. And by degrees in the development of Western democratic societies this has come to incorporate the demand for individual freedom in private life. The growing awareness of self that characterizes the modern individual does not relieve him or her of the need to believe. Indeed, there is now a more urgent need to give a meaning to the experiences of life and to the ultimate questions raised by exposure, now endured in a more personal way, to uncertainty and a sense of incompleteness. Secularization is defined as much by the private and individualist appropriation of fundamental truths of belief as it is by the challenging of the sacred canopies of traditional societies; and, if it is witness to the retreat of so-called irrational beliefs, it manifests itself no less in the individual need to construct a system of meanings on the basis of aptitudes and interests, aspiration and experience, within which day-to-day existence can itself take on meaning.

Hence, the modern rationale of the individualization of belief does not imply the end of religion but a vast reconstruction of the institutional systems of believing and of the regimes of authority associated with them. Identification of such forms of reconstruction is today at the centre of academic reflection on religious modernity. And it is no exaggeration to say that the path thus followed by sociological thought has found a major theoretical source in the work of Peter Berger, and its constant receptiveness to the new problems raised by the transformations in the world have made it all the more valuable. *The Sacred Canopy*, published in 1967, won immediate recognition both as a brilliant continuation of the thought given to the future of religion in modern societies by the founding fathers of sociology and as giving decisive impetus to contemporary sociological reflection of religious modernity. University departments of sociology the world over have pondered Berger's insistence on the character, at once objective and subjective, of the complex process by which modern societies break their links with the dominant religious systems that organize the life of tradition-bound societies.

At the same time as religious institutions find themselves gradually rejected in their claim to administer the different spheres of human activity, thereafter governed by game rules that are specialized and autonomous, so does individual consciousness free itself from the hold of the dominant codes of religious meaning which gave traditional societies their symbolic armature in the form of collectively accepted norms and shared values. At the same time as scientific and technological rationality compels general recognition of its procedures of experimentation and verification in establishing fundamental truths, individuals lay claim to the power of autonomous decision-making in every register where previously a norm issued from above had theoretically undivided sway. The political sphere is the one in which the construction of the individual in modernity is most decisive, a construction that infiltrates the field of morality and even that of religious faith. The autonomous believer who displays his or her freedom of adherence, and his or her ability to assume responsibility for moral choice, has become the central figure in our religious modernity. And it can only be conceived (in the philosophical as in the sociological field) insofar as one takes full and proper account of the meaning individuals themselves attach to an autonomy that deprives them of the symbolic supports within an authoritative tradition. Embarked on such a course, individuals acquire a colossal measure of freedom.

Following a line of reasoning that stems directly from Weber, Berger acknowledges the dominant role played by Christianity, and in particular by a Protestant version of Christianity, in this course. But he underlines that this liberty is at a price, both psychological and social. The loss of traditional ethical markers, the collapse of codes of collective meaning and the erosion of the social bond resulting from the individualist atomization of meaning-systems make anomie a major threat to our societies (Berger, 1977a). In losing all heteronomous moral foundation, the political order finds its legitimacy only in the consent granted by citizens, a consent that is constantly renewed, thus fragile, permanently threatened with being misappropriated or forcibly outlawed. The modernity that confronts us is both a conquest and an ordeal, and the major question for the sociologist, as for the citizen, has to do with the forms of social system that can take over after the disintegration of the shared certainties that structured individual and collective experience in tradition-bound societies.

For the reason that they are individualized societies, modern societies are called upon to find the forms of mediation capable of evolving common values and norms without which no human society can exist. How and with what social and symbolic resources can they succeed in this? The whole of Peter Berger's reflection on religion bears the mark of a primary preoccupation with the ability of modern societies to produce an order which can form a basis for social nexus.

It has been suggested that this central concern for social order categorizes Peter Berger unequivocally as a conservative thinker. But, from a sociological viewpoint at least, what is at issue in his reflection does not first and foremost have to do with ideological and political options. More fundamentally, it concerns the future of society itself and its ability to withstand the threat of chaos and to fill the vacuum left by the massive certitudes furnished by the major religions. Furthermore, it addresses the question of the evaluation and regulation of alternative solutions that individuals are prompted to develop so as to confront, with the means at their disposal, the loss of meaning following on the depletion of the dominant meaning-systems (Berger, 1977a; Berger and Luckmann, 1995). Weber may be the clearest theoretical source of Berger's sociology, but the tone of his questioning in many ways echoes the anxieties of Tocqueville or of Durkheim as to the future of democratic societies faced with the implications of renouncing – and this after all is what makes them democratic – the notion that there is a transcendent basis for social order.

A reappraisal of the theory

Some years after he had put forward the most coherent and comprehensive analysis of the direction taken by Western modernity which the sociology of religion has produced, Peter Berger took a lead among those who had undertaken a radical reappraisal of the standard hypothesis of secularization. The modifications he proposed, whereby its relevance was restricted to western Europe, appeared to give credit to the notion that the theory had undergone reversal, and that the basis of a sociology of religious modernity for which *The Sacred Canopy* (1967) had been an established authority for twenty years was being challenged. Certainly, with the growing place he has given to comparative international studies and the ample evidence thus produced of the social significance of religious phenomena across the planet, Berger has developed a timely critique of the current trend in sociology – of whatever school – to universalize and instance as a general law of social evolution processes that are specific to that Western culture which sees itself as the laboratory and the matrix of universal history. The comparison between socio-religious developments in Europe and in North America has led him into as yet more radical questioning of the classic problematics of the loss of religion in the modern world. It has revealed the inner disparities in the supposed process of secularization, not merely with respect to the vitality of religious beliefs but also with regard to the continuing influence of religious institutions in the public arena, and this at the very centre of the Western sphere. Thus in the narrower confines of north-western Europe, the all-embracing theory of the inescapable loss of plausibility facing the dominant religious systems in modern societies was reduced to more modest proportions.

Consideration of the terms of this reappraisal produces at least two responses. The first has to do in a general way with the methods of validation produced by the social sciences, and the major role that must in this respect (given the lack of any means of experimental verification) fall to comparison. From this viewpoint, the path followed by Peter Berger in sociological inquiry is not split between a secularist and an anti-secularist Berger. It is a lucid invitation to exercise methodological caution and constantly return to the paradigms that research furnishes. The second response has to do with the actual substance of the reappraisal that Berger has carried out and claims responsibility for. Does it involve abandoning the initial perspective, so calling into question the irreversible nature of the historical process of secularization? Peter Berger has made the point that its irreversibility had become questionable, with the qualification that this has more to do with the indefinite projection of the process in the future than with its determinable historical reality (Berger, 1977a, pp. 160, 187, 189–90). Several textual references suggest a finer and a less linear perception of problems involving secularization, touching on its phases, its rhythms, its possible reversals and its inconsistencies (Berger *et al.*, 1973; Berger, 1977a). Early on, Berger provided evidence of differentiated resistance on the part of the various institutional areas to the expulsion of religious norms and references. If the economic sphere is no longer religiously invested, the political sphere, which is first and foremost the arena for the modern construction of autonomy, still maintains token roots in the world of religion by way of a civil religion, itself of little substance and vulnerable to the effects of the modern relativizing of every vision of the world.

But the sphere of the family is still to a large degree under the sway of the stock of symbols deriving from religion, more precisely those relating to Christian ritual. Hence the propagation of secularization is neither constant nor similar in degree in its effect on society. A finer analysis might with impunity go further and allow that religious or spiritual renewal may accompany the dislocation of the dominant religious codes of meaning. The intense emotionalism of certain charismatic-type religious currents, the immediacy of conversion that prevails on a mass scale in mega-churches, and the syncretic acclimatization and assemblage of Eastern spirituality practised within groups in the West are illustrations of such inconsistencies in the secularizing process (Hervieu-Léger, 1993). Secular modernity causes the proliferation of *ersatz* religions (Berger, 1977a, p. 160). Furthermore, and simultaneously, pluralism saps the foundations of secular myths (that of progress, for instance) which stem directly from modernity. Thus, if one cannot speak of a reversal of the process, analysis reveals greater subtlety, and, in particular, a degree of contextualization which precludes one from positing secularization as a historical law. Such contextualization is also the necessary starting point for a new approach towards making religious modernity more intelligible.

To what extent can one speak of the secularization of European culture?

The question to be discussed here springs from Peter Berger's remarks on the state of religion in western Europe, the only geo-cultural area (perhaps with Canada) to which, in his view, the ideal-typical model of secularization implying the expulsion of religion can be applied in contrast with the rest of the world (the United Sates included).

Observation suggests that his opinion is largely justified. Nowhere else but in western Europe has denominational religion become so eroded. Religious practice has foundered, the clergy face a crisis of recruitment, the churches no longer exercise effective political influence. Added to this, belief in a personal God has declined, the articles of Christian faith, if known at all, are disregarded, and the autonomous expression of a personal moral consciousness has replaced the ethical prescriptions of religious systems.

All the indicators give ample evidence of the deepening inroads made by secularization in European societies. The proposition remains valid whether one takes the objective aspect of the trend, the secularization of institutions, or its subjective aspect, the impact secularization makes on consciousness, leading individuals to abandon codes imbued with religious meaning. With the exception of Ireland and of Italy where the quasi-monopoly of religion enjoyed by the Roman Catholic Church limits – but only to a degree – the erosive effects of pluralism, all west European countries show similar inescapable tendencies that point to the institutional deregulation of religion and the individualization of beliefs on a massive scale (Davie and Hervieu-Léger, 1996). The subjective self-assembling of beliefs, the disconnection of the structural link between religious belief and denominational membership, the crisis in the transmission of religious identities from one generation to the next, the free access of individuals to the symbolic resources of different available traditions, and the mobility with which individuals appropriate these resources – all of these factors have come together to constitute a general pattern.

The mobile figure of the pilgrim who sets a free course on a spiritual path that is freely chosen, and the figure of the convert whose choice of religion is dictated by personal interests and aspirations, now afford an outline ideal-typical description of religious attitudes in Europe. Together they have taken the place of the classic figure of the practising follower of fixed faith, which represents stable community membership and the transmission of religious identities. Just as the temporal and spatial reach of religious observance has shrunk, so has this figure now become relatively negligible (Hervieu-Léger, 1999).

Naturally, there are differences of degree in different parts of Europe. In Scandinavia, in Britain, in the Netherlands and in France the collapse is massive and its first signs appeared before the First World War. In Spain, the upheaval is recent and extremely sudden. It corresponds directly to the moment when, following the long isolation of the Franco period, Spain returned to the fold of European democracies. In Italy, which in so many ways exemplifies high modernity, the process appears to have been retarded by the sheer might of social and cultural – but to a lessening degree political – supervision still exercised by the Catholic Church, whose apparatus and personnel remain relatively abundant. Such differences are largely to be explained in terms of the histories of the countries concerned, and there is virtually nothing here to contradict the general diagnosis of secularization. Rather, the picture confirms Peter Berger's perception of Europe as a special case, and one significant enough to justify making it the principle of a descriptive sociology of religion (or rather of the absence of religion) among Europeans.

Observers of the profound secularization of European societies, and the extent of the religious emancipation of consciousness, find some explanation within a religious history of politics, which puts the stress on the concrete role played by Christianity in Europe as a 'religion allowing an exit from religion' (Gauchet, 1985, Ch. 2). It provides an approach that reveals the fundamental differences between the case of Europe and that of the United States, though originating in the same politico-cultural matrix. Two classical analyses suggest themselves as useful here.

First, there is that of Tocqueville (1981; orig. 1840), dealing with the emergence of democracy in the United States and in France. Here he refers to the fact that in America 'a sense of religion and a sense of freedom are closely linked one to the other', whereas in the context of France the Enlightenment could find expression only in opposition to religion, personified in this case by the Catholic Church which was inseparably associated with the *ancien régime*. And second, there is that of Ernst Troeltsch (1912), responding critically to the prevalent notion that worldly religious individualism born of the Reformation was directly responsible for the emergence of the modern concept of the individual, thus paving the way for the arrival of democracy (see p. 635). Luther undoubtedly developed an ethic of work in the practical world in affinity with the development of capitalism, but as an ethical system it is in contradiction with the modern system which recognizes and magnifies the autonomy of worldly realities. Nor does the radical religious individualism of Calvin imply sanctioning the autonomy of the individual, and it is in contradiction with the rationalist and positive individualism of the Enlightenment.

Protestant modernity did not emerge fully developed from the theology of the Reformation; rather, it is integral to the historical experience of the neo-Calvinist Puritan communities which emigrated to the New World, and which were obliged, in part in order to manage the conflicts that developed between them, to draw all the political consequences of the theological value accorded to the free and deliberate adherence of their members to the community. The fundamental principle of the equality of each of the members within the community and of the equality of each community one to another took shape in this context. The religious genesis of American democratic experience marks a fundamental separation between the United States and European societies. The United States immediately became constituted as a modern nation by incorporating a religious history that gave theological legitimacy to the autonomy of politics. European societies constructed their political modernity over a long time period through the emancipation of political authority from the tutelage of religion. Allowing for very different historical and national contexts as for clearly contrasting paths towards secularization, they all experienced a gradual or a brutal emancipation of the political sphere implying, as it did in different ways, deliverance from the domination of religious authority. The historical path taken by political autonomization with regard to religion constitutes thereby, and beyond the obvious diversity of national histories, the matrix of a process that typifies modernization implying as it does the repression, the marginalization and even (as in the case of France) the exclusion of religion. Given modalities that vary widely, the process involves inseparably both institutions and consciousness (both the objective and the subjective dimension of secularization). A reconstruction of the process provides Berger's thesis of a 'European exceptionalism' with its most effective support.

If one acknowledges this historical exceptionalism with regard to Europe (which is truly intelligible, let it be said, only in comparison with the equally exceptional case of the United States), can one then infer that Europe has a cultural specificity which establishes itself in the void left by religion? This is not a conclusion one can readily jump to. The impossibility of building – in this alleged homogeneous secularized field – a 'Europe of religion' able to assume, on a continental scale, the direction of the spiritual and religious reconstructions favoured by the advance of institutional deregulation (Willaime, 1996b) must give ground for caution. The validity of the theory of secularization in the terrain of Europe is established in a negative manner, with the acknowledgement that institutional religion has collapsed. In such a perspective, the extent of the loss of power to mobilize sustained by Christian churches continues to be the main indicator of European secularity.

Yet this tells us nothing of the evidence for spiritual renewal which continental Europe is experiencing, nor does it tell us anything about the degree of cultural permeation that religion continues to exert on these societies at a time when church attendance is minimal and the churches' teaching falls on increasingly deaf ears. This consideration may lend weight to Berger's objections to the general and irreversible nature of secularization in modern societies.

Accordingly, in view of the complexity of the process of the loss of religion in areas where it actually applies and is readily verifiable, that is to say in western Europe, it would seem to be necessary to restate the problem of secularization in its different dimension. One may summarize this by making three propositions:

1   All modern societies are, from the viewpoint of their political constitution and their normative and axiological organization, societies that have 'exited from religion'. The grand religious visions which provided society with codes of meaning binding on each and all have been impaired by pluralism and the rationale of individualization brought about by the autonomy of the person. This is the essence of the perspective developed by Peter Berger in *The Sacred Canopy* (1967).

2   The process of 'exiting from religion' is in no sense to be equated with the renunciation of belief. Secularization is not the end of belief but the movement by which the elements of belief break free of the structures prescribed by religious institutions. As such, the movement is neither uniform nor irreversible; its extent and its timespan vary with the course history has taken in the societies concerned. The comparability study that follows from this proposition shows that only in western Europe has the institutional deregulation of believing become a pervasive cultural phenomenon. This is the significance of the revision undertaken by Peter Berger, a revision which in no way invalidates the

first proposition, but which requires sociological evaluation to be put in a historical setting, to be relativized.

3   Inside Europe – the zone that represents maximum validity of the theory of secularization as thus understood – institutional deregulation does not compose an area that is uniform from the religious viewpoint. Above and beyond the generally attested upsurge of individual, diffuse and differentiated religiosity, the cultural structures shaped (in part at least) by different religious histories continue to organize common references, shared meanings and specific institutional rationales. The permeation of culture by religion offers powerful resistance to the process of institutional deregulation. It is a major factor in local resistance to the uniformization of Europe and, in the wider context, to a process of cultural globalization whose reach is considerably overestimated.

To take up our argument again, the theory of secularization as an exiting from religion is entirely valid if it is applied within a religious genealogy of the autonomization of politics and of the individual in modern societies. From the viewpoint of a sociology of believing, it constitutes a local and limited theory of the deinstitutionalizing of religion. But it is altogether powerless to furnish the basis of a theory of the relationship between religion and culture in Western societies.

Incomplete cultural secularization: reflections based on the French case

To give substance to this differentiated approach to the possible dimensions of secularization (or of non-secularization), one needs to be able to make it operate in a particular terrain. Here France affords a highly promising subject. Nowhere else in Europe does the theory of exiting from religion seem to fit so neatly. France is certainly the country in which the historical process of the dissociation between religion and politics, which characterizes all modern countries, has involved the greatest conflict. The historical symbiosis between the Catholic establishment and the absolute monarchy gave to the process of modernization, achieved none the less with the support of a section of the clergy, the dimension of a genuine religious conflict which cut through the Church itself. The radicalization of the opposing positions during the first five years of the Revolution beginning in 1789 meant that for both sides the adversary must be eliminated. The triumph of the Republic required the humiliation of the Church. One half of France triumphed conclusively over the other. The construction of *laïcité* – the French form of secularism, a system of radical separation between religion and the political sphere – is the outcome of the confrontation which gave no quarter to any form of compromise. The 1905 Act of Separation which was voted in in a climate of civil war paradoxically constituted an instrument of mediation enabling the pro- and anti-religious passions which had reached a climax in the closing years of the nineteenth century to be regulated and gradually calmed. In the new religious order begun in 1905, religion was considered to be a private matter: religious liberty was one among the recognized liberties. The state guaranteed to every citizen the right to profess a religion if he or she had one, but religion itself was considered to be a strictly personal and optional matter. The Republic itself 'neither recognizes, nor provides waged employment for, nor grants funds to, any religion' (Article II of the 1905 Act). Thus the privatization of religion in France, as well as being the end product of a cultural process manifest in all other modern societies, was the result of a deliberate policy. The Catholic hierarchy remained bitterly opposed to the settlement until, first, the rallying of Catholics to the Republic and, second, the shock of the First World War induced it to come to terms with a religious settlement to which it is now greatly attached.

Thus the process of objective secularization, here implying enforced secularization of institutions as a whole, took on in France a comprehensive and definitive character. The process of subjective secularization, signifying the religious emancipation of consciousness, was more gradual, albeit profound. On the eve of the Revolution, and despite significant regional differences, Catholicism, the fount and foundation of social and political life in the *ancien régime*, remained as the matrix of individual attitudes and behaviour and the structure of belief – at least for the rural population, which formed by far the largest sector. A large part of the urban bourgeoisie and of the aristocracy, those who were influenced by the ideas of the Enlightenment, sided with the *philosophes* in rejecting religious obscurantism and ecclesiastical supervision. The nineteenth-century alliance of the Church with the counter-Revolutionary party was to produce throughout the century a major cross-positioning in regard to the Church (Le Bras, 1945, pp. 61–5). The Catholic establishment gave moral and political support to the conservative and reactionary forces with the aim of recapturing the social eminence it had enjoyed before the fracture caused by the Revolution. The bourgeoisie returned to religious practices at a time when the common people, first in the cities, then in the country, tended to abandon them definitively, maintaining only the links that mark the major rites of passage.

On the eve of the Second World War, the French in their majority attended a church service only when the bell rang for them: baptism, marriage, funerals and on other special occasions. The rest of the time the churches were deserted, the number of priests dwindled, the fabric of parish civilization disintegrated. At the close of the twentieth century, Catholic observance in France is among the lowest in Europe. The weekly attendance at mass is under 8 per cent; there is a constant drop in the number of Catholic baptisms and marriages (for all that the figure for church funerals remains more or less stable); and the number of priests continues to shrink.

There were 45,000 priests in France after the Second World War, there are now 20,000; taking account of the age structure, there will be no more than 5,000 to 7,000 by 2005; since 1959, more priests have died each year than have been ordained. The diminishing number of clergy marks the continuing crumbling of a religious civilization.

At the same time, in common with the rest of Europe, the self-assembling of beliefs and observance is spreading, and even the small core of Catholic faithful display considerable liberty in the way in which they appropriate the articles of their faith just as they do the moral prescriptions of the Church. 'Are the French still Catholic?' was the question that supplied the title of a book published by four sociologists at the end of the 1980s (Michelat *et al.*, 1991). The reply, backed up by a series of surveys on the beliefs held by the French, was plainly negative. Thus, if we look no further than these data, the picture on all sides is of a France as highly secularized as could be imagined by those who take the most radical position in regard to the theory of the loss of religion, a sort of ideal type of modern secularity: as much in the institutional domain as in the domain of consciousness.

Yet if the story were to end here a fundamental feature would be lacking: namely the permeation of culture by Catholicism in a country where reference to the beliefs, norms and values imparted by the Roman Catholic Church is negligible. To measure the significance of this secularized Catholicity in present-day French society, one must consider the effect of the far-reaching record of history whereby, in a dialectical fashion, a religion became assimilated into a culture and at the same time incorporated it. Emile Poulat, as a historian of French Catholicism, dwells fluently on this dual movement. On the one hand,

> in a society in which the soil was the basis of the economy and the source of nobility, Christianity took on a rural aspect which outlasted the passage of the centuries and the profound changes in the means of production ... This constituted a major influence on ecclesiastical organization and had a profound impact on the Catholic mentality, both in its popular, traditional and syncretic forms and as represented in official liturgy and teaching, spirituality and even canon law.
>
> (1960, pp. 1168–79)

On the other hand, the Church constituted, on the basis of its own preaching, a body of culture in a society, 'that is both penetrated by it and cherishes it as its source': 'Christianity has succeeded in permeating and in shaping in detail the entirety of the daily lives of a population.' Of this there remains, following the *laïcisation* of institutions and the modern emancipation of consciousness, a '*Christianitude* ... a habitus which has left a profound mark on even the most resolute non-believers' (Poulat, 1982, Ch. III).

Herein lies the most striking paradox of secularization in its French form. Whereas all the evidence points conclusively to individual and collective indifference to that Catholic establishment, mentalities continue to be shaped by a cultural matrix that has been created over centuries by Catholicism. *Laïcité*, secularism in the form it has taken for historical reasons in France, in order to put an end to control exercised by the Church and to the obscurant oppressiveness of religion, itself fits within this mould. The system it instituted rests principally in a confessional definition of religion itself based on a dual premise: on the one hand, the private character of individual choice in matters of religion; and, on the other, the essentially ritual and religious means by which such choice is normally assumed to express itself in a collective manner. This dual assumption governs the context in which religious activity in France is accredited by the state. Its working in fact receives a perfect illustration in the specifically French model of consistorial Judaism set up by Napoleon in 1808. This requires a renouncing of the national element in the Jewish identity, a renouncing that is inseparable from the full integration of Jews into the French nation, which gives concomitant recognition to Judaism as one of the 'official religions of France'.

In order for Judaism to be reckoned as one of the religions accredited by the state, it had to be constituted as a religious body of common belief, a confession, having a central authority and a particular form of worship. In other words, it had to adopt an organizational model that replicated that of the Catholic Church. By the terms of the Act of 1905, the French Republic no longer officially recognizes any form of worship. But it perpetuates a confessional conception of religion that defines the religious community by reducing it in the last instance to the assembly of the faithful gathered for an act of worship. As it happens, this confessional definition of the religious community, which is compatible with the assimilationist model of national identity inherited from the Enlightenment and from the French Revolution, corresponds admirably to the ritual institutional model of the Catholic Church as it functions in a parish civilization in which the act of gathering to celebrate mass is the cornerstone. Indeed, it is directly derivative. Thus is revealed the affinity that exists, behind their historical confrontation, between a Catholic mechanism of religious authority which is both hierarchical and territorially appointed, inseparable from a strict division of religious tasks between priests and laity, and the universalist administrative model which the Republic implemented in every sphere.

It is not merely because of its historical dominance in the life of the nation that the Roman Catholic model was constituted, in the context of *laïcité*, as the organizational reference of every religion. It is also because the ritual institutional construct that it embodies contains implicit reference to the ritual institutional construct of the Republic itself. *Laïcité* took on the social and symbolic force of the Catholic establishment by symmetrically confronting it with its own social and symbolic system – the territorial network of state schools corresponding to the network of parishes: the authoritative figure of the schoolmaster confronting that of the priest; the representative body of the community of citizens facing that of the Catholic communion, and so on. The Republic was able to fight and conquer the might of the Catholic Church by opposing it with the countermodel of a genuine civil religion comprising its pantheon, its martyrology, its liturgy, its myths, its rites, its altars and its temples (Nora, 1996). The confessional definition of 'religion within the limits of the Republic' (this is a parody of Kant's definition of 'religion within the limits of reason alone') imposed on the Catholic Church and on all religious institutions, conforms also to the same mirror-image. In fact, it borrows its references from the Catholic model with the aim of containing its pretensions. This paradoxical affinity may be considered as one of the keys to the secular (*laïque*) reconciliation which in the course of time came about between the erstwhile adversaries. Further, it helps one to understand the difficulties France has in giving full recognition to Islam, which has become the second most important religion in the country in terms of its following, numbering around 5 million, but which has no central institution that is in a position to negotiate with the state. And it throws light on the problem posed by the regulation of sects in a country where religious pluralism can only be conceived in terms of the confessional model that organizes it.

'France is a secular (*laïque*) country whose culture is Catholic': Jean-Paul Willaime's (1996a, p. 154) excellent formula sums up perfectly the paradox of secularization in its French form. On the one hand, a religious loss, which is as much subjective as objective, whose depth, extent and antiquity admit of no argument. On the other, the preservation of a system of Catholic-encoded culture which even now continues to be remarkably compelling. The character of many of the questions that are a matter of public discourse in France, which on the surface appear to have little or no connection with religion – questions touching on the quality of food, on the need to subject science to ethical controls, on the nature of industrial relations or the future of rural life and the countryside – can only be properly understood in the light of the permeation of culture by Catholicism. In fact, as an activity the religious encoding of culture, functioning above and beyond the manifest process of the loss of religion, works differently, but equally cogently, all over western Europe, whether in Scandinavia, Britain, Germany, Belgium or Switzerland, and for similar but stronger reasons in Italy and Ireland. There is insufficient space here to develop examples. The case of France, however, is particularly illuminating because the exclusion of institutional religion from any social role would appear to be more thoroughgoing than elsewhere. But in every European country, the nature and style of politics, the substance of public debate or social problems, the definition of public and private responsibility, the concept of citizenship, attitudes to nature and to the environment, and equally the rules that govern civilized behaviour and so on – all this takes shape in contexts of history and of religion whose influence remains potent. This is so not because religious institutions still possess a real normative capability (we know that this is something they have lost everywhere), but because the symbolic structures they have shaped preserve, above and beyond the loss of beliefs and the collapse of observances, a remarkable potency to permeate culture. In these conditions, it is difficult to consider Europe – even north-western Europe – as an area where secularization is uniform and irreversible.

Can one still speak of secularization? For the notion to preserve some semblance of heuristic relevance its validity requires a dual qualification. In terms of extent first, in line with Peter Berger's view of Europe as its only valid field of application; then of density, remarking that even in this arena it fails to reach down into the deeper layers of culture. One may as well admit that in the final analysis it cannot be taken very far.

Part IV
Signals of transcendence

9 Berger's vision in retrospect

Richard K. Fenn

The precarious vision and the sacred canopy

Of all the sociological images that Peter Berger has given us, two, I suggest, will be a permanent part of the disciplinary lexicon. One is the notion of 'the sacred canopy', a world of meaning that transcends the passage of time and anchors this world in the next. The other image has to do with the experience of the world as anything but anchored in the sacred: the 'precarious vision' in terms of which the social order seems to have little if any foundation at all. The first image requires an openness to the role of religious ideas in social life; the second image requires the sociologist to suspend belief in approaching the mysteries of the social world. One works, as Berger points out, without the assumption of the existence of God (1997a, p. 209).

However, it is this very self-emptying of the sociologist, this relinquishing of religious presuppositions, that allows one to see beyond the surface of the reality, as it were, to the other side of the mirror. The vision of the other world is given only to those who are willing at first to dispense with it, just as the world of the comic, by focusing on the mundane in a new way, opens up a prospect of absurdity or transcendence (1997a, p. 207).

Once this other-worldly vista opens up, the sociologist becomes the religious visionary who can see beyond the flux of everyday life to the world that gives it shape and meaning. The vision of the sacred canopy, so to speak, is given only to those who are willing at first to take seriously the world of everyday life and to ask how it comes to be what it is. Granted that originally the world of taken-for-granted religious meanings arose from the mundane exchanges between husbands and wives, parents and children, soldiers and citizens, torturers and victims. Still it recedes from view as the world takes on its own momentum and offers its own justifications. It becomes a distant and elevated set of symbols and ideas, assumptions and commitments, without which everyday reality would be mundane. Herein lies the paradox that Berger has given us: there is no this-world, so to speak, without an other-world with which to give it coherence and perspective. However, from the vantage-point of the other-world, this one melts away.

When the sociologist is given a vision of this other-world, the world of everyday life suddenly appears to be fragile, tenuous, dependent and derivative. One sees the idea behind the reality, and the reality itself becomes a bit shadowy and ephemeral. Everyday life is seen once again as the flux that it really is, although it has become a flux that has found a way to give itself the symbolic clothing of the given and the inevitable. Certainly the world beyond the cave of everyday life is the one from which light and life emerges, and it is the only world worth living for. Those who see it are transformed. They can no longer take seriously what passes for the sacred in this world. What they once thought was *la vie serieuse* is not so serious after all. Hence Peter Berger's apt notion of 'redeeming laughter' that saves the individual from being taken in by the appearances of normality or seriousness.

In *Redeeming Laughter* (1997a), for instance, he points out that the world can be looked upon as relatively absurd. Indeed, to be a good sociologist one must not take for granted the ordinary if one is to make any sense of it at all. That is because there is really nothing ordinary about it. On the contrary, the world of everyday life is based on another world of hidden meanings, taken-for-granted assumptions, and unconscious fantasies, not to mention cultural fictions and the ghosts of dead beliefs. All these function to make the world of business or family, of politics or entertainment, what it is.

To understand the world of everyday life, therefore, one has to see it from the outside. Typically the sociological outsider, then, is one who is in a particularly good position to question what others take for granted. From the viewpoint of the stranger one can see the hidden premises of everyday life. That allows the sociological observer to imagine what might be and to see the arrangements of any society as particularly *ad hoc*, strange, or even absurd. Thus it is quite remarkable that two people can understand each other perfectly when what is actually put into words offers only a hint of what is meant. Without the other world of assumptions and taken-for-granted meanings, the mundane and obvious aspects of social life would be patently strange, ambiguous or even absurd.

Berger's vision of the world is thus fundamentally a religious one, although it has largely been secularized. That is, he does not need to evoke the presence of angels to account for the unseen aspects of social life; he simply discusses the ways in which sociologists have gone about the business of disclosing the implicit meanings and taken-for-granted assumptions without which social life would grind uncomfortably to a halt. There is less to the observable world than meets the eye. Berger's paradoxical view of social life thus undermines the view that the sociologist's world is open to careful inspection and is therefore observable by someone else whose observations can be used as a check on the sociologist's own perceptions.

The extension of the sociological imagination

Public time, private time

In the years since Berger first put forward his notions of the precarious vision and the sacred canopy, the world has become much more amenable to the suggestion of sociological paradox. Modern societies are now host to a wide range of individuals who can step outside the world-as-it-is in order to see it as temporary or provisional. In part that is because the world of everyday life has now been split into two parts. The one is existential, deeply personal, and may be known to only a few persons or to none other than the individual herself. The other is organized according to the temporal rhythms of bureaucracies and institutions, of large-scale systems and of nation-states. Thus the public world is orchestrated by the fiscal year or the tax year, or by the cycle of elections and of the market-place. Even everyday life is organized according to the schedules of doctors and lawyers, of production and consumption, of the provision of services and the demand for payments of various kinds. It would be a mistake to underestimate the extent to which individuals themselves experience the burden and the pressure of these multiple and sometimes overlapping or conflicting time pressures.

Individuals, however, also live in other time zones that have relatively little to do with the schedules of the hospital or the court, or with routines of social workers or the schedule of the production line. These other time zones have to do with the anniversaries of one's birth or of a death in the family; they concern the individual's sense of where he or she is in life and how far one has yet to go to fulfil one's hopes or dreams, goals or objectives. There is an existential set of times that mark the days on which a tragedy occurred or that define the duration of suffering and hope, aspiration or despair. If the world, to use Berger's seminal notion once again, seems 'precarious', it is because one experiences the times of the public sphere as having little if any resonance with the times of one's own life. If the bell tolls, so to speak, in the village square or on the production line, it may well be tolling for someone else. The clocks that sound their periodic beeps or the bells that ring at the closure of the stock market do not resonate very deeply into the individual's heart or psyche. Even stockbrokers and people with pagers also have to remember anniversaries, worry about the life they are not yet leading, wonder how many years they have left, or count the weeks remaining for their radiation treatments or until their divorces become final. To live in these personal time zones it is not necessary to have a calendar or a watch, and few if any of them are marked by institutional observances of any kind.

I am arguing that the personal experience of time is increasingly freed from public constraints and rhythms, but this freedom comes with a certain increase in the loneliness with which individuals experience the passage of time. The liturgies that once placed the vicissitudes of everyday life in a larger context of public reminiscence and celebration are insufficient, even when they are still observed, to orchestrate the full range of personal encounters with the passage of time. In other words, the experience of the ecstatic has become quite ordinary. One always lives in two worlds at once: a world of deadlines and schedules, and a world, far more intimate, of personal memory and expectation. To alternate between these two worlds is relatively easy. The mind wanders from one to the other in a fashion that may make either world seem provisional and contingent, unnecessary or strange as the case may be. The 'other' world is always there, manifesting itself in ways that can excite the wonder of anyone who has learned to see beyond the immediate and who appreciates how extraordinary or questionable, how distant or irrelevant, the less immediate world may very well be.

No longer is the sociologist the one who is peculiarly able to see the common sense world as anything but common-sensical or who questions the assumptions that sustain it. Others, many others in fact, now may lay claim to the role of a religious seer or prophet who points to the fragility and precariousness of the social order or, for that matter, of the interior world of largely personal concern. It is not only to the sociologically gifted that the world may seem to be artificial or arbitrary, contrived or counterfeit, unnecessary or contingent, and temporary if not wholly doomed. Anyone may see in a society's beliefs or practices a mirror image: a set of ideals that in everyday life may be reversed, but that none the less are a hidden substance that lies in, with, and under the forms of everyday greetings and exchanges, purchases and promises, votes and offerings.

Pentecostal vision

Why are so many now blessed with a second, sociological insight that enables them to see through the appearances of everyday life to the other world that sanctifies and yet also may undermine this one? This paradoxical vision is due in part, as I have suggested, to the differentiation between the worlds of public and private time. However, there are other relevant factors than the separation of the rhythms of personal life from the schedules of the public sphere. As the work of David Martin has shown us, those who are possessed of gifts of the spirit have a particular ability to break the spell of what passes for reality and to see this world in terms of another one. That ecstatic bit of separation from a taken-for-granted existence is now the experience of millions of Pentecostals who in increasing numbers are to be found not only in Latin America and Africa but in the parts of Europe that are recovering from the disintegration of the Soviet empire. Those whose grasp of the social order has been marginal have long had a tendency to see the world as precarious; those for whom the larger society has lost its authority or credibility, as in eastern Europe and the former Soviet Union, are equally likely to be able to stand outside the social order and to imagine another, more stable and inviting one.

However, as Martin (1990; 1996) has argued, it is not sheer marginality *per se* that is conducive to the vision of this world as precarious. It is the gift of charisma that has undermined social orders that have long been taken for granted. That was also Max Weber's point about the unsettling effects of charisma. Various kinds of authority, whether rational or traditional, could be upset by the advent of the charismatic who claim to derive their calling from sources of inspiration and authority not readily available to those who manage the status quo. Charisma is often radically secularizing in its effects. As David Martin has reminded us, priests lose their power to speak for God; the sacraments become signs pointing beyond themselves to another world; duties to landowners, however reinforced by the church, become optional and their observance decadent. The times are no longer owned and controlled by those who set the deadlines for the payment of taxes and tribute. Those endowed with charisma are suddenly coming in to a time-zone of their own, in which the days of this world are numbered and their own future is far more expansive than any they had previously imagined. The past also falls to the axe of charisma, as old obligations are fulfilled or forfeited and new duties undertaken.

Charisma has other secularizing tendencies, of course. Martin notes that those who free themselves from the past and from various forms of peonage or from subservience to dictators now have new obligations that require a new sense of responsibility and rationality. Those newly endowed with charisma also have unprecedented opportunities that require increased rationality. They must concern themselves with the relation of means to ends, and of present actions to the future. The poor become literate and many eventually become professionalized. As they save for the future and for their children's education, they acquire a new sense of what is possible for them and required of them. The times become increasingly full both of danger and of opportunity. The relation of the past to the future hinges on what they do from moment to moment. No wonder they become eschatologically inclined. That inclination itself is a sign that what they do in this world has begun to matter.

Wherever charisma moves, old forms of the sacred lose their mystery. Scholars no longer have a monopoly on interpreting sacred texts; believers do it for themselves. Priests no longer have a monopoly on distributing the means of salvation. Believers have their own unmediated access to divine grace. Churches no longer have a monopoly on sacred times and places. Believers find this world full of opportunities for obedience and grace and lose a great deal of their respect not only for ecclesiastical but for secular authority. Indeed, those who have received charisma are sometimes thought to be antinomian since they understand themselves to be in a new relation to the law. Not only the law of religious institutions but that of the state comes under the judgement of those whose obedience is now given to a higher and more invisible Lord. This new freedom, however, is bestowed on those who take responsibility for the discipline of their own emotions. Of course, some spiritual movements have resulted in the violent overthrow of the church's disciplinary systems and of secular authority. Typically, as Martin (1990) has shown us, those newly authorized by the Spirit to take control of their own lives do so by curbing their violence and addictions, saving their money and educating their children. New opportunities open up, then, and social networks become more complex and resourceful.

Thus charisma is not only a source of the re-enchantment of social systems; it also has long been a major force for secularization, at least in the sense that it has little reverence for old forms of religious authority. To live by the Spirit is to assume that even sacred days such as the Sabbath were made for human beings: not the reverse. Life in the Spirit entitles one to meet human need when and as that need appears, with scant regard for religious inhibitions and proscriptions. One touches whoever requires healing without regard for taboo or consequences. Like Eros, charisma may break down old boundaries that had been held to be sacred. It is therefore not a coincidence that the breaking down of the Iron Curtain and other barriers against the movements of people in Europe has coincided with a rise in popular religious movements, laicized spirituality, and pilgrimages to places of popular devotion. These movements, however, have removed the aura of the sacred from the state and from all those who claim charismatic authority. Even Vaclav Havel has become an object of popular scepticism or even of derision.

The sacralization of the mundane

Under the aegis either of charisma or of the sociological imagination, the world that is revealed to have been resting on taken-for-granted meanings now becomes aware, like the sociologist, of the other side of the looking-glass. People otherwise caught up in the mundane can also peer through the mirror that formerly offered only a set of reflections on this world. That mirror instead now offers a window to the other world. That is, everyone becomes a seer and a visionary, an ecstatic or a prophet, who sees through the images of this world to the shape of the next. This world becomes other-worldly, and prognostication, foresight and insight, fundamental questioning and the suspension of belief become *modi vivendi* for all people some of the time and some people all of the time.

Under these conditions the old dualisms lose their relevance and their meaning. The line, for instance, between this world and the other world becomes problematical when this world becomes filled with possibility. If everyday life brings us to the threshold of the unforeseen or the hitherto impossible, the other world becomes immanent if not entirely mundane. Similarly, the boundary between society and the person becomes tenuous and permeable, as societies become the stage on which individuals engage in self-disclosure; or the arena in which individuals strive for prominence if not mastery.

Microsoft is not merely personified in Bill Gates; Bill Gates is institutionalized in Microsoft. Even those who otherwise have no hope of leaving a mark of their presence on the national stage now have access to enough bombs and guns to draw national attention to themselves for months at a time; witness the shootings at Columbine high school by two boys intent on notoriety and with grandiose ideas of their place in national history. The boundaries between social structure and social process also become difficult to identify or define, as structures become relatively fluid and processes are cybernetically structured. As GM and Ford will now place their bids for supplies and services on the Internet, their internal processes of acquisition and contracting become manifest and continuous: structure and process becoming one. It is difficult in a cybernetic social system to know where one organization begins and another ends: their boundaries are increasingly permeable to the flow of information and ideas.

Enough has been written about global social systems to underscore the same point when applied to nation-states. The insides and outsides of social systems become more like the sides of a Mobius strip: continuous and alternating. Where is the line now drawn between the family and the economy, between home and work? Where is the line drawn now between business and politics, or medicine and insurance? Where is the line now drawn even between church and state or between one nation and another, between the alien and the citizen, or between the neighbour's child and the terrorist? One does not need to engage in ecstatic states of consciousness or to alternate between a taken-for-granted and a more 'precarious' vision in order to imagine, if not wholly to understand, what is happening. Paradox, ambiguity, inconsistency, and contingency have become facts of everyday life.

In the end, then, the oblique and paradoxical viewpoint of the sociologist, who first looks at the world as though God did not exist, becomes the common-sense view of many regardless of their belief in God. The taken-for-granted world is no longer taken for granted. Instead it becomes clearly the result of a myriad decisions and distractions that might never have been. Contingent on human action in the past, it becomes even more contingent in the future. As the Internet makes it possible for information and people to come together in wider networks of communication, it is easier not only to find the right book or toy, but to negotiate novel ways of solving problems, or to imagine other ways of enduring chemotherapy or of preparing for one's last days without pain or unnecessary anguish. The eschatological becomes a suitable subject for ethics committees in hospitals, where doctors and other professionals sit down at the same table with the relatives and friends of a dying patient to prepare for the end.

It is only in the preparation for the end that there is a coming together of the existential and the professional, the deeply personal sense of time and the schedules of medicine and the law. It is then that the 'other' society, to which the seer originally pointed, becomes part and parcel of the existing social order. However, as the social order becomes increasingly permeated with the unprecedented and the possible, it also becomes subject to choice and open to revision. Whereas Berger speaks of the alternation between viewpoints, there is less and less need for an ecstatic break with everyday life. That is because everyday life itself opens on to a sea of possibility, at the far shore of which is, of course, death itself.

It is no accident that what Freud once thought to be a religious experience open to a few is now increasingly mundane. Contemplating such an array of uncertainty and possibility can give one an oceanic feeling as well as a longing for a reunion with the elements. The visionary posturings of venture capitalists and software designers suggest that they do not have to look through a mirror dimly to perceive a world of alternative possibility; they are already initiated into the future and embody its possibilities. So also do those who live in a world of telecommunications and soaring investments; they are not likely to be persuaded that one has to long for the future. A feeling that life is full of infinite possibility, that the horizon is at best undefined, makes it difficult to distinguish between heaven and earth. The problem is to avoid being left behind as the future begins.

The same sense of impinging possibility can also heighten one's existential anxiety. The possibility of becoming redundant increases with the pace of social and technological change. More to the point, one becomes increasingly aware that one's body may be harbouring processes that are lethal. Whether because of a genetic predisposition to later illness or because of damaged DNA that can be silently designing small and undetectable tumours in one's pancreas, the presence of death becomes more immanent, if not imminent. To hold simultaneously a view of this world as unproblematic, solid, and ongoing and a view of this world as being at best flimsy and ephemeral, if not wholly absurd, is simply a way of coming to terms with a very complex and uncertain set of realities. That means that the services of a sociological visionary, who first empties himself of notions about another world, only to find them once again when querying the immediate and mundane, are becoming redundant as every individual becomes his or her own ecstatic and visionary.

If there is still a dichotomy that works, it may be the one that separates the existential experience of time from the public calendar and from the schedules of institutions and organizations. Granted that in some hospitals there has been a rapprochement between institutionalized and personal encounters with the end of one's lifetime. For the most part, however, the two spheres of time exist side by side. In waiting rooms outside a doctor's office or the judge's courtrooms it becomes especially obvious that institutions operate on schedules that are ignorant of and indifferent to the individual's experience of the moment. A lifetime can be reviewed as one waits for the judge to appear or for one's appointment with the doctor to be kept. As I have already suggested, the church's liturgies are lacking that which could consummate an individual's private or personal experience of grief or loss on public occasions of collective reminiscence and aspiration.

Nowhere has this differentiation between public and private time zones been more apparent than in the public celebrations of the end of one millennium and the beginning of the next. Despite the fever of apprehension surrounding possible Y2K disruptions or possible acts of terrorism, the vast majority of people have been relatively calm. Despite the huge public outlays on fireworks and feasts on the occasion, many hotels found that they were still looking for customers as the end of the millennium approached: so many were in fact staying at home. As Frank Rich put it in his *New York Times* column on New Year's Day 2000:

> The more I heard the word 'millennium' and the more I tried to wrap my mind around it, the more I found my own thoughts hewing to the small in scale. Rather than ponder whether the printing press or the microchip was the invention of the millennium, or whether Adolf Hitler or F.D.R. should be marketed as the man of the century, I found myself measuring what was near to me, right at this very minute, right at home.
>
> (p. A31)

The Sacred reduced to the sacred

There are many, of course, who would disagree with my general argument that sociological dichotomies, including the one distinguishing this-worldly and other-worldly orientations, are no longer useful or relevant. They might cite the conventional sociological dichotomy separating the sacred from the profane. Even to discuss this dichotomy, however, we need to be clear about what the words mean. In this discussion I therefore wish to draw a line separating the Sacred from the sacred. By the Sacred I refer to the sum total of possibilities that at any time lie beyond the understanding and control of a particular society. These are the possibilities for life and death, for sickness and health, for maturity and arrested development,
for relationships among the living and the dead, for social isolation, for satisfaction and frustration, for ownership and control of the natural environment, and for the understanding and discipline of the large area of the emotions that remains unconscious.

By the sacred without the capital 's', I mean to refer to all the ways in which the (capitalized) Sacred is brought within the sphere of understanding and control. Note the reduction that is inherent in this transition from the unknown to the recognizable and accessible forms of the sacred. When the world beyond, the Sacred, with all its potential for horror, fascination, and benediction, is brought under control, whether under the auspices of priests or in the visions of a shaman, it becomes the sacred. Salvation, in other words, is offered under certain conditions by those who are in a position to fathom mysteries and provide safe access to the world of possibility.

Note that of all these mysterious possibilities, it is death that provides the most universal and problematic source of mystery. Whether approached as an object of terror or fascination, the possibility of death at any place or time is thus reduced to the certainty of death at particular times and places. Once the Sacred is embodied in the sacred, only the high priest can enter the holy of holies, and only those who have passed the required tests for purification can enter the innermost courts of the temple; all others will die. Conversely, those who follow the prescribed routines for purification and sacrifice are guaranteed life. This do and you shall live. With the reduction of the Sacred to the sacred, those who have a particular saviour can be sure of access to the sources of life; all others have death. Shamans enter into the sort of contact with corpses that would otherwise be polluting and perhaps fatal to the less spiritually adept. The world of spirits and of the departed is itself accessible only to those who have been purified from mundane preoccupations and unworthy motives. The reduction of the Sacred to the sacred is just what one would expect of any social system.

The more the Sacred is reduced to the sacred, the more it is focused in particular times and places, people and events. That focus is precisely what allows a society to claim that it is offering protection against uncertainties and threats that would otherwise confront the individual or community at any time or place. By focusing the sacred in shrines and shamans, in priests and charismatic figures, and in times that memorialize momentous events, a social system is able to claim that it is reducing the sources of terror to manageable proportions. In these reductions the sacred offers a certain fascination, but only at the cost of protecting the individual from the terror that would otherwise occur if the Sacred were to be apprehended directly.

Few, if any, can withstand the encounter with the Sacred. Some, such as Moses, survive and are able to produce laws that the rest of the society must follow if they are to be entitled to receive not only certain satisfactions but also the protections offered by the society against ultimate terror and death itself.

Conversely, the sacred may be less focused and more diffuse. In its more diffuse forms, therefore, the sacred offers more direct access to the Sacred: more access to the sources of life and satisfaction but also a closer encounter with danger and death. The more diffuse is the sacred, the more possible it is for any time or place to offer heightened opportunities for fulfilment and satisfaction; life itself becomes sanctified. However, the diffusion of the sacred also heightens the possibility that the individual may encounter danger or death: rivals for sexual satisfaction, toxic substances, angry spirits, alien microbes, and mortal enemies.

There has been a trend in Western societies over the past three decades towards a greater diffusion of the sacred and with it a tendency to enchant the mundane world of everyday life: witness the widespread belief in angels. Such a belief transforms the moments of everyday life into times that may – or may not – bear sacred significance. Of course, the belief in angels may reflect a growing popular need for spiritual fulfilment or for defence against excruciating social pressures for conformity and productivity, or a primitive attempt to recover immediate access to the sources of one's own being. The more individuals are aware that the world is insensitive to their own existential concerns, the more they may be inclined to believe in the invisible, ubiquitous, and saving presence of another being.

The more the Sacred is reduced to the sacred, the less mystery there will be in any given society. The disenchantment of the universe to which Weber ascribed so much of the process of secularization begins whenever the Sacred is reduced to particular possibilities for satisfaction and fulfilment or to specific liturgical defences against danger and death. The reduction of incalculable possibility to particular recipes for salvific belief and action is the first step in the process of removing mystery from the universe. By contrast with the Sacred, the world of sacred beliefs and practices is relatively lacking in uncertainty and mystery.

The sociological distinction between the sacred and the profane depends for its relevance on the existence of sharp social boundaries between those who qualify for eternal life under the auspices of the sacred and those whose lives will have no memorial. Under these conditions, the world of the profane is an open book. Thus, the more the sacred is focused in particular times and places, persons and events, practices and procedures, the less will other times and places, and so on, be the objects of fascination and veneration. Because they exist outside the occasions and locations where the sacred is focused, they are by definition and social consensus quite profane. As the space before the temple *(pro + fanus)*, the profane is open to inspection even by those who lack any spiritual qualification.

In modern societies, however, the line between the sacred and the profane is largely blurred. Under these conditions there is not only an increased openness to the possibilities for communication with strangers, aliens, and spirits, but also an increased awareness of possible threats to existing institutions and ways of life. Therefore, the more the sacred is diffused, the more will individuals and communities have a heightened sense of possibility and danger over a wide range of situations and circumstances. The enchantment of everyday life caused by increased opportunities for communication and satisfaction is accompanied by a heightened awareness of ambiguity and uncertainty in communications, relationships, understandings, and basic agreements. These heightened possibilities may cause reactionary movements to demand literal readings of the Scripture or to return to a strict construction of such documents as the US Constitution. Under these conditions, furthermore, anxiety over death may focus on a wide variety of potential dangers from microbes and terrorism to environmental and interplanetary catastrophes.

Conversely, because the sacred is diffuse it will be increasingly difficult to obtain agreement on whether any understandings are sacred or profane. The Constitution itself, or the understandings shared in private between doctors and patients, may or may not be regarded as sacred and can be profaned by being opened to public inspection either by the media or by courts of law. Furthermore, the more diffuse forms of the sacred are relatively accessible. One speaks privately to one's own angel instead of going to a shrine where a medium or a priest mediates sacred presences, perhaps for a fee or an offering.

The more that sacred is focused in specific times and places that are under the ownership and control of professional elites or institutions, the more the Sacred is subject to mediation. Where the sacred is highly accessible, of course, it is far more direct and immediate. At the extreme of diffusion, of course, there is no mediation necessary. It is therefore helpful to think of the sacred as undergoing a process of dis-intermediation.

Perhaps a secular example would help to clarify the notion of dis-intermediation. Let us take the case of banking. Where investment is centralized in a single major bank, those who have access to the centre are able to invest their capital in various industries or securities through the banking institution and through the elites that control the flow of capital. Those far from the centre may sew their capital into their mattresses for security or invest it in real estate or livestock: fixed securities that are vulnerable to fire and theft and whose value depends on distant market or demographic forces that are very difficult to know and to control. Brokers and middlemen mediate access to the market, but the rancher and farmer, panhandler and speculator have no direct access of their own. As the process of dis-intermediation reaches the other end of the spectrum, however, dairy farmers are on-line to the futures market and the average investor can eliminate brokers entirely through the use of websites on the Internet.

In the same way, then, access to the sacred has gone through a process of dis-intermediation. Formerly restricted to religious specialists, the Sacrament was given only on occasion to the laity. Groups that administered their own sacraments or claimed access to the sacred through their own piety or ecstatic visions were treated as heretics and subjected to ostracism or the use of lethal force. With the Reformation and its emphasis on the priesthood of all believers, access became somewhat more democratized but was still controlled by a local clerical elite. Indeed, the left wing of the Reformation claimed that believers could have access to the sacred without the ministrations of the clergy; the laity's own untutored understanding of the Word would be enough to place them in the way of revelation. Although frequently attacked as 'individualism', this demand for unmediated access to the sacred has allowed the periphery to demand and slowly to gain access to the electorate and the market and not only to Word and Sacrament.

Conclusion

If sociologists now live in a world in which their conventional dichotomies no longer seem to make much sense, that is no fault of Peter Berger's. On the contrary, his notions of a sacred canopy and of a precarious vision have entered into commonplace sociological usage. The utility of these notions, however, is diminished in part because of the processes of de-differentiation and dis-intermediation that I have just mentioned. Furthermore, the increasing uncertainty and complexity of a world in which ideas and people move with increasing freedom through media such as the Internet makes the precarious vision seem ordinary rather than ecstatic; and the notion of a sacred canopy no longer offers a vantage point from which to understand everyday life. That is because modern societies have largely eroded the distinction between the sacred and the profane, the mundane and the ecstatic, the ordinary and the extraordinary.

When the sacred finally loses its aura, the world of everyday life becomes all there is. Its meanings are open to inspection. Its commitments can be discussed and revised, negotiated and renegotiated. The mysterious other world that allowed contracts to be made and promises fulfilled, that allowed parents to send their children off to die for their country in good conscience: this becomes the material for discussion and debate, for talk shows and on-line chat rooms. It is only a short step from seeing through to the other side of the mirror to looking once again with clear eyes at the world that formerly had seemed to be inevitable: a world, however, that no longer looks as if it were the only possible way to be. Institutions lose the benefit of the doubt. Sacrifice becomes questionable, and calls to sacrifice ignoble.

10 Berger and New Testament Studies

David G. Horrell

Introduction

In the early 1970s New Testament scholars began to rekindle an interest in the social dimensions of early Christianity.[1] Social questions were by no means new to the agenda for historical studies of early Christianity – they had been prominently addressed in diverse ways much earlier in the century, by scholars such as Adolf Deissmann, Shirley Jackson Case, Shailer Mathews, and Karl Kautsky – but for a variety of reasons they had come to be somewhat neglected. By the 1970s, it seemed to a number of scholars that New Testament studies, in its focus on the development of early Christian theology, had rather lost sight of the social realities in which those theological ideas were enmeshed. In Robin Scroggs' (1980) oft-quoted words, 'too often the discipline of the theology of the New Testament (the history of *ideas*) operates out of a methodological docetism, as if believers had minds and spirits unconnected with their individual and corporate bodies' (p. 165). The aim of those who sought to revive an interest in the social aspects of early Christianity was, again in Scroggs' words, 'to put body and soul together again' (p. 166). In 1973 a group was established under the auspices of the US-based Society of Biblical Literature to study the social world of early Christianity (see Smith, 1975). In Germany, the 'sociological' approach to the New Testament was almost single-handedly brought to prominence by Gerd Theissen, who published a series of now classic articles between 1973 and 1975.[2]

As scholars sought to develop their understanding of the social dimensions of early Christianity it was natural that they should turn to the social sciences – themselves expanding in the 1960s and 1970s – for resources to help them in their task. Indeed, in the succeeding decades New Testament scholars have drawn upon a wide variety of theories, models and methods, from sociology, anthropology, social psychology and allied disciplines, in their attempts to illuminate the context and character of the earliest Christian movement. What have come to be known as 'social-scientific' approaches are now well established and widely employed in the field of New Testament studies.[3] And since 1972, when his co-authored theoretical treatise (Berger and Luckmann, 1996b) was (to my knowledge) taken up by a New Testament scholar, Peter Berger's work has remained among the most widely used theoretical resources – and for good reason, as we shall see below. In this chapter I shall first outline some examples of the ways in which Berger's work has been employed in studies of the New Testament. These are, let me stress, only selected examples from what could be an extensive list. Then I shall reflect on both the significant gains and the critical questions that seem to me to remain.

The use of Berger's work in New Testament studies

From the 1970s up to the present, two of Berger's works have remained by far the most frequently drawn upon in New Testament studies: the classic theoretical treatise, *The Social Construction of Reality*, written with Thomas Luckmann and published in 1966, and *The Sacred Canopy*,[4] published by Berger in 1967 and in which he applies the theoretical perspective from the co-authored work specifically to the subject of religion.

The first person to notice the significance of Berger's work for understanding the community-forming role of the New Testament writings was Wayne Meeks, in an article published in 1972. Here Meeks sets out to investigate the enigmatic motif of Jesus' descent and ascent in the Gospel of John. He maintains that the motif must be understood in terms of the social function which it performed: as a part of the Johannine 'symbolic universe' it served to make sense of the history and experiences of the community for which the evangelist wrote, a community which had suffered the painful trauma of separation and isolation from the synagogue. Drawing on Berger and Luckmann's work, Meeks (1972) suggests that the depiction of Jesus in the fourth gospel serves both to create and to reflect the symbolic universe of a sectarian community which has rejected 'the world' and, in a sense, constructed a new one: 'Faith in Jesus, in the Fourth Gospel, means a removal from "the world", because it means transfer to a community which has totalistic and exclusive claims ... If one "believes" what is said in this book, he is quite literally taken out of the ordinary world of social reality' (pp. 70–1). Meeks therefore concludes that:

> One of the primary functions of the book [*sc.* John's Gospel], therefore, must have been to provide a reinforcement for the community's social identity, which appears to have been largely negative. It provided a symbolic universe which gave religious legitimacy, a theodicy, to the group's actual isolation from the larger society.
>
> (p. 70)

Another pioneering work applying social-scientific perspectives to early Christianity was John Gager's 1975 study *Kingdom and Community*. Gager used a wide range of social-scientific studies – on millennarian movements, cognitive dissonance, the routinization of charisma, and so on – to illuminate various aspects of 'the social world of early Christianity' (the subtitle of the book). One of Gager's (1975) basic theoretical foundations is taken from Berger's work, namely the view of religion as 'the human enterprise by which a sacred cosmos is established' (p. 9, quoting Berger, 1967). Clearly indebted to Berger, Gager further describes religion as 'that particular mode of world-building that seeks to ground its world in a sacred order, a realm that justifies and explains the arena of human existence in terms of the eternal nature of things' (p. 10). As a new religion, Gager sees early Christianity primarily as a project of 'world-construction', with 'world-maintenance' emerging as a task once such a movement survives the 'traumatic period of its birth' (p. 10). In a somewhat similar vein, Howard Kee (1980) also acknowledges the stimulus of Berger's work in his approach to early Christianity as a constructed 'sacred cosmos', though he takes his direction more substantially from the work of Alfred Schutz and Thomas Luckmann on *Structures of the Life-World* (1973) (see Kee, 1980, pp. 23–6, 30–53).

A rather different appropriation of Berger's ideas is found in Theissen's 1983 essay on 'Christology and Social Experience' (Eng. trans. Theissen, 1993, pp. 187–201). Taking up Berger's notion of 'plausibility structures' (see Berger, 1970, pp. 50–4), an idea less frequently appropriated by New Testament scholars, Theissen explores how various aspects of Paul's Christology are rendered plausible by social realities of the context in which they were expressed. He examines what he calls 'position Christology', which 'interprets the Christ-event on the analogy of a radical change in social position', and 'participation Christology', which 'works with physiomorphic (or physioform) metaphors', primarily 'the image of the body' (1993, p. 189). According to Theissen, the (limited) opportunities for social mobility in the Roman empire, for example through the manumission of slaves, provide a plausibility basis for early Christian talk of changed position and status for believers. For instance, the one who is a slave is called a 'freedperson of Christ' (1 Cor. 7.22). Correspondingly, Paul's ideas about believers together forming 'the body of Christ' (Rom. 12.5; 1 Cor. 12.27) are meaningful because of the widespread use of the metaphor of the body to describe society.

Berger and Luckmann's theoretical treatise (1966b) provides one of the major theoretical resources for Philip Esler's (1987) exploration of the social and political motivations of the theology of Luke–Acts. Esler focuses particularly on the concept of legitimation, specifically the legitimating function of the symbolic universe. One clear example of this form of legitimation, Esler suggests, is the way in which the author of Luke–Acts (known simply as Luke) 'takes great pains to present Christianity as a faith with a past ... Luke creates a symbolic universe which orders history in such a way as to provide a past, present and future for his Christian contemporaries' (p. 19).[5] Linking these ideas with social-scientific studies of sectarianism, Esler interprets Luke–Acts as an attempt – written for the members of the 'sect' itself – to legitimate the existence of what had originally been a Jewish reform movement but had recently 'acquired a sectarian status in relation to Judaism' (p. 65).[6] Esler then interprets various themes in Luke–Acts in terms of their legitimating function. For example, Luke's portrayal of open table-fellowship between Jewish and Gentile Christians is intended to legitimate this (controversial) practice in the churches of Luke's day: Luke re-writes history so as to summon Peter and James, as well as Paul, in support of this custom (see pp. 71–109; Acts 10.1–11.18; 15.6–29). Another example is Luke's positive portrayal of Rome, for which Esler offers the explanation:

> that among the members of Luke's community were a number of Romans serving the empire in a military or administrative capacity, and that part of Luke's task was to present Christian history in such a way as to demonstrate that faith in Jesus Christ and allegiance to Rome were not mutually inconsistent.
>
> (p. 210)

Some of the theoretical resources central to Esler's approach were taken up by Margaret MacDonald (1988) in her study of the process of institutionalization in the Pauline churches. Once again Berger and Luckmann's work (1966b) (and Berger's 1967 monograph) is, in MacDonald's own words, 'of primary significance' (p. 10). Along with Berger and Luckmann's theory, MacDonald employs Weber's notion of the routinization of charisma and a Troeltschian church-sect typology. She considers the Pauline letters of the New Testament as attempts to construct, maintain and protect a symbolic universe which shapes and orders the belief and practice of the Pauline communities. Along with a majority of scholars, MacDonald regards a number of the epistles attributed to Paul as pseudonymous compositions written some time after Paul's death. Hence she is able to use the Pauline epistles as evidence for a process of institutionalization over a period of time spanning somewhere between 50 and 90 years. MacDonald treats the genuine letters of Paul as reflecting a stage of 'community-building institutionalization'. At this stage in the Pauline movement, 'the [symbolic] universe is in the process of solidifying ... much ambiguity surrounds the question of how members of the community should act and how beliefs should be interpreted. Institutionalization is relatively free to proceed in different directions' (p. 84). With Colossians and Ephesians, written by close associates of Paul around, or shortly after, the time of Paul's death (p. 3) we witness a phase of what MacDonald calls 'community-stabilizing institutionalization'. Here, while the original symbolic universe was transformed, it also gained 'new objectivity as it passed into the hands of a new generation ...

Institutionalization had been set on a more definite course' (p. 157). Finally, the Pastoral Epistles (1 Timothy, 2 Timothy, Titus), written in the early second century (p. 4), represent a stage of 'community-protecting institutionalization'. Heresy and deviance have become pressing problems and the writer's energies are devoted to protecting the church from what are perceived as destructive forces. Stress is placed on the authority of leaders and the need for sound teaching and right conduct: 'In the Pastoral Epistles, the tools of the creative theologian are pushed aside and all attention turns to preservation and protection of existing beliefs' (p. 234). During this period, then, MacDonald concludes, the Pauline churches have moved from their sectarian beginnings towards something closer to Troeltsch's 'church'-type institution, and their originally charismatic form of leadership has been routinized and institutionalized. In short, her study traces 'the transformation of the early church from its loosely-organized, charismatic beginnings to its more tightly-structured nature in the second century' (1988, p. 235).

In very recent monographs too a number of authors have appropriated Berger's work in the formulation of their own approach. For example, Raymond Pickett (1997) draws on *The Social Construction of Reality* in his examination of the ways in which Paul's presentation of Jesus' death on the cross in his Corinthian letters serves to construct and shape the social praxis of the early Christian congregations at Corinth. Pickett explains that his concern is to move beyond social and historical description to an analysis of the 'social impact' that 'a text, or symbol within the text, was designed to have in the realm of social interaction' (pp. 34–5). Here theological symbols and ideas are examined as part of a symbolic universe which shapes and orders human relationships.

Berger's notion of world-construction is important in Edward Adams' (2000) investigation of Paul's use of the terms 'world' (*kosmos*) and 'creation' (*ktisis*) to construct a particular view of the world for his converts and thus shape their interaction with it. However, Adams also raises certain criticisms of Berger and prefers to draw more detailed theoretical resources from the field of critical linguistics (see pp. 23–5).

Significant gains

There are, then, a considerable number of recent studies of the New Testament which have employed Berger's work as a fruitful and important resource for developing new and distinctive understandings of the earliest Christian texts and communities. As Adams (2000) has recently stated: 'Berger's notion of the symbolic universe is now firmly established as a standard heuristic tool in New Testament studies, being widely employed by interpreters' (p. 6). What is it about Berger's work that has encouraged such wide and diverse use, and what have been the gains from this interdisciplinary fertilization?

First, Berger offers a way of approaching the New Testament – or any other religious phenomena, for that matter – sociologically, but without reducing the significance of the religious content to mere epiphenomena, products of social or material determinants. New Testament scholars have rightly been wary of forms of 'reductionism',[7] such as are found in some versions of historical materialism (though not in Marx himself),[8] where religious or spiritual ideas are seen merely as the reflection of specific configurations of socio-economic relationships. Berger and Luckmann (1966b), by contrast, while regarding all 'knowledge', including religious traditions, as a human product (a stance which naturally also raises theological questions),[9] take the constructed cosmos of meaning with great seriousness as a (perhaps *the*) central human achievement in the making of society. Without such a cognitive construction there would be only chaos and anomie: '*All* societies are constructions in the face of chaos' (p. 121). The universe of meaning, humanly produced, is never explained away or reduced to a socio-economic basis, even though it is acknowledged to be enmeshed in and influenced by its material context. Berger maintains that human beings *need* 'meaning', just as they have essential material needs.[10]

Second, with the notion of religion as a 'sacred canopy', a symbolic universe, Berger offers a way of bringing together theological and sociological concerns. The 'content' of the symbolic universe is precisely that 'body of theoretical tradition' which theologians are concerned to elucidate and to develop. But by viewing this body of tradition *as a symbolic universe*, within the theoretical framework set out in *The Social Construction of Reality*, our attention is drawn to the fact that such a body of 'ideas', or 'knowledge', shapes and orders human life. It not only creates a framework of meaning and significance, but also determines the boundaries of right and wrong, structures human relationships and actions. From the perspective of Berger and Luckmann's sociology of knowledge, there is an inextricable connection between theological ideas and social practice. It is not surprising, then, that this theoretical framework was seized upon by those concerned precisely to 'put body and soul together again' in their studies of earliest Christianity.

One further consequence of this theoretical perspective is to blur the boundaries between, and to broaden the scope of investigations into, aspects of New Testament 'theology' and 'ethics'. Under a traditional model it is easy to identify the specifically 'theological' and 'ethical' sections of, say, a Pauline letter such as Romans or Galatians: after an extended theological argument Paul gives specific exhortations about Christian conduct. And studies of ethics may be clearly distinguished from studies of theological or doctrinal topics such as Christology, or eschatology. But once the whole body of theological tradition in the New Testament is viewed as a community-shaping symbolic universe any such distinction between ethical and theological portions of the documents becomes somewhat (though not entirely) artificial. For even thoroughly 'theological' ideas about God, Christ, the Spirit, convictions concerning righteousness and salvation, and so on, all serve to structure the identity and interaction of the Christian community. The whole symbolic universe gives meaning and shape to human life. Hence authors such as Pickett (1997), briefly mentioned above, using this perspective, examine how particular theological symbols or ideas shape the social praxis of the early Christian communities.

Berger's work has also provided a stimulus to study the ways in which theological ideas legitimate particular social practices and patterns of social interaction (as in Esler's (1987) work: see above). Once again this brings the study of theology down to earth, so to speak: one is led not only to investigate the structure, logic or history of some specific idea, but also to ask about what pattern of conduct and relationships, what position of authority, whose interests, it serves to legitimate. Such questions are fundamental to any attempt to investigate theology *critically*, since they help to focus attention on its *social impact* or implications, and, moreover, on the crucial issues of power and ideology: who says what to whom, and in whose interests?[11]

In short, for those who seek to develop a social-scientific perspective on the New Testament, Berger's work provides some basic *desiderata* which are, it seems to me, likely to remain of central importance. The conception of a symbolic universe which shapes the lives of those who inhabit it provides a theoretical framework which takes the theology of the New Testament seriously but which opens up sociological questions about how this universe orders and legitimates certain patterns of social life and interaction. From this point of view early Christianity is indeed a project of world-construction — not *ex nihilo*, to be sure, but with long-established traditions from its religious and cultural parent, Judaism; yet certainly a new and distinctive creation, which shaped and ordered human lives in a distinctive manner.

Critical questions

However, along with the important gains that Berger's work has brought to New Testament studies there are also critical issues to be considered. I am not primarily concerned here with the 'theological' issues, to which Berger himself has previously responded (see note 9), raised by the view of New Testament theology as a human construction;[12] rather it is the issues relating to the practice of social-scientific, or socio-historical, method that I intend to explore.[13]

My first question concerns the use of the notion of legitimation. While I am entirely persuaded that this is an important concept with which to explore questions about the social purpose or impact of theological texts, it seems to me that it can be used to present such texts as forms of post-practice reflection, rather than as ideas which may have played a causal role in establishing certain forms of practice in the first place. Indeed, this sequence of practice followed by legitimation derives from Berger and Luckmann's analysis, where a form of social interaction subsequently has to be justified or explained to a third party, or a new generation, and hence gives rise to forms of legitimation (cf. Berger and Luckmann, 1966b, pp. 110–22; Berger, 1967, pp. 29–36). So, for example, Esler sees Luke as engaged in an attempt to legitimate the practice of mixed table-fellowship (see above). Francis Watson (1986) regards much of Paul's 'theology' as serving a 'social function': to legitimate the sectarian separation of the Pauline law-free congregations from the Jewish synagogues. For Watson, Paul's decision to turn to the Gentiles in mission and to preach a gospel free from the demands of the Jewish law (circumcision and so on) came about for merely pragmatic reasons; his theology is a legitimating ideology which is intended to undergird the state of separation between Pauline sect and 'parent' Judaism. In this essentially functionalist analysis (Paul's theology serves a social function) it seems that the view of Paul's theology as legitimation obscures any appreciation of the possibility that theological convictions may have played a key role in initiating and establishing the forms of social practice that remained controversial and thus subsequently needed to be (further) legitimated. For example, the baptismal tradition that 'there is no longer Jew or Gentile ... you are all one in Christ' (Gal. 3.28; cf. 1 Cor. 12.13; Col. 3.11) seems highly likely to have played a part in establishing the practice of mixed table-fellowship at Antioch and elsewhere, although clearly the practice proved controversial and thus led to further arguments and attempts to legitimate it (see Gal. 2.11–21). I am not, let me stress, meaning to imply that the concept of legitimation is not of considerable importance, but there is a danger that its use as an interpretative tool can lead to texts being interpreted primarily as attempts to legitimate already existing forms of social practice. The social practices themselves are thus left initially unexplained, emerging for merely accidental or pragmatic reasons.[14] Here one sees the need for what Berger himself has emphasized as characteristic of social life, namely an appreciation of its dialectical and diachronic character, in which, over time, ideas and social practices interrelate, with ideas serving to initiate, shape and legitimate various forms of social life, which are themselves always enmeshed in an ongoing and ever-changing process.

My second concern arises from the *way* in which Berger and Luckmann present the objectivity of the social order in their attempt to grasp the ongoing dialectic of externalization, objectification and internalization. While they seek to do justice to the fact that the social order is only ever a human construction, and one which is continually in the process of production, so to speak, their theory *presents* the social order as something which attains a form of objectivity and which can be threatened, protected, and so on.[15] This focus on the objectivity which the social world attains can lead to a neglect of the extent to which this world is continually being reproduced and hence transformed, in and through human action, and may lead also to a portrayal of *change as threat* (cf. Berger, 1967, pp. 29–32). Despite their aims, then, I question whether Berger and Luckmann's theory of the social construction of reality grasps adequately the relationships between action and structure, reproduction and transformation.[16] This theoretical perspective can itself serve as an ideological legitimation of the status quo: first, because it presents as a solidified 'object' what is in fact a fluid, contested, and continually reproduced set of customs and conventions, and second, because it portrays 'challenges' to the dominant social order as threats which may unleash the dreaded forces of chaos and anomie.[17] As I suggested in 1996:

> The fact that a social order may be experienced as 'coercive power' by many is not necessarily to be explained by the notion that it is 'externalised' and 'objectified' but rather by the fact that certain groups have power and others do not. Berger and Luckmann present as a feature of the construction of social reality what is in fact a feature of the unequal distribution of power ... The labelling of some forms [of the symbolic order] as 'deviant' may be a strategy of dominant social groups to portray themselves as defenders of the social order while stigmatising and externalising others.
>
> (Horrell, 1996, pp. 42–3)

What is implicit in the above quotation is my third concern, expressed in Anthony Giddens' terse comment that Berger and Luckmann's approach 'completely lacks a conception of the critique of ideology' (Giddens, 1979, p. 267 n. 8). What I understand by this is that there is no systematic attempt to explore 'the ways in which meaning (or signification) serves to sustain relations of domination', to use John Thompson's definition of ideology (Thompson, 1984, pp. 4, 130–1). To what extent does a particular symbolic universe sustain the interests of particular social groups or classes? How are specific relations of domination concealed as 'natural' and inevitable in a specific symbolic order? And how might the presentation of alternatives as threats to the very fabric of human society serve to legitimate ideologically the maintenance of a conventional pattern of social relations? In short, while Berger and Luckmann focus on the construction of the social order and its maintenance in the face of threats as a sine qua non for human society, there are also critical questions to be asked about the ideological dimensions of this process: about the distribution and exercise of power, the legitimation of sectional interests, and the strategies used to marginalize critique and alternatives in any specific form of the social order.

These critical concerns may be illustrated with reference to the New Testament.[18] In her study outlined briefly above, MacDonald (1988) uses Berger and Luckmann's work (1966b) to provide the fundamental theoretical framework for her investigation into the process of institutionalization in the Pauline churches. According to MacDonald, the Pastoral Epistles represent a stage of 'community-protecting institutionalization', where the author is concerned to protect the community and its symbolic universe from the threat presented by heretical or deviant forms of teaching. Here Berger and Luckmann's theoretical perspective converges closely with the perspective presented by the author of the Pastorals. First, just as Berger and Luckmann present the symbolic universe as an objectified body of tradition, so too the Pastorals' author presents his own teaching as a faithful presentation of Pauline doctrine (cf. 2 Tim. 1.13–14; also 1 Tim. 1.1–20). What this author therefore conceals is the extent to which his instruction is actually a transformed form of Pauline teaching, just as Berger and Luckmann's (1966b) notion of objectification can conceal the extent to which the social order is continually being reproduced and transformed. Second, just as Berger and Luckmann present challenges to the dominant social order as threats which may induce chaos and anomie, so the Pastorals' author presents his opponents as nothing but 'despicable deviants'[19] whose teaching threatens to undermine the very existence of the churches (see e.g. 1 Tim. 4.1–3; 2 Tim. 3.1–9; Titus 1.10–16). Using a theoretical perspective derived from Berger and Luckmann's work seems therefore to lead to confirming the ideology of this conservative author, rather than penetrating it critically. Questions should be asked about the ways in which both the 'opponents' *and* the author of the Pastorals are promoting particular forms of the Pauline tradition and about the power-struggle which this reflects; about the ways in which the Pastorals' author uses his form of Christian teaching in the service of particular social interests, to keep subordinate social groups – primarily women and slaves – firmly in their place (see 1 Tim. 2.11–15; 6.1–2; Titus 2.1–10); and about the attempt to marginalize alternative viewpoints by *labelling* them as heretical and threatening. Somewhat ironically – since she expresses some sympathy with those whose voices were marginalized and silenced (MacDonald, 1988, p. 238) – MacDonald's theoretical framework does not give conceptual space to such questions. This illustrates for me why the important theoretical resources provided by Berger and Luckmann's theory need to be woven into the framework of a more critical social theory, in order to facilitate a critical sociological analysis of the early Christian movement.

Conclusion

Berger's theoretical work – and especially his treatise co-authored with Luckmann (1966b) – has been widely influential in recent social-scientific study of the New Testament. There are, I have suggested, good reasons for this influence, for Berger's conceptual framework has provided a valuable way of appreciating the New Testament texts as theology, but as theology which – produced by human beings – constructs a meaningful human world and shapes the human conduct which takes place within that 'world'. The gains from this reconceptualization will be lasting. However, I have also raised some critical concerns about the shortcomings of this theoretical framework which illustrate why I think that its valuable insights need to be incorporated into a critical theory which gives more space to issues of power, interests and ideology. Of course, the broader challenge to New Testament specialists seeking to develop a sociological understanding of early Christianity is to avoid any simple adoption of this or that model or theory, popped into their shopping trolley during a brief dash through the social-scientific supermarket, and instead to adapt and refine their theoretical resources so that they are appropriate for the task of investigating the ancient texts that form their primary object of study. It should not be surprising if *The Social Construction of Reality* (1966b) and *The Sacred Canopy* (1967), published over three decades ago,[20] and written by sociologists whose primary field of empirical study is the contemporary world, need careful and critical appropriation in order to contribute to contemporary studies of the New Testament and its world. But the fact that these works have inspired – and continue to inspire – such a range of scholarly studies of the New Testament is ample tribute to the creativity and scholarly acumen of Peter Berger. In my particular field of study, though in some ways far removed from that of Berger's own, his considerable influence will continue to be felt for some time to come.

Notes

1 For a more detailed overview of the developments sketched here, and a summary of current debates in the field and prospects for future development, see Horrell (1999a).
2 These essays were collected together and published in Theissen (1979). English translations are available in Theissen (1982; 1993).
3 A representative collection of the range of work produced between 1973 and 1997 may be found in Horrell (1999b).
4 Published in the UK under the title *The Social Reality of Religion* (1969c).
5 Cf. Berger and Luckmann (1966b): 'The symbolic universe also orders history. It locates all collective events in a cohesive unity that includes past, present and future' (p. 120).
6 This model, drawn from Esler's work and without explicit reference to Berger and Luckmann, is applied to Paul's letters by Watson (1986).
7 This issue has often been discussed when considering the merits and dangers of using the social sciences in biblical exegesis. See e.g. Holmberg (1990, pp. 149–50) and Malina (1982, pp. 237–8).
8 Cf. the comments of Berger and Luckmann (1966b, pp. 17–18) and Giddens (1971, pp. 205–23).
9 Questions to which Berger himself has responded: see Berger (1967, pp. 179–88) and (1970). For discussion of the theological implications of Berger's work, see also Cairns (1974); Gill (1974; 1975, pp. 29–34; 1977, pp. 16–22).
10 See e.g. Berger (1974a); also Wuthnow (1986, pp. 126, 136, etc.).

11 According to Berger (1963b), one of the basic questions from the sociological perspective is 'Says who?' (p. 80). The discipline has a fundamentally 'unmasking tendency' (p. 51) in questioning that which is conventionally taken-for-granted. In the study of religion, where people claim to speak of the divine will, and so on, 'unmasking' this claim to power by asking, 'Says who?' seems to me of particular importance.

12 But for a recent attempt to place *theological* interpretation at the heart of New Testament studies, see the work of Francis Watson (e.g. 1994).

13 For further detail on the following ideas, see Horrell (1993; 1996, pp. 39–45). Philip Esler has responded to my critique of Berger and Luckmann in Esler (1998); for my response, see Horrell (2000).

14 Berger (1986b) himself has seen the same problem, stating that legitimation 'is one of the few terms in *The Social Construction of Reality* (and, consequently, in *The Sacred Canopy*) that I would prefer to reword today ... "Legitimation" suggests that the social structure legitimated is indeed prior, logically as well as chronologically, to whatever the legitimating ideas are. This is generally distortive, and particularly so in the case of religion' (pp. 229–30).

15 Cf. e.g. Berger and Luckmann (1966b, pp. 76–7; Berger and Pullberg, 1966, p. 63; Berger, 1967, pp. 11, 24–5).

16 Hence I have preferred in my own work to adopt a framework which, while indebted to Berger and Luckmann, takes its orientation from Anthony Giddens' structuration theory (see Horrell, 1996). On the similarities and differences between these and other attempts to resolve the fundamental theoretical issue of the relationship between human action and social structure, see Bhaskar (1979, pp. 39–47) and Gregory (1981, pp. 10–11).

17 It is notable that Berger has become more clear and explicit about what I think it would be fair to call his conservative proclivities (cf. e.g. 1986b, pp. 223, 225–6; 1991). My reading and critique of *The Social Construction of Reality* (1966b) may therefore perhaps be nearer the mark than the interpretations of those who see in it a radical analysis of society. Berger writes: 'When *The Social Construction of Reality* and other early writings of mine were taken as a warrant for the various Utopian eruptions of the late 1960s and early 1970s, this was due to a profound misunderstanding ... I may have "moved to the right" on specific political issues, but it is they who misread radicalism into these early writings. It was never there, either objectively or in intention' (1986b, p. 223).

18 For a more detailed presentation of the critique outlined here, see Horrell (1993).

19 To use the felicitous phrase of Lloyd Pietersen (1997).

20 Though Berger's view, at least in 1986, was that: 'Of all the books I wrote or coauthored during the earlier part of my career, this [*The Social Construction of Reality*] is the one that I would change least if I were to revise it today' (1986b, p. 222).

11 Berger's anthropological theology

Bernice Martin

I've always had a weakness for divinity.

(Berger, 1975, p. 38)

Introduction: on being a modern Protestant and a sociologist

In an essay he wrote in 1998 for a Christian journal, Peter Berger summed up the intellectual conclusions of a lifetime. He begins with a typically arresting first paragraph:

> In the course of my career as a sociologist of religion I made one big mistake and had one big insight (arguably not such a bad record). The big mistake which I shared with almost everyone who worked in this area in the 1950s and 1960s, was to believe that modernity necessarily leads to a decline in religion. The big insight was that pluralism undermines the taken-for-grantedness of beliefs and values. It took me some time to relate the insight to the mistake. And it has only been very recently that I understood the implications for the position of Protestantism in the contemporary world.
>
> (1998, p. 782)

Berger's argument is that while modernity as such does not invariably mean secularization – Europe is exceptional rather than exemplary in this respect since 'most of the world today is as religous as it ever was and, in a good many locales more religious than ever' (ibid.) – the pluralism that tends to come with modernity affects the basis of belief. It is not so much that people believe less, or believe different things, but rather that they believe in a new and more uncertain fashion. In the past people on the whole believed what others who inhabited the same 'life-world' and belonged to the same 'plausibility structures' believed, and they held those beliefs with a more solid and unquestioning sense of their reality than is possible in contexts which reveal the contingency of these life-worlds and religious traditions by forcing them to jostle for place in the cultural free-for-all which is pluralism.

The long-term consequence of pluralism, Berger suggests, has been the cultural necessity of living with inescapable uncertainty in a world where people seem to need a degree of certainty in order to function as humans at all. Human consciousness is paradoxically constituted in that it is a lack of existential, if not ontological, certainty and security, especially in childhood, which breeds intolerance and a sometimes murderous distrust of all who are different. This contradiction, built into the foundations of pluralist cultures, gives rise to a chronic oscillation between nihilism and fanaticism, between a vertiginous relativity and a susceptibility to the claims of the many competing purveyors of absolute certainty.

Berger proposes the Lutheran formula, *sola fide*, as the only way out of this impasse. Knowledge – whether tangibly empirical, abstractly philosophical or the certainty we take for solid knowledge because it comes from the unexamined, subterranean layers of the life-world – has no need of either belief or faith. The role of faith is to undergird belief in precisely those uncertain areas where we cannot call on knowledge. In the West today few people any longer rest their religious affirmations on claims to certain knowledge, though three assertions of absolute certainty, deriving from past religious history, live out a contested afterlife in inauspicious pluralist contexts. These are: absolute certainty of the truth of the scriptures; of the tradition of the church; and of personal religious experience. All three have been seriously weakened by the modern human sciences: 'the certainty of the institution by historical scholarship; the certainty of the text by the findings of biblical criticism and the certainty of inner experience by psychology and the sociology of knowledge' (1998, p. 792).

What remains is the option of 'epistemological modesty' about truth claims (Berger is here quoting his colleague Adam Seligman who coined the phrase in discussion at a conference on 'Tolerance in World Religions' in 1998) and a position akin to the classic Protestant view of the sacrament of the eucharist as neither mere human commemoration nor a miracle of transubstantiation:

> It seems to me that the same understanding of the presence of God in the world – 'in, with and under' its empirical elements – can be applied to the institution of the church and the Biblical text. Such an approach to religion can, with some justice be called relativizing. But it is well armored against that extreme of relativization that falls over into nihilism, for it is founded on faith in God who is truth. We may not know what this truth is; we may only get glimpses of it here and there; but in that faith we can never give up the notion of truth.
>
> (Berger, 1998, p. 793)

Churches based on this kind of believing may be 'weak' institutions, in the sense that they are full of what Berger calls 'uncertainty wallahs', but they show considerable resilience not least because their individual members are there out of choice. And choice – what in an earlier work he called 'the heretical imperative' (Berger, 1979a) – is the unavoidable doom and blessing of those living in pluralist cultures. He even speculates that such churches, which have 'institutionalized permanent reflection' are more likely than the 'strong' 'triumphalist' ghettoes of certainty to be places where the presence of the 'kenotic', 'self-emptying' Jesus may be found, 'where people are unsure of themselves, groping for a few glimpses of truth to hold onto, even where it seems the roof is about to fall' (1998, p. 796).

I begin with Peter Berger, 'uncertainty wallah', and his lucid and economical summary of his considered position on these matters, in order to place in the context of his long-term preoccupations the two books on which this chapter will concentrate, his remarkable novel, *Protocol of a Damnation* (1975), and *A Rumor of Angels* (1969a) [English edition, *A Rumour of Angels*, 1970)] which he described as an exercise in 'anthropological theology'. Together, these two works constitute Berger's first systematic attempt to find a way through the problems which the relativizing tendency of pluralism poses for Christian belief. They are Berger's proposal for a modernized grounding of faith to underpin belief in a world where knowledge can no longer do the job – using these terms in the sense he spells out in the 1998 essay. The problem, as we shall see, however, is Berger's itch to join up the triangle formed by the three concepts and bring 'knowledge' back in as the basis of 'faith' even though he has already recognized the difficulty of such a move, not least because his own work in developing the sociology of knowledge has rendered it problematic. But this is to anticipate.

Both *Protocol* and *Rumour* lie somewhat at a tangent to Peter Berger's strictly sociological work, but at the same time they represent a fundamental strand in his thinking and a deeply serious response to the dilemmas anatomized in his sociology of religion. If we are to give these two books their proper place in the Berger *oeuvre* we need to relate them both to the continuities and to the major changes in his thinking, particularly the crucial revisions which characterize his work in the course of the 1960s.

Peter Berger has never made any secret of being a believing Christian formed in the European Lutheran tradition, as well as being a professional sociologist. He does not separate these two personae except heuristically for the purposes of methodological clarity and intellectual candour, but rather allows the Christian and the sociologist to fire questions at each other. The processes he analyses in the wider culture are also part of his own religious and intellectual biography. They leave him (in common with the rest of us) no uncontested territory on which to stand where the problems he grapples with as a sociologist have not already invaded the ground he occupies as a believer. Both as Christian and as scholar he counters the dilemmas of cultural pluralism – how to sustain belief despite the erosions wrought by the plural market in life-worlds; how to salvage reason and objectivity from the wreckage of the intellectual drift to relativism – by recommending empirical thoroughness and 'methodological agnosticism', though both prove difficult to sustain with consistency. And while he makes no claim to theological expertise – indeed he often explicitly disclaims it – he tends to use both his experience of being a contemporary Protestant believer and his sociological knowledge to run a reality check on theological formulations.

Berger has been strikingly consistent in worrying at the implications of pluralism and the problems and potentialities which emerge once the taken-for-grantedness of social (and religious) reality has been disturbed for whatever reason. Indeed, this issue forms a connecting thread running through the whole of Berger's writings. Diverse though his subject matter may seem, the ambiguous dual legacy of pluralism is the enduring theme extending from the early sociology of religion, through the ground-breaking work in the sociology of knowledge with Thomas Luckmann (1966a), the analysis of contemporary consciousness and the work on marriage and the family with Brigitte Berger and Hansfried Kellner (1973), to the role of cultural change in economic and political development which has mostly absorbed his energies in recent years.

During the 1960s Berger gradually but, in the event, dramatically, shifted his position on the significance of disturbances in the taken-for-granted and adjusted his perspective on the relationship between religious commitment and sociological argument no less decisively. By the end of the 1960s he was a distinctive and hugely influential voice. He has sustained the position then arrived at with little further modification up to the present. A brief overview of the distance travelled in that momentous decade may provide a useful backdrop to the concerns of this chapter.

In 1961 Peter Berger was a passionately committed Lutheran who wanted to use sociology to reveal the disjunction between the true Christian vision – radical, prophetic, bringing judgement and proclaiming a bitterly bought Kingdom – and the institutional churches inhabited by comfortable Americans. In *The Precarious Vision* (1961a) he contrasts the core Christian message with the array of 'comforting social fictions' in which the church is so implicated and embedded that they are commonly mistaken for Christianity itself. In *The Noise of Solemn Assemblies* (1961b) he proposes a programme for deploying sociology as the 'acid' applied to the 'alloy', the church, to distil the precious metal of the true faith from the dross of the church's social, cultural, political and psychological 'functionality' in 'our OK world' (Berger 1961b, p. 118). Berger is clear that the Christian vision, though 'precarious' and shot through with paradox, is *inherently* athwart the interests of social convenience, personal comfort and acceptance of the – of *any* – status quo. His is a prophetic Christian reading signalled from the outset even in the title borrowed from Amos' denunciation of the Hebrew cultus and his prophetic call to righteousness and justice. In these two books one perhaps overhears the impatience not just of a young man but of an Austrian, who grew up amid the conflagrations of Nazism and a world war, who finds the unshaken complacency of mainstream American churches in the 1950s a goad and the precariousness of the radical Christian vision in the face of social inertia all too apparent.

At this point Berger is still preoccupied with the *restrictive* weight of the taken-for-granted in both individual and institutional life and the huge effort required to shift it in order to pursue God in ecstatic metaphysical encounter and in the search for the justice of the Kingdom. Even so, he has already glimpsed the effects of pluralism out of the corner of his sociological eye. Thus he writes (1961b) that 'There are many Americans, young and not-so-young, who have "left home". And many have learned that they "can't go home again"'... in the sense of returning to the taken-for-granted social reality of their past' (p. 118). And he declares in a ringing passage that it is now possible:

> to break ecstatically through the confines of an American biography ... and to break through the taken-for-granted character of an American religious upbringing ... It is possible to be free as an American ... to enter on a passionate search for truth in America ... That such spiritual adventure has its social and psychological risks is but a measure of its authenticity ... religion is out of place on those occasions when Americans try to shake off the weight of the pretenses of social propriety.
>
> (ibid. pp. 118–19)

His view of the institutional church is severely negative. 'Any situation in which the church exists in a culture without noteworthy tension provides a danger signal', he declares (ibid., p. 132). The current danger signals include 'this-worldliness, moralism, success, activism, conformity to cultural norms and suppression of metaphysical concerns' (ibid.). Furthermore, the church's – admittedly legitimate – concern with liturgy is no excuse for its neglect of social engagement: 'liturgy is not the key to the Kingdom of Christ. The key is obedience in faith and action. As Dietrich Bonhoeffer once put it during the Nazi era, only he who cries out for the Jews has the right to sing Gregorian chants' (ibid., p. 176).

Reading again these 1961 texts, it is not difficult to see why so many young campus radicals of the 1960s looked to Berger as their guru – to his irritation and disgust, it should be said. His brilliantly accessible introductory textbook *Invitation to Sociology* (1963a), still a bestseller, was and remains appealing to apprentice sociologists precisely because of the vividness and clarity with which he reveals as culturally *constructed*, and thus alterable, so many 'social facts' which had seemed immutable. Indeed Berger, together with his fellow Austrian, Thomas Luckmann, in their immensely influential collaboration, *The Social Construction of Reality*

(1966a), delivered the *coup de grâce* to those reductionist versions of classical sociology, Marxist and functionalist alike, which, preoccupied with their own intellectual Cold War in the 1950s, had lost sight of the social potency of individual actors. More than any other single text, it familiarized the mass of Anglophone social scientists with the German phenomenological tradition and united it with mainstream Weberian scholarship in a powerful synthesis. This enabled a new generation to restore the human person to the heart of sociology, not as the impotent cipher of implacable structures and impersonal processes but as the creative agent of cultural construction and *re*-construction. *The Social Construction of Reality* was a prime constituent in the turn to culture as the crucial locus of analysis in the social sciences. It also served as a handbook on the liberating potential of sociology, in particular of the sociology of knowledge. Indeed, Berger was still stressing this point in *A Rumour of Angels* (1969a): 'While other analytic disciplines free us from the dead weight of the past, sociology frees us from the tyranny of the present. Once we grasp our own situation in sociological terms, it ceases to impress us as an inexorable fate' (p. 62).

Nevertheless, by the middle of the 1960s Berger had also become concerned about certain negative effects of that kind of 'liberation'. His 'big insight' about pluralism as solvent of the taken-for-granted (with or without a little help from sociology) also brought a realization of the increased difficulty of sustaining a religious vision in face of incipient intellectual relativism and the increasing fragility of Christian institutions in the competitive market in world-views. Churches, which in 1961 had been castigated as the distorting mirror of the Christian message, had gradually taken on the aspect of threatened bulwarks against loss of belief, rickety but precious 'plausibility structures'. At the end of the 1960s Berger had not yet resolved these worries by positively embracing uncertainty and fragility as he does in the 1998 essay. He still felt the pressure of pluralism as a probable presage of secularization and certainly as a problem for individual believers seeking places where they might share or jointly create a Christian life-world with others of like mind. (He makes the same point about marriage as a necessary but precarious exercise in '*nomos* construction' in a famous and often reprinted essay (Berger with Kellner, 1977).)

Towards renewing the foundations of faith: the reaffirmation of transcendence

In 1967 Peter Berger published *The Sacred Canopy: Elements of a Sociological Theory of Religion* (which appeared as *The Social Reality of Religion* in Britain in 1969), applying the perspective developed with Thomas Luckmann to the field of religion. As he notes in the preface to *A Rumour of Angels* (1970), it 'read like a treatise on atheism, at least in parts' (p. 9). The language of sociological discourse, including the phenomenological vocabulary of 'cultural construction', even when deployed by so lucid a prose stylist as Peter Berger, tends to have implicit Feuerbachian overtones when it comes to religion. The human person may be back in focus but where is God? Is He just another cultural construction? How is the sociologist who is also a believer to write about 'divinity' or 'the supernatural' without sounding reductionist? Is the reductionist implication in the language in fact inseparable from 'methodological agnosticism'? These were the problems which prompted Berger to write the two books which are the primary focus of this chapter, his novel, *Protocol of a Damnation*, written in 1965–6 but not published until 1975, and *A Rumor of Angels* (1969a). Both were bold ventures going well beyond the accepted territory of professional sociology. It is true that Berger had published an earlier comic novel under the pseudonym of Felix Bastian, but *Protocol* was an altogether more serious and ambitious work. *A Rumour of Angels* was an equally daring experiment in which Berger, the religious seeker after truth, and Berger, the sociologist of religion, stuck out their shared neck and attempted to derive the beginnings of an 'inductive theology' from the materials of the human sciences.

In fact, as he explains in the Afterword to the novel, the two books are facets of the same enterprise:

> [*Protocol*] was begun in Ascona in the summer of 1965, finished in New York in the summer of 1966. As it later turned out, it opened up for me the central theme of my *Rumor of Angels* (1969). This theme, which occupies me as much today as it did then, could be described as the apparent inevitability of some sort of Christianity.
>
> (1975, p. 208)

The arguments first propounded in *Protocol* and *Rumour* were, perhaps, given an additional urgency by Berger's sense, at the time, of impending secularization, though, curiously enough, despite the heavy emphasis in the conclusion of *Rumour* on secularization as the force which was causing 'the divine fullness' to 'recede' (Berger, 1970, p. 118), earlier parts of the book hint that he was already beginning to wonder whether secularization was as inevitable as all that (p. 39). Even when he later fully corrected that one 'big mistake' about secularization, he felt no call to revise the essential argument of the novel and of *Rumour*. Indeed, in the 1990s he went back to these ideas and further developed them in the Noble Lectures delivered at Harvard in 1991–2, published in book form as *A Far Glory* (1992), and extensively elaborated as one strand of the argument in *Redeeming Laughter* (1997a). These ideas, first formulated in the second half of the 1960s, were Peter Berger's attempt to use an empirical method to shore up the threatened foundations of faith. He has persisted in the enterprise undaunted, despite his clear recognition that the sociology of knowledge (to which he and Luckmann had made such a decisive contribution) had further compounded the difficulties on which so many previous attempts to put faith on a rational basis through the use of a sceptical and empirical method had already foundered.

Like his compatriot and fellow Lutheran, John Updike – a novelist with a well-documented 'weakness for divinity' (Yerkes, 1999) – Peter Berger had decided by the mid-1960s that the sense of the 'transcendent', of something 'beyond', was an inescapable given of human cultures and that to seek it outside everyday reality was to look for it – whatever 'it' is – in the wrong place. Rather than working like a conventional theologian from Christianity as revelation, he would interrogate the anthropological record ('in the continental sense' of 'systematic inquiry into the constitution and condition of man' (Berger, 1970, p. 66)) for the evidential basis of a theology. It must be an objective, 'non-psychological' (ibid. p. 40) index of the persistence of belief in 'the transcendent'. He uses the latter term, following Rudolph Otto, to mean 'belief that there is *an other reality* and one of ultimate significance for man which transcends the ordinary reality within which our everyday experience unfolds' (Berger, 1969a, p. 14).

That 'disenchantment of the world' postulated by Weber and putatively derived from the same advance in the human sciences which has knocked the feet from under religious certainty, Berger (1970) describes as 'a grim joke' played by humanity on itself: 'There is nothing very funny about finding oneself stranded alone, in a remote corner of a universe bereft of human meaning – nor about the idea that this fate is the outcome of the mindless massacre that Darwin, rather euphemistically, called natural selection' (p. 45).

The almost visceral evocation of a naked existential terror which humans keep at bay only by creating society, culture and religion, surfaces in all Berger's work on cultural construction as a hedge against the encroaching void. It is vividly present, for example, in his discussion of the 'nightmare' aspect of 'marginal experiences' (Berger, 1967, pp. 42–4). The authenticity of such terror in the author himself is never left in doubt.

What he then does in *Rumour* is something which, if he did not hate the pretensions of 'postmodern' theorizing so much, one might be tempted to describe as a smart postmodern move executed long before such things were commonplace. In a famous chapter 'Relativizing the Relativizers', he turns the tables on Enlightenment secularist argument. We must follow the logic of relativity through to its end, he writes. Thus,

> When everything has been subsumed under the relativizing categories in question (those of history, of the sociology of knowledge or what-have-you) the question of truth reasserts itself in almost pristine simplicity. Once we know that all human affirmations are subject to scientifically

graspable socio-historical processes, *which affirmations are true and which are false?*

(Berger, 1970, p. 57)

Once *all* perspectives have been relativized, Enlightenment secularism loses its own privileged status and can be seen as a bullying intellectual fashion from which we are entitled to free ourselves.

Religious phenomena may indeed be *projections* of human imagination but the important question is how far they are *also reflections* of a wider 'encompassing reality'. Berger uses the example of mathematics to illustrate his argument. Mathematical order is both an observed feature of the physical universe and a propensity of the human intellect. This does not mean that the former is a mere projection of the latter. Because humanity is part of the cosmos it is hardly surprising if human intellect and the material universe share a propensity for mathematical order. Hegel and Feuerbach are accordingly turned to face one another, each reflecting the other on equal terms and showing religion as simultaneously projection and reflection.

Theology must, therefore, begin with phenomena which, whatever else they may be, will also be human projections: 'The theological decision will have to be that "in, with and under" the immense array of human projections there are indicators of a reality that is truly "other" and that the imagination of man truly reflects' (Berger, 1970, p. 65).

Berger finds these 'indicators' in what he calls 'signals of transcendence'. The list he offers is not presented as definitive or exhaustive, and it is clearly not the fruit of some encyclopaedic trawl through empirical, anthropological evidence, but rather a distillation of personal experience and humane reflection. The first form it took was as a novel, a fictional narrative, rather than the set of abstractions it has become in *Rumour*, and the sequence, as I shall argue below, is significant. The other term Berger uses interchangeably with 'signals of transcendence' is 'prototypical human gestures'. One glimpses, both in the phrase and in some of the examples he uses, the possibility of a very different text which might have emerged if these 'gestures' had been considered as the repertoire of liturgical language or the basic units of an artistic and symbolic vocabulary. That, however, would have been a qualitatively different exercise, too far, perhaps, from Berger's ambition to find an incontrovertibly empirical and evidential grounding for faith.

Berger's first signal of transcendence is the human propensity for order. The argument from order has several strands not easily subsumed into a unified argument since the concept of order, as Berger deploys it, encompasses the physical laws structuring the material universe, the gestures by which humans exercise and express symbolic control over the social and physical world and a conviction of the human meaningfulness and essential benevolence of the cosmos. Both in *Rumour* and in *A Far*

Glory (1992) the argument from order centres around lyrical and moving descriptions of a mother reasssuring a frightened child that the world is safe and 'in order'. Indeed, Berger argues that the human role which most fundamentally represents this conception of order is that of parent, the person who *constructs* a safe world for a child even in face of the inevitability of death and destruction. In an echo of his earlier argument about the upheaval in the taken-for-granted being a way of 'leaving home' the argument from order asserts the possibility of 'going home again'. The problem here is that while Berger is hearing Mother (*sic*) Julian's 'all shall be well and all manner of things shall be well', the sceptic may well contemplate cosmic order and come to quite other conclusions, for example, like Thomas Hardy's, in the poem 'Before Life and After', that it is only the need to attribute human meaning to an orderly but impersonal cosmos which spells trouble.

> A time there was – as one may guess
> And as, indeed, earth's testimonies tell –
>   Before the birth of consciousness
> When all went well ...
>
> If something ceased, no tongue bewailed
> If something winced and waned, no heart was wrung
> If brightness dimmed and dark prevailed
>   No sense was stung
>
> But the disease of feeling germed
> And primal rightness took the tint of wrong ...
>   (Hardy, 1976, p. 277)

More optimistic than Hardy, Berger asserts that at the centre of the process of becoming fully human, at the core of *humanitas*, we find the experience of trust in the order of reality (1970, p. 74). This is, of course, a more universalized version of the dilemma he discusses in the essay from which we began (Berger, 1998): the primal, existential need for certainty in an objectively uncertain world. As Berger (1970) uses it, the concept of order rather easily mutates into benevolence or the principle of love: 'In [the supernatural] frame of reference the natural world in which we are born, love and die is not the only world but only the foreground of another world in which love is not annihilated in death, and in which, therefore, the trust in the power of love to banish chaos is justified' (p. 75). The modality of the language has become recognizably Christian.

The second signal of transcendence is the argument from play. Play constructs an 'enclave' in which the serious world and its chronology (always 'living towards death') is suspended. Moreover, (and with the proviso that 'distorted' play can employ and entail pain), 'joy is play's intention'. 'The time structure of the playful universe *becomes eternity* ... When adults play with genuine joy, they momentarily regain the deathlessness of childhood' (1970, p. 77).

The third is the argument from hope. Humanity displays a persistent tendency to hope even in the midst of suffering and impending death. Man is a being who says 'no' to death and pain, his own and others'. 'There seems to be a death-refusing hope at the very core of our *humanitas*' (Berger, 1969a, p. 83). This is something more than a 'childish' failure of Cartesian honesty. We are not all Candides: 'religion vindicates the gestures in which hope and courage are embodied in human action – including, given certain conditions, the gestures of revolutionary hope and, in the ultimate irony of redemption, the courage of stoic resignation' (1970, p. 84). Once again the language here has more than an overtone of the Christian, particularly in what is taken for granted by the phrase 'the ultimate irony of redemption'.

The fourth signal is the argument from damnation. The claim is that:

> there are experiences in which our sense of what is humanly permissible is so fundamentally outraged that the only adequate response to the offence as well as to the offender seems to be a curse of supernatural dimensions ... There are certain deeds that cry out to heaven. These deeds are not only an outrage to our moral sense, they seem to violate a fundamental awareness of the constitution of our humanity.
>
> (1970, pp. 84–5)

They are not merely evil but 'monstrously evil'. We refuse a perspective of moral relativity to excuse their perpetration. (There is an intriguing but not wholly disarming passage in *A Far Glory* (1992) in which Berger wryly imagines the deliberations of a group of Aztec priests before their 'sacred massacre' of a group of children: it is a recognition of a problem rather than the solution to the difficulty posed by the huge variability over time and space of the deeds that are *self-evidently* 'monstrously evil' (p. 158).)

Thus,

> Just as certain gestures can be interpreted as anticipations of redemption so other gestures can be viewed as anticipations of hell (hell meaning here no more or less than the state of being damned, both here and now and also beyond the confines of this life and this world) ... Just as religion vindicates the gesture of protective reassurance, even when it is performed in the face of death, so it also vindicates the ultimate condemnation of the countergesture of inhumanity, precisely because religion provides a context for damnation.
>
> (Berger, 1970, p. 88)

Finally, there is the argument from humour. The familiar view of humour as discrepancy is here expanded to encompass 'the discrepancy between man and the universe' (1970, p. 90). Accordingly:

> *The comic reflects the imprisonment of the human spirit in the world*
> ... Humour not only recognizes the comic discrepancy of the human condition, it also relativizes it, and thereby suggests that the tragic perspective on the discrepancies of the human condition can also be relativized. At least for the duration of the comic perception the tragedy of man is bracketed. By laughing at the imprisonment of the human spirit, humour implies that this imprisonment is not final but will be overcome, and by this implication provides yet another signal of transcendence – in this instance in the form of an intimation of redemption. I would thus argue that humour, like childhood and play, can be seen as an ultimately religious vindication of joy.
>
> (ibid.)

Again the concept of redemption appears as a core feature of the argument.

There is a certain problem in Berger's insistence that these signals of transcendence have a primarily metaphysical rather than ethical character. Moral criteria infiltrate all the arguments because in every case what is at issue is the problem of evil, the inevitability of death, the ubiquity of pain and loss, the whole familiar list of chronic conundrums about mortality and the human condition. The argument from order, in particular, fails to eliminate the moral dimension since it has less to do with the regularities in the ordering of the cosmos than the question of whether the cosmos is 'ultimately' benevolent towards individual human beings, a 'home', whether the 'encompassing reality' is (good) parent-like or indifferent to all our fates. The argument from hope confronts the same underlying issue. Humour and play, as Berger expresses it in *A Far Glory* (1992), are 'redemptive experiences' which 'supersede the tragic dimensions of the human experience' (p. 139). The argument from damnation seems to be inherently moral in assuming a class of absolute evils, not precisely specified but certainly including the torture and killing of children. Yet the gesture of damnation is not extrapolated into a universal, relativity-defying moral *system* and the reader is left with an uneasy sense that the argument from damnation is dangerously dependent on the self-evident validity of 'moral outrage' in a way that leaves it open to the psychological or cultural reductionism that Berger has been at pains to deny. Berger's reply to these demurs might well be that the derivation of a universal moral *content* was precisely what he was seeking to avoid in insisting on the metaphysical rather than the ethical significance of these persistently recurring signals or gestures (in the context of highly various moral systems) as intimations of 'another reality'. Yet the ethical character of that 'other reality' is surely the crux. A certain unease with his argument seeps through Berger's own prose and is acknowledged as an open problem in *A Far Glory* (1992).

In *Rumour* (1970) Berger presents his outline of signals of transcendence as little more than a tentative suggestion of categories within which 'man's experience with himself and with reality' (p. 105) might be organized. A 'rigorous empirical analysis of these experiences in terms of both a historical anthropology and a history of religion' will have to be undertaken as a preliminary to a theology which begins only 'at the point where the transcendent intentions in human experience are treated as *realities* rather than as *alleged realities*' (p. 105). The second part of the proposed programme will be to 'confront' the various religious traditions of the world as repositories of different projections/experiences of 'the divine fulness' (p. 118), giving no privileges to Christianity in the process. In a revealing aside he speculates about a possible third search for signals of transcendence in 'for instance, the creations of Bach or Mozart, of Gothic Cathedral builders, or of Chagall, Hölderlin or Blake (to mention names at random)'. He adds the telling observation: 'as yet we can hardly conceive of the procedures by which this particular confrontation might be realised' (p. 108). The arts, it seems, evade interrogation through the empirical methods he has just advocated as the route to an 'inductive theology'. What this passage inadvertently highlights is how far *Rumour* really is from the 'rigorous empirical analysis' Berger is ideally advocating and how much it resembles the artistic response to the human condition – a leap of imaginative apprehension which is an illumination, perhaps even an epiphany. It is a statement of faith.

If we regard the argument in this light, its occasional shortcomings of logic and its definitional sleights of hand (as in the relegation of those manifestations of play and humour which signify not joy but sadism, malice or vengeance, to the category of 'distortions'; or in the unacknowledged slippage between different meanings of the concept of order; or the apparent inconsistencies in the claim to be dealing with metaphysical rather than ethical phenomena) become unimportant. Rather than a scientific sifting of empirical data, it is a searchlight picking out those aspects of the human cultural response to the problem of ultimate meaning which, for Peter Berger, point towards the transcendent.

In fact, when Berger returned to these matters in the 1990s, he did not embark on his impossibly vast programme of 'rigorous empirical analysis' of the anthropological record and systematic 'confrontation' of the religious traditions (notwithstanding the chapter in *A Far Glory* (1992) comparing the insights of 'Jerusalem' and 'Benares'). Instead he expanded on his original meditation on the 'signals of transcendence' in much the same fashion as in *Rumour*, using many more examples from the arts, especially European literature, notably a long excursus in the Noble Lectures on the significance of the novel through a discussion of Robert Musil's *A Man without Qualities* (Berger, 1992, Ch. 4), and drawing on a wide range of literary source material in *Redeeming Laughter* (1997a), his extended development of the argument from the comic. Indeed, in *A Far Glory* (1992) he admits that his method is not quite as empirical or scientifically inductive as he had sought to present it in *Rumour*. He acknowledges that all the phenomena he lists as signals of transcendence are ambiguous and susceptible of being explained in purely secular terms. Accordingly:

> To see these experiences as sign-posts towards transcendence therefore is itself a decision of faith. There must be no illusion about this, no manoeuvre to bring in the hoary proofs of the existence of God by the back door. But the faith in these signals is not baseless, nor is it a mental *acte gratuit*. It takes my experience seriously and dares to suppose that what this experience intends is not a lie.
>
> (1992, p. 140)

Nor, one must suppose on Berger's behalf, is it a mere piece of psychological or cultural reductionism. In a later part of the same passage he goes on to describe the consequences for consciousness of making the leap of faith almost as an act of intellectual will (the recurring term 'intention' as used in the previous quotation has a similar import to the term 'act' applied to belief). Thus:

> On the other side of a Christian act of belief the world discloses itself as a sacramental world; that is, a world in which the visible reality contains many signs of the invisible presence of God. Christian faith not only affirms that God will not abandon us, but that He has left scattered evidence of that promise in all sorts of places ... God plays a vast game of hide-and-seek with mankind ... He gives more than a few hints as to where He is hiding.
>
> (1992, pp. 142–3)

In revisiting these issues Berger does explore more fully some of the problems and paradoxes left unresolved (and in some cases unacknowledged) in *Rumour*, notably the relation of religion and moral action, including the problem of political action. Religion and morality are 'linked but not *necessarily* linked' and the relation is indirect (1992, p. 193). Every religious tradition 'shapes conscience' within a religiously affirmed morality, but the direct translation of theology into ethics 'does not work'. Some moral certainties are easier to achieve than religious certainty, he argues; for example, 'I know torture is wrong, I don't simply believe it' because it has been 'disclosed as wrong' over the centuries of the Christian tradition (p. 198). Yet he has moved away from his early easier certainty in *The Noise of Solemn Assemblies* (1961b) that the Christian vision is inherently athwart social convenience. The original Pauline position, based on 'the new being in Christ', is precarious and vulnerable, he argues, because it is based on a faith which radically shifts the individual's perception of reality. It has given way because of its precariousness, more particularly under the pressure of pluralism, to two 'false securities', legalism and Utopianism, both of which simplify and systematize moral options. He rejects both in favour of a version of Weber's ethic of responsibility:

> In the sphere of political action, especially, this means accepting the fact that there are situations where it is morally unavoidable to get one's hands dirty, even bloody ... Christian faith mandates an overriding concern for our neighbours, *not* for the purity of our selves. More than that, the latter concern is a morally deplorable self-indulgence, especially when coupled with a lack of thought for the consequences of our supposedly pure actions.
>
> (1992, p. 208)

On this basis, he concludes, one can adopt an ethic of responsibility even if one is convinced of the absolute evil that torture represents. What precisely this means for the argument from damnation, or what, if any, limits the apparently utilitarian calculus of the consequences for our neighbours of our moral choices places on the operations of *realpolitik*, is left unspecified. (Nor is it self-evident how such a moral calculus precisely squares with the libertarian individualism which characterizes Berger's championship of free-market capitalism and his furious opposition to self-appointed moral entrepreneurs in matters of sexual conduct, smoking, and so on.) The issue of where the line is drawn between the necessarily dirty hands which come with an ethic of responsibility and cosmically unforgivable implication in 'monstrous evil' is the issue at the heart of Berger's novel, so it is of some moment that he leaves it more ambiguous in *A Far Glory* than in *Rumour* or *Protocol*. Berger's comparison between the position of, say, General Pinochet and that of the (fictional) German executioner damned in the novel would probably clarify the issue if he could be persuaded to make it.

Two final aspects of Peter Berger's preoccupation with signals of transcendence are worth brief comment before we finally turn to the novel. The first is his intellectualism, something which from time to time occurs to Berger himself as a problem; and the second is the utter dominance of something resembling the Jewish creator God (though not in His most vengeful Old Testament guise) and the insignificance of the other two persons of the Christian trinity in his theological thinking.

Towards the end of *Rumour* (1970, pp. 108–9) there is a passage in which, having proclaimed the necessity of a vast empirical research programme to renew the intellectual foundations of faith, he bethinks himself that it ill becomes a proto-theologian working from the premise that the materials of theology must come from everyday life, to ignore ordinary morals and assume that a small cadre of intellectuals can make or break the faith. If faith *is* to be renewed the initiative must come from, indeed may already be germinating in, the grass roots, he concedes. To Peter Berger's eternal credit, his respect for truth in this and certain other striking instances has prevailed over his own first thoughts. Perhaps most of all Western sociologists of religion, he has kept his eyes skinned and his ears cocked for these grass-roots religious renewals: he was not only one of the first to doubt the inevitability of secularization while it was still accepted sociological dogma, but he detected signs of the Pentecostal upsurge in developing societies in the 1980s before it had been noticed by any of the area specialists and others under whose noses it had already been growing for a couple of decades. From his texts of the early 1960s through to his current writings on religion, Berger has been consistent in his conviction that 'God is truth' – a phrase to which he constantly reverts – and that, therefore, the pursuit of truth is a spiritual as well as a professional intellectual necessity, however bleak the truths that may have to be confronted *en route*.

This implacable search for truth has also, however, taken him to the margins of Christian orthodoxy (though in that he is hardly unusual among modern Protestants). In the Preface to *Rumour* he admits that, while considering himself a Christian, he has 'not yet found the heresy into which my theological views would comfortably fit' (1970, p. 10). The Lutheran heritage, however, is very clear. Berger's 'transcendent' seems to be a teasing sort of *deus* not-quite-*absconditus* who plays a deliberate game of hide-and-seek with his human creation. Though this God plants traces of his existence in his cosmos, Berger sees nothing special in the life and death of the historical Jesus as part of the system of clues to the transcendental mystery: 'the redeeming presence of God in the world is manifested in history but is not given once and for all in the particular historical events reported on in the New Testament' (1970, p. 115). Incarnation and the redemption of the cross are not, therefore, at the heart of Berger's theology, even of his theology of redemption. The central place is occupied by the parent-like love of God experienced in human history and community:

> The redemptive community of Christ ... will be there implicitly wherever the redeeming gestures of love, hope and compassion are reiterated in human experience. It will become explicit wherever these gestures are understood in relation to the God who both created and redeems the world, who may well have been 'in Jesus', but who is ever again present in human imitations of redemptive love.
>
> (1970, p. 116)

I have suggested above that Berger, as he more than half acknowledges in *A Far Glory* (1992), is engaged in something more reflexive and subjective, and less scientifically empirical and methodologically agnostic than he initially suggests, and the fact that the genesis of his ideas about signals of transcendence took the form of a novel adds weight to that view. Let us finally come to Peter Berger's theological novel and see how his ideas play out as story and what sort of God lurks behind the cosmic arras.

A literary construction of transcendence: *Protocol of a Damnation* (1975)

John Updike once remarked that human self-consciousness is 'an existential desperation which all men being mortal feel': the need 'to make sense of it all' gives rise not only to religion but to the modern novel (Yerkes, 1999, p. 12 *et seq.*). For Peter Berger too, the threat of meaninglessness fuels the whole human enterprise of culture, all the more urgently once pluralism strips away the prophylactic of the taken-for-granted and exposes the underlying cosmic anxiety at the root of the human condition. In *A Far Glory* (1992, p. 105) Berger argues that the novel is *par excellence* the literary form which delineates modern Western individualism and maps modern self-consciousness. The novel might therefore be not unapt as a vehicle for exploring transcendent meaning in contemporary life. Further, Judaism and Christianity – which have not only shaped the vision of divinity addicts such as Updike and Berger but to a significant degree have moulded modern Western consciousness itself – are, at bottom, *stories*. They are essentially narratives of redemption in history which lose some of their multifaceted meaning when they are turned into abstract theological argument and systematized as sets of beliefs and dogmas. Doing theology by telling stories has a long pedigree and Peter Berger was placing himself in an honourable tradition when he decided to write a theological novel.

Protocol of a Damnation (1975) is a classic realist narrative. The main technical trick of this type of novel is to pile up naturalistic detail in order to ground the reader in a taken-for-granted everyday truthfulness. In this sense, creating the complete fictional world of a novel enabled Peter Berger to 'cancel' or 'bracket' some of the erosions of pluralism. He constructs an enclave of play in which his own cognitive writ runs, his distinctive vision of truth is established without rivals, at least for as long as the reader is immersed in the reading and complicit with him. This constructed taken-for-grantedness of the realist novel can even override elements which demand the suspension of disbelief. Berger exploited this feature to gloss over the one implausibility in his plot. One of his characters, a young Polish girl, Olga, becomes ill whenever she is close to a place in which some gross cruelty – the 'monstrous evil' of Berger's argument from damnation – has taken place in the (fairly) recent past. (The problem of how long the effect of such evil clings to a spot is one of the more curious features of this plot device. I think, however, we may suppose that Berger himself does not regard Olga's susceptibility as an empirically implausible invention: in *A Far Glory* (1992) he comments *en passant* on 'presences that still brood' over the pyramids of Mesoamerica and adds: 'I, for one, would not like to say that they are merely memories of all the human anguish that called out from the sacrificial platforms' (p. 158).) The sheer pleasure involved in entering the protected bubble of a narrative gives the novel as a form a persuasiveness which has certain obvious advantages by comparison with the intellectual effort required to read an abstract academic exegesis such as *Rumour*, however elegantly written. The story touches parts of the self which the intellect alone cannot reach.

The second classic feature of the realist novel – and one which, in its way, exemplifies one aspect of Berger's argument from order – is that as a genre it evinces a regularly patterned sequence: indeed, the anticipation and unfolding of this pattern is a considerable part of the pleasure given by such texts. The classic sequence begins with the construction of an orderly and recognizable world, followed by the introduction of what has been variously termed a 'disruption' or 'enigma' which brings disorder; and finally there is a movement towards resolution or closure which re-establishes order, either that with which the story opened or a new order. Often it is only at the point of narrative closure that the full 'facts' of the story are revealed or made finally transparent to the reader. This model characterizes the whole range of conventionally realist narratives though it applies most explicitly to the sub-genre of mystery or crime fiction to which *Protocol* somewhat approximates.

Peter Berger's novel of the transcendent displays both these classic features, skilfully deployed. It is a first-person narrative couched in the form of a protocol or record of a set of mysterious events which the narrator is, supposedly, setting down on paper for himself in order to lay them to rest. We, the readers, see the whole story through the eyes of this narrator, a seasoned 'God-botherer' who confesses at the beginning that he has spent a lifetime in frustrated pursuit of 'the supernatural' and who intimates that all the events in the protocol are somehow connected with this fact. From the outset there is mystery in the air; cosmic mystery and narrative puzzles are put in play simultaneously. As I noted above, the novel has structural affinities with the classic mystery story, though the death – murder or execution – comes only towards the end as part of the closure rather than as the disruption which is the more typical narrative function of a death in this genre. The mystery lies in the significance of this climactic death – though, in truth, the supernatural curse, the damnation, which precedes it is the real climax of the story and the death itself a mere coda which tidies up the moral loose ends. The identity of those responsible for the death is not definitively established and is anyway not important: the disclosure of the facts which make the death and the damnation *just*, constitutes the real solution to the mystery. Yet there remains one final narrative act of closure even beyond this, that is, the unlooked-for grace of a direct encounter with 'the divine fulness' which comes to the narrator just when he thinks he has put aside for ever his metaphysical ambitions.

This tale of a long-frustrated religious seeker minutely illustrates all Berger's 'signals of transcendence' yet it is not an obtrusively didactic novel. On the contrary, it is a page-turner, both a thriller and a comedy. The reader is impatient to know more, to unravel all the puzzles, but is also content to linger over the humour, ranging from low farce to pungent irony, which characterizes the sub-plots and incidental anecdotes that punctuate the working out of the central mystery and act as brakes on disclosure which build up the narrative tension. The book is often very funny as well as being deeply serious and it is the mixture which gives it something of the character of what Graham Greene called 'an entertainment'. Some of the incidental vignettes are the broadest satire, such as the sharp little caricature of an avant-garde film festival (Berger, 1975, pp. 74–7) in which Peter Berger's delight in a joke at the expense of incoherent pretentiousness and banality is let off the leash. The way in which Berger throughout the book uses the humour of incongruity as a vehicle for exploring the profoundest problems of the human condition, makes his novel an exemplification of his own argument from the comic as signal of transcendence and token of redemption. The very last pages recount the ultimate consummation of the narrator's long love affair with the elusive 'divinity' in the most absurd of circumstances, as he is crammed uncomfortably into a children's railway carriage, riding around a miniature model of Switzerland in a tourist theme park. It is a wholly fitting and satisfying ending.

The book is out of print and hard to obtain so I propose to outline its characters, plot and style in some detail in order to show how it makes the case for Peter Berger's arguments for transcendence.

Protocol of a Damnation concerns a motley group of people thrown together one summer in the early 1960s in Ascona, a picturesque Italian-Swiss tourist resort on Lake Maggiore. As the narrator explains in the first chapter of the novel, ever since the turn of the century when the first vegetarian-naturist colony was set up on Monte Verita, the town has attracted a wide variety of seekers after esoteric knowledge, fringe religious sects and bohemians of every sort. Ascona is a liminal place, a border crossing, the point where the mountains divide German Switzerland from the Mediterranean, where Schwyzerdytch gives way to the Italian tongue: it is a natural magnet for misfits. (Ascona was, indeed, a mecca for the New Religious Movements spawned in the 1960s as it had been for their predecessors, and Berger's well-tuned antennae clearly picked up evidences of the new boom in religious invention which was in its early stages as he began the novel there in the summer of 1965.)

The narrator of the story is Jacob Van Buren, a dour, middle-aged Dutchman with a nice line in ironic self-revelation. He makes an unlikely living as a children's photographer among Ascona's summer tourists though we soon learn of his adventurous and sometimes disreputable history as:

A student of oriental languages at Leiden. An officer in the Dutch merchant marine. An undercover agent for the Allies in Japanese-occupied Indonesia. A gun-runner, a smuggler and, believe it or not, for a while a bookkeeper in a house of ill-repute. In Surabaya to be precise.

(1975, p. 30)

His wife, Isa, 'une brave hollandaise', has only a minor role in the plot though the narrator makes considerable play on their uneasy marriage-of-opposites and their contrasting spiritual biographies in a way that suggests a relevance for the underlying theme of the book. Van Buren presents himself as a virtuoso debauchee, '*Monsieur le diable*', at least in his younger days, though currently he is 'a very tired devil'. He has ransacked the world for a direct encounter with the supernatural, so far to no avail, and this despite spending months in hiding from the Japanese in a fag-end little town in Sumatra towards the end of the war, living in the shed of an expatriate Portuguese mystic who ran a general store, reading his host's few books (St John of the Cross and a couple of modern Portuguese theological texts), though having to piece the meaning of the Portuguese together from a smattering of Latin and French, and relying on his host to explain obscurities during the evenings when they could talk. Even this intense 'attentiveness to the divine' yielded no mystical experience for Van Buren.

Isa, his wife, a sometime mission teacher in Indonesia, respectable Dutch Calvinist and bourgeois *hausfrau*, is, by contrast, regularly visited by visions of the Devil – not sexual but grotesque, as Van Buren is at pains to insist. As the two have grown into middle age he has largely given up 'playing the devil' and she has moved away from her Dutch respectability; in consequence their mutual disappointment has grown. Van Buren's debauchery is reduced to the occasional act of petulant adultery with a compliant local widow, while Isa seeks out women friends among the summer visitors who are in Ascona to find spiritual enlightenment. The Van Buren children are grown, gone and barely missed, at least by their not very paternal father, but the ill-assorted couple has become a social focus for the flotsam and jetsam that washes up in Ascona. In particular, their home is a haven for children neglected by inadequate parents in hot pursuit of their own summer pleasures. The current chick they have taken under their wing is an eight-year-old English boy, Basil, a precocious infant who might have strayed in from a novel by Wodehouse or Waugh. (Berger makes clear both in Van Buren's account of himself and Isa and in one of the comic sub-plots to which we shall come in due course, his belief that national stereotypes have a kernel of truth as well as a capacity to misrepresent the full truth. Basil's prep-school precociousness, his imperial self-confidence and his streak of malice are, perhaps, one such stereotype of Englishness which may appeal more to an Austrian-American than to the English themselves.) The quasi-parental relationship is a theme which recurs in the novel and, not by accident, is the means through which Van Buren finally achieves his mystical experience while taking Basil to 'Swissminiatur'.

The events of the story are precipitated by an accidental encounter between Van Buren and a visiting American, Raymond Dell, who at first seems to be just a professional gigolo, occasional male model and sardonic religious sceptic but who is gradually revealed as, perhaps, one of those angels entertained unawares. He later reveals to Van Buren his own history as a divinity junkie, sometime Methodist seminarian and army chaplain's assistant. It is he who eventually utters the sentence of damnation. Dell is companion for the summer to Dottie La Farge, a wealthy American woman 'of a certain age' who is renting a villa on the slopes of Monte Verita. At Dottie's villa Van Buren meets the rest of the *dramatis personae*. There are the wealthy German entrepreneur, Herr Karstmann and his attractive daughter, Jutta (for whom Van Buren mildly lusts on catching sight of her piquantly, Europeanly unshaven legs); Signor Borelli, mayor of the village of Ombelico in the Gamborogno on the other shore of the lake; Bochalski, a Polish civil servant on some unstated mission from the other side of the Iron Curtain; Olga, a Polish girl who has been befriended in a curiously non-sexual way by the playboy Raymond Dell who is teaching her English; and Professor Langbein, Coptic scholar and leader of a small Gnostic sect known as the Kuschta community.

Dottie is financing a conference in Ombelico (for which Borelli, as mayor, anticipates a rain of dollars) to bring together two warring Gnostic sects, embattled over the interpretation of a Coptic manuscript, the Book of Kimon, which is allegedly in the possession of the second group, the Order of Kimon the Pneumatic, led by one 'Brother' Karpistes who may perhaps have forged the manuscript or even invented its existence. The Kuschta community, which wants direct access to the (perhaps non-existent) Book of Kimon, and is under Dottie's patronage, is headed by Professor Langbein and his competent, middle-aged secretary, Mademoiselle Duferre. Karpistes, leader of the rival group, also has a secretary/assistant, his plain, sharp-tongued young cousin, Mademoiselle Lebrun. He too, has his financial backer, Mr Johnson, a soft-drinks millionaire from Ohio, who has even paid for central heating to be installed in the buildings of the Order, to the disgust of the ascetic Kuschta community. The handful of delegates from each of the two Gnostic communities comprise the usual suspects – schoolteachers, secretaries, bookkeepers, just sufficiently under-educated seekers after spiritual wisdom, endearing in their intensity, comic in their gullibility and their rivalrous spite. What divides the two groups is the question of whether, in the Gnostic quest for the liberation of spirit from matter, the supernatural powers are a help or a hindrance to humankind. Karpistes' group regards these supernatural powers, the archons, as uniformly demonic, while Professor Langbein and his followers reverence the high archon they call Abraxas, as the friend and helper of the human soul. The feud is, of course, a dramatization of Berger's argument from order, based around the question of the benevolence or otherwise of the cosmic order. The last comer to the central story is Riggi, who has been brought in to 'facilitate dialogue' between the two hostile Gnostic groups. Riggi is a professional ecumenical diplomat, a caricature of the self-important technocrat, willing to reconcile any number of incompatible positions by a feat of political skill and public relations sleight of hand. With Raymond Dell as his mouthpiece, Berger has a good deal of malicious fun at Riggi's, and ecumenism's, expense.

The plot unfolds in a series of set-piece events recounted by Van Buren and interspersed with his musings on the supernatural and with a number of sub-plots and diversions which Van Buren sees as somehow related to the main story. The most substantial of these is a comic tale of near-pathological addiction to order. A young man, Franz Tesco, turns up on Van Buren's doorstep from Germany. There is a tradition in his family that his grandfather was an Italian smuggler in the Ticino who fled to Germany to avoid arrest. Tesco is a romantic who wants to 'find himself' by verifying his grandfather's history: he longs to be Italian rather than German though he admits to being 'pedantic' in a suggestively Germanic fashion. He goes to his local brothel every Tuesday and Friday, his 'B' days, and gets unbearably excited and discomfited if he tries to vary the ritual: he dates 'legitimate' girls in alphabetical order, and in the tavern he goes through brands of beer according to a rotating system. What, he asks, does Van Buren make of this? Well, 'In general man's instinct for order is stronger than his sexual instinct. In particular that you have the instinct for order worse than most' (1975, p. 85). Inexorably, it transpires that grandfather, though an *echt* smuggler, was indeed German, Francesco Tedesco – Franz the German!

What connects the sub-plots and diversions, in fact, is their exemplification of one or other of Berger's signals of transcendence not fully covered by the central events of the novel. (The story of Tesco is a pretty equivocal instance of the argument from order.) As a formula this may sound potentially leaden, but it is done with a light and playful touch. Berger's wit and his sharp ear for word play are the key. Van Buren, who perhaps has more than a little of his author's verbal felicity in his make-up, is never less than entertaining even in his most extended metaphysical asides, and his accounts of himself are full of sardonic and ironic observation and wryly humorous self-exposure. The rivalry between the two Gnostic sects is played as a ludicrous comedy with serious undertones, and Professor Langbein and his followers as holy fools – the folly and the holiness inseparable. Karpistes may be an unscrupulous and spiteful fraud though even he is, perhaps, self-deluding as much as merely manipulative.

The opening of the book is a bravura piece of Van Buren comedy at his own expense which sets the tone of the novel and whets the reader's appetite. After a brief – five-page – chapter setting the scene, we are launched into the first set-piece, Van Buren's initial encounter with

Raymond Dell. I quote its prelude at some length in order to do justice to the comic invention of Berger's style. Chapter 2 begins as follows:

> Very probably I would not have become involved in this business at all if it had not been for my wretched tattoos. These date from my years in Indonesia, or what was then the Dutch East Indies, when I was second officer of a coastal schooner. We had to stop over for repairs in a miserable port on one of the Molucca Islands and I was more or less drunk for the three days of our stay. When I came to, back in my cabin, I found that I had contracted gonorrhea. I also found something much worse, spread over both my chest and back. I dimly recall the tattoo artist responsible for this monstrosity, a wily Chinese with a perpetual smile, somehow related, I think, to the Chinese girl who gave me the lesser of these two mementos. On my chest this virtuoso of skin ornamentation had engraved a panoramic view of the city and harbor of Batavia, junks and all, with the Dutch flag bravely flying over the tallest buildings and the name of the capital of our erstwhile Asian empire inscribed at the bottom (around my navel, to be precise) in Gothic letters. The *chef d'oeuvre*, however, was reserved for my back. There can be seen, to this day, an enormous replication of the coat of arms of the House of Orange, flanked by bundles of royal flags and subscribed in huge letters, by the brave words from the Song of William of Nassau (which, of course, is the national anthem of the Netherlands):
>
> 'DEN VADERLANT GHETROUWE
> BLIJF ICK TOT INDEN DOET'

which means: 'To the fatherland I remain faithful unto death'.

I need hardly add that the removal of two tattoos of this size is just about impossible, even with major surgery. Consequently, to this day, my torso has been a walking monument to a defunct Dutch imperialism, an aesthetic and political horror. As the Asian empire of the Netherlands has shrunk, the circumference of my body has expanded, and with it, naturally, the double portrait it carries. I have been truly fat since about the time we lost West Irian to Sukarno, so that the total disappearance of our empire in history coincided with its maximum distension on me. It will readily be understood that this distinguishing physical characteristic (which is described in my passport in a long paragraph of sadistically precise prose, expressing, no doubt, an ultimate wish-fulfilment of policemen's mentality) has inhibited me from frequenting public beaches. I tried it only once after settling in Ascona, on a rainy day when I had reason to think that there would be few people there. So there were, but among the handful was a band of compatriots, all teenagers markedly underprivileged in patriotic sentiment, who congregated around me in a state of mounting hysteria, singing the national anthem and shouting obscenities. I beat them rather badly in the ensuing violence and had the satisfaction of seeing one of them the next day with stitches on his chin, but I did not repeat the experiment.

(1975, pp. 12–13)

This sets up the situation in which Van Buren's curiosity about Raymond Dell as, perhaps, something other than he appears, is first piqued. The occasion is a photo session in Van Buren's studio, where a preening and camp Raymond models beachwear for Laureano, a Milanese in the fashion business, whom Van Buren describes as 'an inveterate pederast'. After the shoot is completed the main party goes off to the beach (the weather throughout the events of the summer is stiflingly hot) while Van Buren pretends to have an engagement out of town in order not to have to expose his torso to ridicule. His general bad temper leads him to take a defiant and absurd soak in the bathtub off his studio, where he is glumly wallowing when Raymond and Laureano return. He overhears Raymond's tactful and gentle rejection of Laureano's sexual overtures. Raymond's charitable failure to humiliate Laureano makes Van Buren curious about the American.

From this point two main plot strands are developed and interwoven: the battle of the Gnostics which in part acts as a device for bringing all the characters together; and the eventual disclosure of the involvement of the German businessman, Karstmann, in acts of 'monstrous evil' as a Nazi executioner with the *Einsatzkommandos* in Poland during the Second World War, his ritual damnation by Raymond, and subsequent murder or execution.

The Gnostic conference is held in the town hall of Borelli's village. It culminates in a farcical disruption of the Kuschta liturgy. A frail and tottery Professor Langbein ritually ascends and descends the rickety platforms representing the several levels of spiritual being, harshly intoning the ritual sentences in Coptic and pausing at the summit to invoke Abraxas. The liturgy is interrupted by a hysterical and furious Karpistes from a speedboat on the lake, bellowing obscenities and ridiculing the Kuschta ceremony through a megaphone. The breakdown of the conference has been precipitated by the arrival of Karpistes' patron, Mr Johnson, who finds Dottie more to his taste than discussions of Gnostic doctrine in the village hall. He and Dottie take off together to tour Italy and when they leave on a Mediterranean cruise the money for the 'Council of Ombelico' finally dries up, the ecumenical fun is over, and Borelli's great expectations for investment in his village are frustrated.

The second narrative strand, which culminates in Karstmann's damnation, is less thickly spiced with comedy. In a series of encounters and conversations the real reasons for the presence of Olga and Bochalski are revealed to Van Buren. Part of Bochalski's professional responsibility is the oversight of the Nazi death camps in Poland which have become centres for historical education. On a school trip to one such camp Olga first showed her acute sensitivity to such places. She was diagnosed as suffering from 'thanatopathy', the fear of death, which she experienced vicariously in any spot 'where in the more or less recent past people have died in great anguish or terror ... It is as if a miasma of anguish were produced in a place' (Berger, 1975, p. 144). Unable to live virtually anywhere in Poland because of this sensitivity, Olga has been invited to Ascona as the guest of a Swiss psychiatrist and here she has been befriended by Raymond. (In the dénouement of the story Olga goes to live on a weather station in the Soviet Arctic where she finds love with a meteorologist who hates urban life: it is an ingenious solution to the knotty problem of locating any place on earth wholly free from the 'miasma' of 'monstrous evil'.) Van Buren hears the story after Olga becomes ill, sweating and screaming in terror on a picnic in the Valle Veddesca close to the spot where, as it transpires, Nazis massacred twenty-five villagers in 1944. She has to be tranquillized and her stay in the area is cut short.

Before he leaves Switzerland with Olga, Bochalski confides to Van Buren that he has been in Ascona as part of his job, which is to track down Nazi war criminals. He had been hoping to find confirmation of suspicions that Karstmann was responsible for one of the mobile extermination units which operated in Poland. Van Buren agrees to pass on any relevant information which may come his way after Bochalski's departure. The evidence emerges at a final party, thrown by Raymond just before he closes up Dottie's villa after the disintegration of the Gnostic Council. Those present, the tail-end of the original group, are Van Buren, Karstmann and his daughter, Raymond Dell and Mademoiselle Lebrun, whom Raymond has liberated from thraldom to her unsavoury cousin, 'Karpistes', by, among other things, teaching her water skiing. (Whether sex plays any part in this liberation is left ambiguous: earlier, Raymond had declared to Van Buren that he never sleeps with women under forty.) At the party Raymond incites Mademoiselle Lebrun to perform a long, sensual, quasi-ritual dance while he plays the drums. The trance-like performance sexually excites Karstmann who is already drunk. When Raymond brings the dance to an abrupt close, he and Van Buren initiate a conversation with Karstmann about politics and metaphysics, provoked by the photograph in Van Buren's newspaper of the 'execution' of a supposed Communist agent in South Vietnam. Van Buren and Raymond regard the 'execution' as barbaric and Karstmann derides their sentimentality. Such events, he argues, are a necessary part of 'the moral price of power', a price which America seems reluctant to face up to. In fact he makes the extreme case for an 'ethic of responsibility', justifying his own activities as executioner:

'I was in the army. I am not even sure I was a National Socialist. I did not enjoy it, but I knew that if I did not do it others would ... Anyway, I don't have to tell you old horror stories. My point to Mr Van Buren was simply this – that one must accept the burdens of power if they happen to land on one's shoulders. There is nothing else one can do. Also it is important that one does what one has to do without enjoyment, only because it is a duty, that one tries to be humane within the limits of what has to be done.'

(Berger, 1975, p. 187)

Karstmann freely tells his own story, insisting that he feels no guilt or remorse, regret perhaps, but guilt is merely 'cowardice *vis-à-vis* the past'. In 1941 he was drafted to eastern Poland to take over command of a detachment of military police from a district commander who was seriously ill. Orders came down to liquidate Communists and Jews. He had the Communists executed in the town square as an example: 'Most of them were denounced by their neighbours, incidentally' (p. 189). The few hundred Jews including around a hundred children were systematically shot in a field in a two-day operation. He had discontinued his predecessor's sadistic practices of torturing Communists and shooting the Jewish children in front of their parents: 'I insisted that families be executed together' (p. 189).

Jutta is visibly shocked and Mademoiselle Lebrun horrified by the recital. Van Buren and Raymond protest that nothing can justify the killing of children. Karstmann replies that it is inherently no different from Americans dropping napalm on villages where they know children are present: both are military necessities: 'Do calm yourself, Mr Van Buren. Your outburst is rather ridiculous. Why don't you just be grateful that the actions of others allow you the luxury of innocence?' (p. 190).

Van Buren moves to hit Karstmann but is restrained by Raymond who offers the German another drink. When the glass is empty Raymond takes it, places round his neck an ecclesiastical stole hanging on the wall as part of the decoration of the villa and smashes the glass on the table at which Karstmann is sitting.

Raymond stood in front of him, erect and unmoving. He powerfully reminded me of Langbein standing before the altar at Ombelico, but the association at once underlined the contrast. Where Langbein had declaimed in the ear-splitting cadences of his ritual diction, Raymond spoke quietly, in a conversational tone, as if he were stating some ordinary fact of everyday life:

'I speak to you with an authority that does not come from myself', continued Raymond. 'It is by this authority that I now curse you. You are already now as one who is dead. You will be separated from joy, from hope and from the community of living men. You will die also and in agony. You will scream but no one will hear you, and no one will grieve over your death. You will not be remembered except in loathing. And by the same authority I damn you, both in this life and in the next. You are separated from redemption, now and forever. Before these witnesses, Karstmann, I sentence you to death and hell'.

(pp. 192–3)

Jutta renounces her father, and Raymond is violently sick. Van Buren asks whether Raymond believes what he said to be true: '"How the fuck should I know?" Raymond spat out savagely. "It had better be. That's all I know. It had better be"' (p. 195).

All the *dramatis personae* quickly disperse leaving only the Van Burens and Karstmann still in Ascona. Van Buren sends a note to Bochalski telling him of Karstmann's 'confession' and some ten days afterwards Karstmann is found dead:

The garage had been turned into a makeshift gas chamber. Karstmann's body was found gagged and handcuffed to the fender of his Mercedes ... Tagged onto the wall of the garage was a typewritten note stating that Karstmann had been executed for the murder of men, women and children in Brzanice, Poland, in September 1941. The note was in German and was signed 'The Brotherhood of Long Memory'.

(pp. 199–200)

Berger the author, like his God, leaves a few ambiguous hints about who might have been responsible. The lack of any sign of struggle suggests that Karstmann, perhaps, knew his executioners (or that he was led to the garage at gunpoint). Jutta asks Van Buren anxiously whether he thinks Raymond had anything to do with her father's death and Van Buren 'denied her question much more vigorously than I had in my own mind' (p. 201); Bochalski writes to regret that Van Buren's letter 'arrived too late for me to take any action' (p. 202). No matter. No one is arrested and Van Buren does not meet any of the protagonists again. Justice has been done.

Around the events of the plot Berger has woven a series of theological encounters and conversations, particularly some intimate exchanges between Van Buren and Raymond Dell, and one significant conversation between Van Buren and Langbein, in which the ideas which later became the argument of *A Rumour of Angels* are given a first expression and through which the events of the novel's two plots are given their significance.

Langbein is in some ways presented as a sympathetic even exemplary figure. He summarizes his history for Van Buren as follows:

'I was a young *Dozent* in early church history. The time was the early years of the National Socialist regime. The Protestant theological faculty, to which I was attached, was torn by the controversy between the so-called "German Christians" who supported the new regime ideologically, and the Confessing Church movement that was opposed to them. I found myself in an uncomfortable position between the two. I was repelled by the brutality of the regime and, perhaps even more, by the vulgarities of its intellectual supporters at the university. The other side, however, based its opposition on a narrow Protestant conservatism, a return to the classic positions of the Reformation, and there I could not go along either. I was driven back to my scholarship. I immersed myself in those early disputes, and the more I did so, the more I found myself attracted to just those positions that the orthodox Christian tradition felt it necessary to condemn'.

(pp. 128–9)

Langbein, thus, embodies the dilemma of the Austrian-German Lutheranism in which Berger himself was, somewhat later than Langbein, theologically formed, and also exemplifies a resolution not so very far from that which Berger himself sets out in *Rumour*. An earlier exchange between Langbein, Bochalski and Raymond Dell shows Langbein as no literalist. Bochalski suggests that Langbein's position is a form of 'cosmic optimism', a term Langbein accepts and relates to Christian soteriology:

'Soteriology – salvation doctrine. The Christians have understood one thing – that man is not alone in his quest for liberation. But they have terribly misunderstood everything else'.

'You mean that Christ is a misunderstood Abraxas?' asked Raymond.

' " Christ", "Abraxas" – these are but names. The important thing is to understand the spiritual realities for which these names stand', said Langbein a little tartly.

(p. 63)

Langbein, Van Buren and Raymond Dell all at one point or other assert the importance of one significant person or event which acts as a continuing influence in the search for spiritual truth and, again in this, one hears Peter Berger's own authentic voice speaking through the fiction. Langbein, however, is not the whole answer to his author's theological difficulties. Another comic digression has Van Buren trying to follow Langbein's instructions for first-stage meditation. His attempt to concentrate on seeing the (postulated) red line around his chosen object of meditation, a bush on the hillside, is constantly intruded upon by his own sexual memories or anticipations (of the 'house of ill repute', of Isa, of the widow), by itches and discomfort, by a mosquito which eventually bites him: 'I looked once more at the meditated-over-shrub, then unbuttoned my trousers and urinated on it' (p. 136). He and Raymond later joke about 'the thin red line of the ethereal around the sauerkraut you were hypnotising' and Raymond voices their shared scepticism: 'any successes in seeing it, or anything else in that territory fall within psychiatry rather than theology' (p. 160). So much for psychological reductionism.

The two most important passages anticipating the arguments of *Rumour* are conversations between Raymond Dell and Van Buren about the nature of the supernatural, the cosmic divine, and its relation to the moral problems thrown up by war and politics, particularly by killing.

The first time Dell and Van Buren meet after the bathtub incident they quickly reveal their common preoccupation with the supernatural. They are both, in Raymond's term, 'Godders': 'you know – God-person – person interested in God ... Once a Godder, always a Godder!' (p. 24). They have a number of subsequent conversations during the 'Council of Ombelico', mostly concerning the argument(s) from order. But there are two particular exchanges which serve to frame the damnation and 'execution' of Karstmann. The first of these does not have an explicit theological reference but signals the problem of indefensible violence and the nature of absolute evil.

As Van Buren drives a party to the film festival Raymond rides with him in front. Raymond is depressed by the report in the morning paper of the bombing by American troops of a Vietcong village containing women and children – just such an incident as Karstmann later equates with his own extermination of Polish Communists and Jews. Raymond tries to get Van Buren to talk about his own war in Indonesia. Van Buren admits it was probably only luck that saved him from killing women and children and declines to say more. He records in his protocol that the memory of his acts of killing and the faces of his victims still haunt his dreams. Raymond tells him that his own army days were spent in postwar Germany as assistant to a Southern Baptist chaplain in the US army. Their shared repugnance at the killing of women and children is established and lays the groundwork for the later discussion.

On the second occasion on which such matters arise, their exchange becomes a full-blooded, drunken theological discussion (a high-class pub debate!) which virtually summarizes the whole substantive argument of *A Rumour of Angels*. It takes place in a louche night club, possibly a brothel (certainly the 'girls' are available for hire), as Raymond drowns his depression after the departure of Olga and Bochalski and Van Buren matches him, cognac for cognac. They exchange their personal histories of struggles with belief. Raymond was once a theological student in 'the worst' denomination, Methodism. In the course of his training he lost faith in Jehova, 'Old Joe', 'the Judeo-Christian product' (p. 156).

'Oh, they take Old Joe and work him over into a sort of boy scout chief, sweet Jesus who's also keen on baseball and all wholesome things. Lately he's even started to use four-letter words. Very non-simpatico'.

(p. 157)

(The novel reader is not, perhaps, expected to tease out contradictions like this double damnation of American Methodism, first for wholesomeness and then for its abandonment.)
Van Buren, too, lost his belief in the Dutch Calvinist version of Old Joe.

'I think I stopped believing in Him when I became a father ... You see, when you become a parent you get to be terribly conscious of how incredibly fragile a child is. That, of course, is why you are afraid. Then, naturally, you think of God who is supposed to be incredibly powerful ... you realize that, empirically, it is quite absurd to expect Him to protect your child or any other. He just doesn't, does He?'.

(1975, pp. 157–8)

Raymond sardonically characterizes this as 'In the Absence of God, the Fatherhood of Man' (p. 158). So far the arguments are in favour of scepticism but they go on to make the case for belief, starting from the need to clear away Old Joe in order to see what he has been obscuring. The Gnostics at least ask the questions in a new way even if they don't have the right answers: 'Once you give up the notion of an all-powerful and all-good God, who, to boot, created the world, you have a quite different set of questions' (p. 159).
They agree that the world is not all bad: Raymond cites the smile of a child and 'what you see and smell after there's been a thunderstorm over the Lago Maggiore' (pp. 161–2). Van Buren asks for more:

'Well, there's what could be called the argument from human gestures. There are some gestures that men make that seem to point beyond themselves. For instance, if you move to protect a child against harm. Or if you turn to someone with compassion. Or if you strike a blow for justice'.

(p. 162)

Raymond elaborates the last instance by a hypothetical case. If he stumbled on a pack of white men about to lynch an American 'Negro', would Van Buren shoot them to save their intended victim? Van Buren replies: Of course, without hesitation. Raymond comments:

'You see, you'd be acting as if your gesture of upholding justice *represented* someone or something else, a justice that is not just part of some particular relativistic background ... in the tacit assumption that there is someone out there, somewhere in the universe, whom you are imitating, a divine gesture of justice to which yours corresponds in some crazy way ... There are some more arguments like this. Some have technical names and, no doubt, are on Riggi's punch cards. And the ones that interest me most are all based on quite common human experiences, *not* on dark and difficult mysteries'.

(p. 163)

Raymond now produces the final argument, 'the argument from hell', 'more convincing than all the others':

'Suppose, just suppose, that right now you had it in your power to decide the fate of one of the men who did the things that make Olga scream twenty years later. Would you condemn him? Read him out of the human race?'
'Yes, I would'.
'Would you have doubts about condemning him?'
'No, I don't think so'.
'*Why?*'
'I don't know. I suppose there are some deeds that just read you out of the human race, period' ...
'Right. In other words, you'd be sure that this individual deserves hell. Do you have a hell at your disposal? ... a real hell, an Old-Joe-type of hell?'
'No, I don't'.
'*But somebody should*', yelled Raymond.

(Berger, 1975, pp. 164-5)

One curious feature of these theological exchanges between Dell and Van Buren (who seem to be aspects of Berger and certainly divide up his arguments between them) is an insistence, even an over-insistence, on the two men's somewhat transgressive sexuality. This sexual theme is interwoven with the theological reflections and embedded in the interaction between these two 'men of the world' who are also divinity junkies, in so persistent a way that it is hard not to see it as making a deliberate point. Raymond Dell, professional gigolo, and Jacob Van Buren, adulterer, virtuoso debauchee and 'tired devil', are the 'Godders' of the story and there is an intimate, cheek-by-jowl relationship between their mystical and metaphyscial concerns and their rather unreconstructed masculine sexuality which the reader is surely meant to see as more than just incidental.

Van Buren's experiment in meditation is continually thrown off course by memories of the Surabaya brothel, of the compliant widow's thighs, of the thighs of Isa, his wife, and, of course, the episode concludes with a piece of small-boy scatological humour as he pees on the supernaturally unyielding bush. The point of all this may be nothing more than that sexuality is more compelling and real than the red herring of meditation, just as the point of the Tesco episode is that the 'instinct' for order is more powerful than sex. But there again the main sexual reference is the brothel. During Van Buren's theological consultation with Professor Langbein there is another sly sexual aside when Langbein asks if Van Buren reads German and Van Buren records his thought that, provided the incentive is good enough, as it is when he reads pornography, his German is adequate. When Borelli reports that Karpistes has abandoned his delegation to go off on a sexual adventure with a young man, Raymond's response is that it is the first nice thing he has heard about the old fraud. The long conversation in the night club, where Raymond rehearses the arguments for the transcendent and the necessity of hell, is periodically interrupted by offers from 'the girls' to the increasingly drunken 'Godders' and it is this which maintains the thin narrative thread and a mildly humorous incongruity in what might otherwise be a rather shamelessly didactic passage. The episode climaxes in Van Buren's removing his shirt and exposing his comically gross and tattooed torso on the dance floor. And, of course, the damnation of Karstmann is prepared by Mademoiselle Lebrun's sweaty abandonment in the dance and Karstmann's drunken arousal. Moreover, in the discussion of executions which leads up to the curse, Raymond reveals that he attended the execution of a soldier for rape, an event which, it is hinted, was the one unjust death which tuned him in to all the others represented by Olga. (If the outrage of the Holocaust is the enormous half-spoken evil underpinning the preoccupations of the book, this detail, like Raymond's lynching example, seems implicitly haunted by an inversion of the moral order depicted in Griffiths' seminal myth-making American film, *The Birth of a Nation*.)

The sexuality portrayed in this book is overwhelmingly presented from a masculine point of view, which is hardly inappropriate given that it is a first-person narrative. Its pre- if not anti-feminist tone may represent Berger's own views but is certainly an authentically realistic detail given the generation and background of Van Buren, and perhaps verisimilitude is its only rationale. Or it may be no more than an expected feature of the hard-boiled thriller genre, a mere epiphenomenon of the narrative form. Yet it does underline the point Berger makes in *Rumour* that 'morality' cannot be read off from metaphysics and it reinforces his condemnation of moralistic churches in *The Noise of Solemn Assemblies* (1961b) and his designation of moralism as one of the characteristic distortions of the Christian message. If it sometimes sounds a little over-emphatic that is probably because Berger wants to make his picture of the everyday reality within which the signals of transcendence are encountered, properly earthy and embodied rather than rarefied or narrowly 'respectable'. And the use of a defiant, transgressive sexuality as a challenge to death is an old theme, of course. Berger's detestation of the sexual illiberalism which pervades America's culture wars is well known. Moreover, the crude moments are balanced, for instance by Raymond's (sexual) kindness to his needy and ageing women patrons and by his (non-sexual) compassion for Olga and even for Laureano. And in a novel it is perhaps acceptable to leave the relations of the sexual and the metaphysical piquantly ambiguous where in an academic text the reader might legitimately expect to have the issue clarified and resolved.

None the less, the portrait of the two metaphyscial heroes with their worldly-wise masculine sexual assumptions, their individualistic sense of personal integrity and their absolutist mission against monstrous evil does have some incongruous (perhaps even intentionally comic) parallels with the action hero/'buddy' duo of mainstream American popular culture, even though the Humphrey Bogarts, Clint Eastwoods and their ilk seldom stray into examining the underlying metaphysics of their vigilante heroics in a naughty world.

There is no doubt that the argument from hell is the signal of transcendence which gets the most powerful and least equivocal expression in the novel. It is the core of the central narrative and the rationale of the book's title and structure. Further, it is presented as inseparable from the principle of cosmic benevolence. At the close of the book Van Buren/Berger makes the argument fully explicit:

> Can one write, within a few pages, about the death of a murderer of children and about the perfect microcosm of 'Swissminiatur'? The thought occurred to me as I was waiting for Basil to come back from the ride ... How can one experience 'Swissminiatur' without remembering Karstmann's garage, and all it represents? A platitudinous question. Perhaps even *the* platitude of our age. But is there not perhaps a less platitudinous question – how can one properly interpret Karstmann's garage without remembering 'Swissminiatur'? I cannot give very clear answers to these questions, not in terms of metaphysics, certainly, or of Riggi's well-ordered systematics. But, at least at that moment, and in the reason of my own heart, Raymond's argument from hell seemed conjoined with his argument from a smiling child in one, meaningful order.
>
> (Berger, 1975, p. 206)

This is the prelude to Van Buren's solitary ride on the children's miniature train from which Basil has just alighted in search of another ice cream, the narrator's momentary reversion to the eternal well-being of childhood and play.

> I looked around as we moved, at the little Switzerland below us and what there was of life-sized Switzerland all around. I could see the blue of Lake Lugano and above it the steep hills. And it was just then, suddenly and almost overwhelmingly, that my heart jumped into my

throat with an almost searing sensation of joy ... and I was filled with the god'.

For the fraction of a moment I asked myself which god it might be. Hardly 'Old Joe', I thought, but conceivably a sort of first cousin of his.

(p. 207)

These, the last words of the novel, show Berger/Van Buren still conscious of belonging to the Judeo-Christian family. This, it seems, is 'the apparent inevitability of some sort of Christianity' to which he refers in the Postscript (1975, p. 208). The paradoxes remain those of the Christian tradition though their distinctively Christian character has been smudged.

It is ironic that when he wrote these two books, *A Rumour of Angels* (1969a) and *Protocol of a Damnation* (1975) Peter Berger, still partly blinded by secularization theory, believed that angels, 'God's messengers as His signals in reality' had been 'reduced to a rumour' (1970, p. 119), but that the argument from hell was so self-evidently powerful that it might convince the legion of doubters that the transcendent was real, true and a moral as well as a metaphysical necessity. Today every bookshop in America has a flourishing angelology section (69 per cent of Americans believe in angels and 32 per cent have personally felt an angelic presence, according to *Time* magazine (see Ramer, 1999)), while belief in hell and damnation withers. The 'uncertainty wallahs' alongside Peter Berger in the Protestant pews do not much like the idea of hell and even those conservative evangelicals who do, tend to regard it as a staging post in the redemption process rather than a permanent punishment for innumerable immortal souls. One lapsed Catholic, reviewing the Evangelical Alliance's document, *The Nature of Hell* (Hilborne, 2000), recently wrote:

Hell ... was a place created by 'the justice of an offended God' to punish people for the sins they committed on earth. It was for the whole of time, for ever and ever ... And you could find yourself consigned to this dismaying prison sentence not for starting an unjust war or stabbing someone to death, but for having sex with your girlfriend. The God that presided over this totalitarian regime was supposed to be a benign and forgiving old party – but how could you square this talk about his divine love with this elaborately forged Ministry of Pain?

(Walsh, 2000, p. 5)

This is essentially Raymond's and Van Buren's objection to 'Old Joe' and, perhaps, part of the rationale for all that defiant sexuality. John Walsh, Catholic unbeliever, concludes:

Don't get me wrong. I don't believe in the place, any more than I believe in Heaven or, come to that, God. But the image of Hell I picked up at three or four ... has stayed with me all my life and probably governed whatever moral sense I possess. The human mind needs absolutes of good and bad as it grows up, and Hell is as absolute as it gets.

(ibid. p. 5)

Walsh's utilitarian paradox – it's a lie, but a useful one – is not Berger's way. Peter Berger continues to wrestle with the problem of getting to the *truth* behind those things it is needful to believe if we are to enter fully into our *humanitas* as poor, forked, naked beings faced with mortality, pain and loss as well as with beauty, love and wonder – and vice versa. Berger's is a more than honourable essay in approaching the central mystery of human life with eyes wide open, rejecting the hollow comfort of what has been taken for granted by previous generations and must now be riddled out. If his answers have no more self-evident validity than those of Professor Langbein or of the contemporary liberal churches we can hardly be surprised.

There is no definitive breakthrough to a new level of theological understanding, no new certainty, but only a very old and urgent pilgrimage through fear, doubt and the desire to find truth and not empty reassurance in the distinctive Christian paradoxes, particularly that there may be meaning and hope even in the most appalling human experiences. After following Peter Berger closely on his pilgrimage, the only proper response is not cool academic assessment but empathy with the pilgrim. R. S. Thomas, in 'The Empty Church' catches just the mixture of melancholia and hopefulness that marks Berger's pursuit of the divine:

> They laid this stone trap
> for him, enticing him with candles,
> as though he would come like some huge moth
> out of the darkness to beat there.
> Ah, he had burned himself
> before in the human flame
> and escaped, leaving the reason
> torn. He will not come any more
>
> to our lure. Why, then, do I kneel still
> striking my prayers on a stone
> heart? Is it in hope one
> of them will ignite yet and throw
> on its illumined walls the shadow
> of someone greater than I can understand?

(Thomas, 1995, p. 349)

Postscript

Peter Berger

Years ago I read Dale Carnegie's classic textbook on American niceness, *How to Win Friends and Influence People* (1981, orig. 1937). I've forgotten everything about it, except for one observation by Carnegie: 'Always remember a person's name, because that is his favorite word in the English language.' True enough. One might add that a rather long manuscript that deals, chapter by chapter, with oneself must be the favourite reading at least of academics. (That would be the PG-rated description. The R-rated description would say that it is the favourite form of cognitive masturbation, at least by academics.) In any case, I confess, possibly not to my moral credit, that I enjoyed the exercise. Thus I must thank Linda Woodhead and all the contributors for having enhanced my summer. I must also thank them for the thoughtful and eminently fair way in which they dealt with my embarrassingly large literary output. The contributors range from individuals whom I have known for many years to some whom I have never met, but it is gratifying that, after having finished reading the manuscript, I did not have to add a single name to my enemy list.

I gave some thought to how to organize this postscript in an intellectually coherent way. I couldn't come up with anything. So I will deal with the various contributions seriatim, in the order in which they appear in the table of contents. If my comments are of unequal length as between the several contributors, this is not to be interpreted as implying invidious distinctions; it simply means that in some cases I didn't have much to add to what is already there.

The first three chapters are *ad hominem* (definitely not in the pejorative sense of the phrase.) Consequently it is more difficult to comment about them, unless by way of sentimental reminiscence. This is very much so with regard to the chapter by David Martin. If I say that I disagree with his generous assessment of my career, I will not be believed; if I say that I agree, I will seem to be insufferably self-satisfied. He and I share a remarkably similar 'homelessness' between sociology and theology, epitomized in the episode he mentions, when I was loudly booed by enraged students when giving a lecture, which he chaired, at the London School of Economics about thirty years ago. Both of us, I think, have found our 'homelessness' both personally difficult and intellectually stimulating, giving us reason to address the 'Father of all mercies' in the words of the General Thanksgiving: 'We thine unworthy servants do give thee most humble and hearty thanks for all thy goodness and loving-kindness to us.' And while I'm on the subject of liturgy let me add that, when some biographer or recording angel will make a tally of David's good deeds, close to the top of the list will be his valiant struggle to protect the Book of Common Prayer from the barbarians who translated it into the language of a mail-order catalogue.

I can say little in response to Thomas Luckmann, who is one of my oldest friends and intellectual interlocutors. I can only agree with what he says about the unusual character of our collaboration. The only other person with whom I have been able to collaborate with comparable ease has been Brigitte Berger, but then, after all, she is my wife. When, many years after Tom and I wrote *The Social Construction of Reality* (1966), we collaborated once more on the book commissioned by the Bertelsmann Foundation which he mentions, we slipped back into the same tension-free exchange of ideas as if time had stood still. I'm particularly pleased that Tom referred to our shared roots in the vanished world of the Habsburg monarchy, which of course we did not experience personally (we are old, alas, but not *that* old!), but which we absorbed in our upbringing and which served as a useful vantage point from which to observe the inanities of our own time. Out of this same world, I think, comes a heightened sense of what our teacher Alfred Schutz called 'multiple realities' (he came from the last generation that actually lived as a subject of the monarchy). I have little difficulty imagining one such reality in which, right now, Tom as a retired k.u.k. general and I as a retired Royal Hungarian bureaucrat, are sitting together in a Kaffeehaus in Meran, reminiscing about the *coup d'état* by which we saved the monarchy in 1910. (For the uninitiated: the initials k.u.k. stand for *kaiserlich und koeniglich/Imperial and Royal*, referring to all the institutions, notably the military, which served both the Austrian and Hungarian parts of the monarchy. I will also quote a statement by Schutz: 'The difference between *Kaffee* and coffee is like the difference between Mozart and Mantovani.')

Before the reader decides that I have lapsed into irreversible senile dementia, let me make one 'serious' intellectual point (not that I would concede that the reality in which Tom and I converse in Meran is any less 'serious'). He mentions it in passing: 'The relation between our book *The Social Construction of Reality* (1966) and much of what passes today under the heading of "constructivism".' To the extent that this term refers to a new appreciation of culture in the development of social institutions (this is notably the case today among a growing number of political scientists and a few economists), neither he nor I have any objections. But when the term is used by a good number of so-called 'postmodernist' theorists something quite different is implied. The difference between these theorists and what we tried to do is glaring: we proposed (correctly, I continue to think) that all human reality is socially produced and interpreted. They propose that all interpretations are equally valid, and some of them propose that there is no reality at all outside the interpretations. Their former proposition is an invitation to solipsism, with coteries of interpreters imprisoned in quasi-Leibnizian monads between which communication is impossible – a recipe for the self-liquidation of science and, beyond that and far more dangerously, for a politics of fanaticism. Their latter proposition fits the clinical description of schizophrenia, whereby the individual is incapable of distinguishing between the real world and his own fantasies (this, by the way, is how Juergen Habermas characterized his radical critics in the debates of the late 1960s).

I have only met Gary Dorrien once, but I'm grateful to him for an earlier appraisal of my work in which he was critical but sympathetic. He is particularly interested in the allegedly conservative tendency in my writings, though he understands that this may apply to my political positions but not to my theological trajectory. This has been a major factor in my 'homelessness' on the intellectual scene: those who agree with me politically have tended to disagree with me theologically, and vice versa: for most of my adult life I have been politically right-of-centre but theologically liberal, which has induced a sort of cognitive sea-sickness in many of my interlocutors. Dorrien is quite correct in saying that, for a while, I found a sort of political 'home' in the so-called neo-conservative movement. I cannot fault him for not having paid sufficient attention to my rather dramatic break from this movement in 1997 over what I perceived (correctly, I believe) as its members' increasing extremism, especially their monomaniacal preoccupation with the issues of abortion, homosexuality (on the former issue I have always been somewhere in the middle, and on the latter decisively liberal.) I cannot fault him, because after all he must have other things to do than noting every twist and turn in my less than orderly biography.

There may be something to the 'postmodernist' view that the author is the last to know, but I'm not persuaded by Dorrien's proposition that 'Berger's shifting theology showed through his objectivistic social science prose'. My theology shifted from the Lutheran neo-orthodoxy of my youth to a self-conscious Protestant liberalism broadly speaking in the tradition of Schleiermacher; this could be seen as a move away from dogmatic order. My sociology, on the other hand, shifted from a sort of existentialist celebration of freedom (especially in my book *Invitation to Sociology* (1963)) to a greater appreciation of the importance of social order. Was this, at least partly, the result of my recoiling from the destructive disorder of the late 1960s? Maybe. But the collaborative efforts that led to *The Social Construction of Reality* (1966) began in the *early* 1960s, and they were the result of a theoretical 'marriage' between the Schutzian interpretation of Max Weber and the Durkheimian tradition in sociology. This had nothing to do with what happened on the streets a few years later. It may, of course, have had something to do with the simple fact of getting older.

Dorrien regrets that I did not engage in more 'interrogations' of recent academic theology. From what I have seen of the latter, especially in its 'postmodernist' versions, I cannot share his regret. He comments at some length on my criticisms of Langdon Gilkey, Schubert Ogden and David Tracy. He thinks that they could have been my natural allies. I rather doubt it, though I'm open to the possibility that I may have misunderstood some of their positions. But these are *tempi passati*, and I have little desire to revive these old debates. In recent years I have found myself in happier theological company, especially with a number of people in German-speaking Protestantism, but that is another story.

With the chapter by Paul Heelas and Linda Woodhead one moves into a more rarified intellectual atmosphere, and I am less tempted to engage in Austro-Hungarian digressions. They have accurately and thoughtfully commented on the argument I made with Brigitte Berger and Hansfried Kellner in our book *The Homeless Mind* (1973). However, I rather disagree with Heelas' and Woodhead's view of what has happened to the counterculture since the late 1960s. The 'relational', 'ecological' and 'cosmic' aspects of this culture, which they see as more recent developments, were present from the beginning. And I disagree with their view that the counterculture has 'largely faded away'. It has not. Rather, it has been *institutionalized*, especially in the cultural elites of Europe and North America, radiating downwards into other classes of Western societies and radiating outwards through miscellaneous agencies of a globalizing Western intelligentsia. What began as a liberating insurgency has become a dreary orthodoxy, exercising remarkable coercive power in a large number of institutions. Let me say that I am sympathetic with a number of features of this culture – notably its remarkable freedom from racial and ethnic prejudices, its tolerance of sexual diversity, and above all what the French sociologist Danièle Hervieu-Léger has called the 'ecumenism of human rights'. But I cannot share in what seems to be Heelas' and Woodhead's enthusiasm for an alleged 'turn-to-life'; my own *attention à la vie* (to use Bergson's phrase) is rather different.

Either Heelas and Woodhead are charitable or they have actually overlooked what, in retrospect, was the most critical omission in *The Homeless Mind*: there was no discussion of capitalism. I'm not sure why this omission occurred; perhaps it was because much of the book was composed while we were spending time in Mexico, where other aspects of modernization were clamouring for attention. Be this as it may, Heelas and Woodhead are correct in bringing the new 'soft capitalism' into the discussion, and I'm glad that they noticed the work of Hansfried Kellner and Frank Heuberger (1992) on this topic (their research was supported by the Institute for the Study of Economic Culture, which I have been directing at Boston University since 1985). Perhaps more than Heelas and Woodhead would, I see this 'soft-capitalism' as an interpretation (or, if you will, a mutual co-optation) of the counterculture and the business culture – a significant development that could not have been foreseen in the early 1970s when the relation between the two seemed more like a class war.

Heelas and Woodhead raise the interesting question of whether the hard distinction between primary and secondary institutions is breaking down. I agree that this should be an area of sustained research. In this connection I would refer to another book coming out of the work of our Institute – Frank Heuberger and Laura Nash (eds), *A Fatal Embrace? – Assessing Holistic Trends in Human Resources Programs* (1994). One of the fringe benefits of being the director of a research centre is that you can get other people to do what you failed to do yourself! I would hesitate to call these phenomena a 'spiritual revolution' and I will politely dissent from the proposition that this calls for a 'gendered' perspective.

I find the discussion of New Age by Colin Campbell thoroughly persuasive. I find his characterization of New Age as a 'theodicy' and as a 'metaphysical monism' very illuminating, and I agree that the latter constitutes a challenge to the view of the self that has been a major product of Western civilization. I particularly like his discussion of how New Age adapted to the Hindu notions of *samsara* and *karma*: what has been a profoundly pessimistic view of the human condition in India has been twisted into an upbeat optimism – reincarnation as a terrible fate to reincarnation as an endless enjoyment of self-enhancing possibilities.

Campbell has previously referred to New Age as a form of 'Easternization' (1999). Our Institute is at present completing our most ambitious research prose yet – a ten-country study of the cultural effects of globalization. This process has usually been seen as a phenomenon of Westernization – an emergent global culture, using the English language and containing elements deriving almost exclusively from the West (indeed mostly from America). There is indeed such an emerging global culture, both on elite and popular levels; the Chilean historian Claudio Véliz has aptly called it 'the Hellenistic phase of Anglo-American civilization', with American English as its koiné. It is not a monolithic or irresistible force, and it encounters different responses in different parts of the world, ranging from supine acceptance to fierce resistance, with important in-between cases of hybridization and synthesis. But there are also movements of alternative globalization, cultural influences originating outside the West and impinging on the latter. Among these movements of 'Easternization', New Age is arguably the most important, and Campbell is one of its insightful commentators.

The chapter by Steve Bruce is the most piquant of the lot, pitting 'early Berger' against 'later Berger'. I'm grateful that, unlike some unfriendly American criticism, he did not identify his own position as 'post-Bergerian' (though his effort 'to save an intellectual hero from himself' reminds me, uncomfortably, of the attempts to rescue the Marx of the *Economic and*

Philosophical Manuscripts of 1848 from the Marx of *Das Kapital*). All this is both charming and flattering, and I almost regret that I cannot agree with him. I must stand by my 'recantation' of secularization theory, for all the reasons that Bruce enumerates and which, I think, he does not successfully repudiate. The comparison between religion in Europe and in the United States *is* strategically important: if modernization and secularization are intrinsically linked, one would have to argue that the United States is less modern than, say, the United Kingdom (which Bruce almost does, when he submits thatmodernization came later in the former – so it did – but it came even later in Sweden, and look what happened *there*). There is indeed, in America as in Europe, an individualization of religion. Robert Wuthnow called it 'patchwork religion', Danièle Hervieu-Léger described it by the Levi-Straussian term '*bricolage*'. The interesting difference is that the American 'patchworkers' continue to go to church and to express often very traditional beliefs (some 40 million of them calling themselves 'born-again Christians'), while the European '*bricoleurs*' do neither. As to the rest of the world, full of massive religious explosions, it won't do to explain this in terms of a lesser degree of modernization (one might call this the 'last gasp theory' of, say, the Iranian revolution). On the contrary, some of the most impressive religious upsurges are occurring in relatively modernized milieus (such as militant Islamism and the remarkable global expansion of Pentecostalism, which is being magisterially studied by David Martin). Those who, in the face of all this, maintain the old secularization theory – Bryan Wilson and Steve Bruce are notable among them – can be admired for their dissent – from what is by now a widespread consensus among scholars of contemporary religion. For all that, they are wrong.

There does indeed exist the phenomenon of secularization, and more specifically the version of it that one may call Eurosecularity. But one cannot assume that this is the normal concomitant of modernity. On the contrary, in a cross-cultural perspective it is the deviant case. As such, it must be mapped and explained. I would argue that this is the most interesting topic for the sociology of religion today. It begins with the dawning suspicion that British intellectuals are more interesting than Iranian mullahs as objects of sociological research.

If I look back on my earlier work, I would say that I was wrong about secularization, but right about pluralism. I misunderstood the relation between the two: the latter does not necessarily lead to the former (*vide* the American case). What pluralism does (and there I was right) is to undermine all taken-for-granted certainties, in religion as in all other spheres of life. But it is possible to hold beliefs and to live by them even if they no longer hold the status of taken-for-granted verities. In other words, I would now say that pluralism affects the *how* of religious belief, but not necessarily the *what*. Bruce understands my position on this very well, but he thinks that, in the longer run, it will be impossible to combine a religious attitude with uncertainty, even if in the short run, for people coming out of a restrictive dogmatic milieu, this may be attractive. As he puts it eloquently, 'an open prison seems like a welcome release to someone who transfers from a high security prison'. Eventually, he argues, the 'cultural capital' of the generation that was still brought up in dogmatic religion will be exhausted and all religion will wilt away, at least in the highly developed societies. This argument takes us into the area of futurology and I suppose one could emulate Chou Enlai who, when asked what he thought of the results of the French Revolution, replied that it is too early to tell. At this point, though, I see no reason to agree with Bruce and the other non-recanting secularization theorists.

Grace Davie, along with her friend and collaborator Danièle Hervieu-Léger, is among the most interesting sociologists of religion writing today. Her portrayal of European exceptionalism in the area of religion is very persuasive. Here she argues that, over and beyond the phenomenon of 'believing without belonging' which she used before in interpreting the religious situation in Britain, the *churches* in Europe continue to play an important role in society, despite the fact that diminishing numbers of people attend their services or profess their official creeds. This is the phenomenon of 'belonging without believing', to which she attaches the very useful concept of 'vicarious religion'. (This, by the way, is brilliantly developed in her just-published book *Religion in Modern Europe*, 2000a.) I continue to think that Europe continues to be the one geographical area where the old secularization theory retains plausibility, but Davie's work provides a more nuanced understanding of Eurosecularity.

During the last years I have had frequent occasions to visit Berlin, which may well be the most secularized city in the world. Somewhat to his annoyance, I once told Wolfgang Huber, the bishop of the Protestant *Landeskirche* of Berlin-Brandenburg, that his diocese consists of the world capital of atheism. His church must be called 'weak' by any reasonable criterion. But if anyone wants to have a vivid impression of Davie's concept of 'vicariousness' I would suggest that he visit the famous Gedaechniskirche in the centre of West Berlin, sit down for a while and watch the people who spend time in the church. The experience gives weight to Davie's observation that 'weak churches are less weak if they have the tacit support of considerably wider sections of the population'. (In the German case one may add the remarkable fact that the majority of this population continue to pay their church tax, although a simple bureaucratic step is all that is required to save this expenditure.)

Danièle Hervieu-Léger has understood me better than almost anyone else in the sociology of religion, and indeed at one point understood me better than I did myself. It was on a walk in Cambridge, Massachusetts, a few years ago, when I was saying something about the tension between uncertainty and religious belief, that she said: 'Why do you leave yourself out of your theory?' This was what Alfred Schutz used to call an '*aha* experience', and it set me on a train of thought that led to my present understanding of the relation of pluralism and secularity. Danièle's work for several years now has had as its focus the individualization of belief and the resultant 'vast recomposition of the institutional systems of believing' (most recently in her as yet untranslated book *Le Pèlerin et le converti*). I fully share her view that this leads to a far-reaching problem of social order; this view does not necessarily make either her or me a 'conservative thinker' (though I would accept that title for quite different reasons). I'm also grateful for her statement that my intellectual path was 'not split between a secularist and an antisecularist Berger', but rather (thank you, Danièle!) 'a lucid invitation to exercise methodological precaution'.

But is Europe secularized? And if so, how and why? Danièle and I agree that Europe is a special case. Like Grace Davie, she has a nuanced view of this, and it is my impression that her view is still developing, as indeed is mine. (As I like to tell my students, one of the benefits of being a social scientist, as against, say, a theologian or philosopher, is that one can have as much fun when the empirical evidence falsifies one's theories as when it supports them.) I have for a long time made a distinction between institutional secularization and the secularization of consciousness; I still think that this is a useful distinction (it has been somewhat amplified in José Casanova's recent work). But Danièle adds a third dimension, an important one – the secularization of culture. Speaking about France (but the point can easily be extended to other countries) she proposes that there exists a cultural Catholicism there which persists even among people who don't attend Catholic services or profess Catholic beliefs. This is not quite the same as Davie's 'vicarious religion'. It is the permeation of a culture by, as it were, a certain religious cognitive style, by certain habits, even by a constellation of emotions. Danièle has recently ventured the hypothesis that this too is vanishing, thus adding a third dimension to the secularization process (at least in Europe).

The last three contributions in this volume move back from sociology to more theological considerations. I have had some difficulties understanding the argument in the chapter by Richard Fenn. I follow his thoughts about the relation between the 'precarious vision' of sociology and a religious view of the world: both the sociological imagination and what he calls 'the Spirit' undermine the conventional, everyday definition of reality (the one that Schutz has called the 'paramount reality'). But Fenn also argues that this liquidates 'social dichotomies', as between the sacred and the profane, and between the other-worldly and the this-worldly. I cannot follow him there. He also seems to believe that the 'precarious vision' has lately become 'ordinary rather than ecstatic'. I don't understand why this should be so. Perhaps, like Heelas and Woodhead, Fenn overestimates the cultural transformation of the past few decades. To be sure, there is a heightened sense of precariousness in any period of rapid social and cultural change, but I don't see any evidence to the effect that the generation that has come to maturity since the cultural earthquake of the 1960s has the sort of 'precarious vision' that Fenn endorses.

The chapter by David Horrell was a big surprise for me. I have been familiar with the work of my friend and colleague Howard Kee, but I had no idea that *The Social Construction of Reality* (1966) had the effect on other New Testament scholars described by Horrell. Needless to say, I'm greatly pleased! His explanation of this influence makes sense: New Testament scholars apparently like a sociological approach that is not reductionist – that is, an approach that takes the social foundations of religion seriously, but that does not reduce religion to an epiphenomenon that simply reflects underlying social forces. In this approach, I would claim, I continue to be an orthodox Weberian! I was puzzled for some time by the fact that an Islamic publishing house in Indonesia put out one translation after another of my principal books in sociology and religion, until I visited Indonesia and had some conversations about this. I then discovered that here were Muslim intellectuals who liked my approach (despite its Christian character) for precisely the reasons for which, according to Horrell, New Testament scholars like it.

Horrell mostly approves of my view of how religion relates to the 'symbolic universe' of human societies, but he has some criticisms. One of these I accept: the concept of 'legitimation', as I used it in my earlier work in the sociology of religion, tends to suggest that religion is always a phenomenon *post festum*, reinforced social structures that were there before it. I did not intend such an interpretation, but Horrell is right in saying that the term 'legitimation' implies this. I have used it much more cautiously in recent years. Two other criticisms I do not accept. I do not see how my concept of objectivation leads to a static view of society. Not at all. Any 'objective' social reality is the result of the ongoing externalization of human meanings – a highly dynamic phenomenon indeed. Nor would I accept Antony Giddens's criticism, which Horrell endorses, that my approach contains no critique of ideology – that is, that it overlooks the place of power and vested interests in the social construction of reality. Again, no. Already in the early book with Thomas Luckmann there is the recognition that not all definitions of reality are equally powerful. Put simply, my definitions of reality, *nebbich*, are less likely to have an impact than those of the Pope or the World Bank. It is possible, of course, that Giddens and Horrell have in mind ideologies that I have not paid attention to, but that is not a methodological issue. I don't know what Horrell means when he recommends that my approach be augmented by a 'critical theory'. If he means by that phrase what it has meant in the Frankfurt School and other neo-Marxist circles, then I would heartily disagree – not least because these people have always exercised their critical acumen in dealing with the ideologies of others, hardly ever turning it back on their own ideology.

And so I come to the last chapter, the one by Bernice Martin. I read it with very great pleasure indeed, and not only because it deals mainly with my second novel, *Protocol of a Damnation* (1975), which almost nobody else has read. (Nobody *at all* has read the first one, *The Enclaves*, published ten years earlier under the pseudonym Felix Bastien; if Bernice Martin had difficulty getting a copy of *Protocol*, this is nothing compared to the difficulty of finding a copy of *Enclaves*. Whatever successes I have had in my life, none has been as a novelist!) Bernice has fully understood the link between *Protocol* and *A Rumour of Angels*, which was published four years later. She may be right that I had to write the novel first and that *Rumour* is itself more of an artistic than a theoretical response to the problems raised in the novel – which is, quite simply, how it is possible to believe in God. As she puts it very plausibly, 'the story touches part of the self the intellect alone cannot reach'.

I was intrigued by her observation about the salience of sexual themes in the novel. I had not paid attention to this before, and I had not intended this salience when I was writing the novel. I had been much more conscious of another salience, that of fatherhood: almost all the male characters in the novel are either fathers or father-surrogates, and the problem of theodicy, which is central to the novel, is precisely that of the fatherhood of God. The biographical context of the latter salience is easily explained: I had recently become a father! As to the former salience, there is the simple fact that I was very young when I wrote the novel. But there is a more objective consideration: sexuality is one of the major forces resulting in ruptures of ordinary, everyday reality, and as such it has an affinity with the ruptures brought about by religious experience. This is not an original perception. In the novel the orgiastic dance of Mlle Lebrun precedes the rupture which necessitates Raymond's act of damnation.

I cannot think of an elegant conclusion to these observations. I can only repeat my thanks to Linda Woodhead and the other contributors for having taken my work so seriously (perhaps more seriously than I take it myself!). I can only hope that they enjoyed writing this book as much as I have enjoyed reading it.

References

Peter Berger: books (including co-authored works)

Berger, Peter L. (1961a) *The Precarious Vision: A Sociologist Looks at Social Fictions and the Christian Faith*, Garden City, NY: Doubleday.

— (1961b) *The Noise of Solemn Assemblies: Christian Commitment and the Religious Establishment*, Garden City, NY: Doubleday.

— (1963a) *Invitation to Sociology: A Humanistic Perspective*, Garden City, NY: Anchor Books.

— (1963b) *Invitation to Sociology: A Humanistic Perspective*, Harmondsworth: Penguin Books.

— and Thomas Luckmann (1966a) *The Social Construction of Reality: A Treatise in the Sociology of Knowledge*, Garden City, NY: Doubleday.

— and — (1966b) *The Social Construction of Reality: A Treatise in the Sociology of Knowledge*, Harmondsworth: Penguin Books.

— and — (1966c) *The Social Construction of Reality*, London: Allen Lane.

— (1966d) *Invitation to Sociology: A Humanistic Perspective*, Harmondsworth: Penguin Books.

— (1967) *The Sacred Canopy: Elements of a Sociological Theory of Religion*, Garden City, NY: Doubleday.

— (1969a) *A Rumor of Angels: Modern Society and the Rediscovery of the Supernatural*, Garden City, NY: Doubleday.

— (1969b) *The Sacred Canopy: Elements of a Sociological Theory of Religion*, London: Faber and Faber.

— (1969c) *The Social Reality of Religion*, London: Faber and Faber.

— (1970) *A Rumour of Angels: Modern Society and the Rediscovery of the Supernatural*, London: Allen Lane.

— (1973) *The Social Reality of Religion*, Harmondsworth: Penguin Books.

—, Brigitte Berger and Hansfried Kellner (1973) *The Homeless Mind: Modernization and Consciousness*, New York: Random House.

— (1974a) *Pyramids of Sacrifice: Political Ethics and Social Change*, New York: Basic Books.

— (1974b) *Religion in a Revolutionary Society*, Washington DC: American Enterprise Institute for Public Policy Research.

—, Brigitte Berger and Hansfried Kellner (1974) *The Homeless Mind: Modernization and Consciousness*, Harmondsworth: Penguin Books.

Berger, Peter L. (1975) *Protocol of a Damnation: a Novel*, New York: Seabury Press.
— and Richard J. Neuhaus (eds) (1976) *Against the World for the World: The Hartford Appeal and the Future of American Religion*, New York: Seabury Press.
— (1977a) *Facing Up to Modernity: Excursions in Society, Politics, and Religion*, New York: Basic Books.
— (1977b) *Pyramids of Sacrifice: Political Ethics and Social Change*, Harmondsworth: Penguin Books.
— (1979a) *The Heretical Imperative*, Garden City, NY: Anchor/Doubleday.
— (1979b) *Facing up to Modernity*, Harmondsworth: Penguin Books.
— (ed.) (1981) *The Other Side of God: A Polarity in World Religions*, Garden City, NY: Anchor Books.
Berger, Brigitte and Peter L. Berger (1983) *The War over the Family*, Garden City, NY: Anchor/Doubleday.
Berger, Peter L. (1986a) *The Capitalist Revolution: Fifty Propositions about Prosperity, Equality, and Liberty*, New York: Basic Books.
— (1987) *The Capitalist Revolution: Fifty Propositions about Prosperity, Equality, and Liberty*, Aldershot: Wildwood House.
— (1992) *A Far Glory: The Quest for Faith in an Age of Credulity*, New York: Free Press.
— and Thomas Luckmann (1995) *Modernity, Pluralism and the Crisis of Meaning*, Gütersloh: Bertelsmann Foundation Publishers.
— (1997a) *Redeeming Laughter*, New York and Berlin: Walter de Gruyter.
— (ed.) (1999) *The Desecularization of the World: Resurgent Religion and World Politics*, Grand Rapids, MI: Eerdmans.

Peter Berger: articles

Berger, Peter L. (1963c) 'Charisma and Ideological Innovation: the Social Location of Israelite Prophecy', *American Sociological Review*, 28 (6), pp. 940–50.
— and Thomas Luckmann (1963) 'Sociology of Religion and Sociology of Knowledge', *Sociology and Social Research*, 47, pp. 61–73.
— (1964) 'Some General Observations on the Problem of Work', in Peter Berger (ed.) *The Human Shape of Work*, New York: Macmillan, pp. 211–41.
Luckmann, Thomas and Peter L. Berger (1964) 'Social Mobility and Personal Identity', *European Journal of Sociology*, 5, pp. 331–44.
Berger, Peter L. and Stanley Pullberg (1966) 'Reification and the Sociological Critique of Consciousness', *New Left Review*, 35, pp. 56–71.
— and Thomas Luckmann (1966) 'Secularization and Pluralism', *International Yearbook for the Sociology of Religion*, 2, pp. 73–86.
— (1977c) 'Secular Theology and the Rejection of the Supernatural: Reflections on Recent Trends', *Theological Studies*, 38 (1), pp. 45–55.
— and Hansfried Kellner (1977) 'Marriage and the Construction of Reality', in Peter L. Berger (ed.) *Facing Up to Modernity*, New York: Basic Books, pp. 27–47.
— (1980) 'From Secularity to World Religions', *The Christian Century*, 97, pp. 44–8.
— (1986b) 'Epilogue', in James Davison Hunter and Stephen C. Ainlay (eds) *Making Sense of Modern Times: Peter L. Berger and the Vision of Interpretive Sociology*, London and New York: Routledge and Kegan Paul, pp. 221–35.

Berger, Peter L. (1988) 'Moral Judgment and Political Action', *This World*, 21, pp. 4–7, 15–18.

— (1990) 'Reflections of an Ecclesiastical Expatriate', *The Christian Century*, 107: 24 October, pp. 964–9.

— (1991) 'The Serendipity of Liberties', in Richard John Neuhaus (ed.) *The Structure of Freedom: Correlations, Causes, and Cautions*, Grand Rapids, MI: Eerdmans, pp. 1–17.

— (1997b) 'Against the Current', *Prospect*, March, pp. 32–6.

— (1998) 'Protestantism and the Quest of Certainty', *The Christian Century*, 26 August–2 September 2, pp. 782–96.

General

Adams, Edward (2000) *Constructing the World: A Study in Paul's Cosmological Language*, Edinburgh: T. & T. Clark.

Ammerman, Nancy (1997) *Congregation and Community*, New Brunswick, NJ: Rutgers University Press.

Bäckström, Anders and Jonas Bromander (1995) *Kyrkobyggnaden och det Offentliga Rummet*, Uppsala: Svenska Kyrkans Utredningar (with a summary in English).

Barker, David, Loek Halman and Astrid Vloet (1992) *The European Values Study 1981–1990: Summary Report*, London: The Gordon Cook Foundation on behalf of the European Values Group.

Bhaskar, Roy (1979) *The Possibility of Naturalism: A Philosophical Critique of the Contemporary Human Sciences*, Brighton: Harvester.

Bloch, John (1998) 'Individualism and Community in Alternative Spiritual "Magic"', *Journal for the Scientific Study of Religion*, 37, pp. 286–302.

Bonhoeffer, Dietrich (1971) *Letters and Papers from Prison*, Eberhard Bethge (ed.), New York: Macmillan.

Brierley, Peter (1997) *Religious Trends 1998/99*, No. 1, London: Christian Research.

— (1999) *Religious Trends 2000/01*, No. 2, London: Christian Research.

— (2000) *The Tide is Running Out*, London: Christian Research.

Brown, Peter (1967) *Augustine of Hippo*, Berkeley and Los Angeles: University of California Press.

Bruce, Steve (1982) 'The Student Christian Movement: A Nineteenth Century New Religious Movement and its Vicissitudes', *International Journal of Sociology and Social Policy*, 2, pp. 67–82.

— (1999) *Choice and Religion: A Critique of Rational Choice Theory*, Oxford: Oxford University Press.

Cairns, D. (1974) 'The Thought of Peter Berger', *Scottish Journal of Theology*, 27, pp. 181–97.

Campbell, Colin (1999) 'The Easternization of the West', in Bryan Wilson and Jamie Cresswell (eds) *New Religious Movements: Challenge and Response*, London: Routledge.

Campbell, Matthew (2000) 'Cry God for Sales as the Bard Goes Centre Stage in US Boardrooms', *The Sunday Times*, 9 January, p. 25.

Carnegie, Dale (1981) *How to Win Friends and Influence People* (revised edition), New York: Simon and Schuster.

Casanova, José (1996) *Public Religion in the Modern World,* Chicago: University of Chicago Press.

Chambers, Paul (2000) 'Factors in Church Growth and Decline', unpublished PhD thesis, University of Wales.

Collins, Sylvia (1997) 'Young People's Faith in Late Modernity', unpublished PhD thesis, University of Surrey.

Cox, Harvey (1965) *The Secular City: Urbanization and Secularization in Theological Perspective,* New York: Macmillan.

Cupitt, Don (1999) *The New Religion of Life in Everyday Speech,* London: SCM.

Dalton, Russell and Manfred Kuechler (eds) (1990) *Challenging the Political Order: New Social and Political Movements in Western Democracies,* New York: Oxford University Press.

Davie, Grace (1994) *Religion in Britain since 1945: Believing without Belonging,* Oxford: Blackwell.

—— and Danièle Hervieu-Léger (eds) (1996) *Identités Religieuses en Europe,* Paris: La Découverte.

—— (1999) 'Religion and Laïcité', in Malcolm Cook and Grace Davie (eds) *Modern France: Society in Transition,* London: Routledge, pp. 195–215.

—— (2000a) *Religion in Modern Europe: A Memory Mutates,* Oxford: Oxford University Press.

—— (2000b) 'Patterns of Religion in Western Europe: An Exceptional Case', in Richard Fenn (ed.) *The Blackwell Companion to the Sociology of Religion,* Oxford: Blackwell, forthcoming.

Davies, Paul and John Gribbin (1992) *The Matter Myth: Beyond Chaos and Complexity,* London: Penguin Books.

de Tocqueville, Alexis (1981) (orig. 1840) *Democracy in America,* New York: The Modern Library: Random House Inc.

Dittgen, Alfred (1994) 'La Forme du Mariage en Europe. Cérémonie Civile, Cérémonie Religieuse: Panorama et évolution', *Population,* 2, pp. 339–68.

Dorrien, Gary (1990) Interview with Peter L. Berger, 26 September.

—— (1993) *The Neoconservative Mind: Politics, Culture and the War of Ideology,* Philadelphia: Temple University Press.

—— (1997) *The Word as True Myth: Interpreting Modern Theology,* Louisville, KY: Westminster John Knox Press.

—— (1999) *The Barthian Revolt in Modern Theology: Theology Without Weapons,* Louisville, KY: Westminster John Knox Press.

Elgin, Duane (1981) *Voluntary Simplicity: Toward a Way of Life That is Outwardly Simple, Inwardly Rich,* New York: Morrow.

Esler, Philip F. (1987) *Community and Gospel in Luke–Acts: The Social and Political Motivations of Lucan Theology,* Cambridge: Cambridge University Press.

—— (1998) 'Review of D. G. Horrell, The Social Ethos of the Corinthian Correspondence', *Journal of Theological Studies,* 49, pp. 253–60.

Estruch, Joan (1995) *Saints and Schemers: Opus Dei and its Paradoxes,* New York and Oxford: Oxford University Press.

Gager, John G. (1975) *Kingdom and Community: The Social World of Early Christianity,* Englewood Cliffs, NJ: Prentice-Hall.

Gauchet, Marcel (1985) *Le Désenchantement du Monde: Une histoire politique de la religion,* Paris: Gallimard.

Gehlen, Arnold (1957) *Die Seele im Technischen Zeitalter,* Hamburg: Rowohlt.

Gehlen, Arnold (1980) (orig. 1949) *Man in the Age of Technology,* New York: Columbia University Press.

Giddens, Anthony (1971) *Capitalism and Modern Social Theory: An Analysis of the Writings of Marx, Durkheim and Max Weber,* Cambridge: Cambridge University Press.

—— (1979) *Central Problems in Social Theory: Action, Structure and Contradiction in Social Analysis,* Basingstoke: Macmillan.

Gilkey, Langdon (1969) *Naming the Whirlwind: The Renewal of God-Language,* Indianapolis: Bobbs-Merrill.

—— (1977) 'Anathemas and Orthodoxy: A Reply to Avery Dulles', *The Christian Century,* 94, pp. 1027–29.

—— (1978) 'Responses to Peter Berger', *Theological Studies,* 39 (3), pp. 486–97.

Gill, Robin (1974) 'Berger's Plausibility Structures: A Response to Professor Cairns', *Scottish Journal of Theology,* 27, pp. 198–207.

—— (1975) *The Social Context of Theology,* London: Mowbrays.

—— (1977) *Theology and Social Structure,* London: Mowbrays.

—— (1999) *Churchgoing and Christian Ethics,* Cambridge: Cambridge University Press.

——, C. Kirk Hadaway and Penny Long Marler (1998) 'Is Religious Belief Declining in Britain?', *Journal for the Scientific Study of Religion,* 37, pp. 507–16.

Gregory, Derek (1981) 'Human Agency and Human Geography', *Transactions of the Institute of British Geographers,* 6, pp. 1–18.

Hadaway, C. Kirk, Penny Long Marler and Mark Chaves (1993) 'What the Polls Don't Show: A Closer Look at US Church Attendance', *American Sociological Review,* 58, pp. 741–52.

Hadden, Jeffrey K. (1987) 'Towards Desacralizing Secularization Theory', *Social Forces,* 65, pp. 587–611.

Hanegraaff, Wouter J. (1996) *New Age Religion and Western Culture: Esotericism in the Mirror of Secular Thought,* Leiden: E.J. Brill.

Hanley, David (ed.) (1994) *Christian Democracy in Europe: a Comparative Perspective,* London: Pinter.

Hardy, Thomas (1976) *The Complete Poems,* London: Macmillan.

Harrison, Roger (1987) *Organization Culture and Quality of Service: A Strategy for Releasing Love in the Workplace,* London: The Association for Management Education and Development.

Hefner, Robert (1977) *Politics and Religious Renewal in Muslim South-East Asia,* Honolulu: University of Hawaii Press.

Heelas, Paul (1991) 'Cults for Capitalism: Self Religions, Magic and the Empowerment of Business', in Peter Gee and John Fulton (eds) *Religion and Power, Decline and Growth,* British Sociological Association: Sociology of Religion Study Group, pp. 27–41.

—— (1994) 'The Limits of Consumption and the Post-modern "Religion" of the New Age', in Russell Keat, Nigel Whiteley and Nicholas Abercrombie (eds) *The Authority of the Consumer,* London: Routledge, pp. 102–15.

—— (1996) *The New Age Movement: The Celebration of the Self and the Sacralization of Modernity,* Oxford: Blackwell.

Heelas, Paul (2000) 'Turning Within', in Martyn Percy (ed.) *Previous Convictions*, London: SPCK, pp. 58–76.

— (2001) 'Work Ethics, Soft Capitalism and "the Turn to Life"', in Paul du Gay and Michael Pryke (eds) *Cultural Economy*, London: Sage (forthcoming).

Hefner, Robert W. (2000) *Civil Islam*, Princeton: Princeton University Press.

Hervieu-Léger, Danièle (1993) 'Present Day Emotional Renewals: The End of Secularization or the End of Religion?', in William H. Swatos (ed.) *A Future for Religion: New Paradigms for Social Analysis*, Thousand Oaks, CA and London: Sage Publications, pp. 129–48.

— (1996) ' "Une Messe est possible": Les doubles funérailles du Président', *Le Débat*, 91, pp. 23–30.

— (1999) *Le Pèlerin et le converti: La religion en mouvement*, Paris: Flammarion.

Herzberg, Frederick (1968) *Work and the Nature of Man*, London: Staples Press.

Heuberger, Frank and Laura Nash (eds) (1994) *A Fatal Embrace? – Assessing Holistic Trends in Human Resources Programs*, New Brunswick, NJ: Transaction Publishers.

Hickman, Craig and Michael Silva (1985) *Creating Excellence: Managing Corporate Culture, Strategy and Change in the New Age*, London: George Allen & Unwin.

Hilborne, David (2000) *The Nature of Hell*, Carlisle: Acute.

Hochschild, Arlie (1997) *The Time Bind: When Work Becomes Home and Home Becomes Work*, New York: Metropolitan Books.

— (1983) *The Managed Heart: Commercialization of Human Feeling*, Berkeley: University of California Press.

Hoge, D. R. (1979) 'A Test of Theories of Denominational Growth and Decline', in D.R. Hoge and D.A. Roozen (eds) *Understanding Church Growth and Decline: 1950–1978*, New York: The Pilgrim Press, pp. 179–223.

Holmberg, Bengt (1990) *Sociology and the New Testament: An Appraisal*, Minneapolis, MN: Fortress Press.

Horrell, David G. (1993) 'Converging Ideologies: Berger and Luckmann and the Pastoral Epistles', *Journal for the Study of the New Testament*, 50, pp. 85–103. Reprinted in *New Testament Interpretation and Methods*, Stanley E. Porter and Craig A. Evans (eds), Sheffield: Sheffield Academic Press, 1997, pp. 102–20.

— (1996) *The Social Ethos of the Corinthian Correspondence: Interests and Ideology from 1 Corinthians to 1 Clement*, Edinburgh: T. & T. Clark.

— (1999a) 'Social-Scientific Interpretation of the New Testament: Retrospect and Prospect', in David G. Horrell (ed.) *Social-Scientific Approaches to New Testament Interpretation*, Edinburgh: T. & T. Clark, pp. 3–27.

— (ed.) (1999b) *Social-Scientific Approaches to New Testament Interpretation*, Edinburgh: T. & T. Clark.

— (2000) 'Models and Methods in Social-Scientific Interpretation: A Response to Philip Esler', *Journal for the Study of the New Testament*, 78, pp. 83–105.

Huczynski, A. (1993) *Management Gurus: What Makes Them and How to Become One*, London: Routledge.

Hunter, George G. III (1996) *Church for the Unchurched*, Nashville: Abingdon Press.

Hunter, James Davison (1987) *Evangelicalism: the Coming Generation*, Chicago: University of Chicago Press.

Inglehart, Robert (1977) *The Silent Revolution*, Princeton: Princeton University Press.

— (1990) *Culture Shift in Advanced Industrial Society*, Princeton: Princeton University Press.

Inglehart, Robert (1997) *Modernization and Postmodernization: Cultural, Economic and Political Change in 43 Societies*, Princeton: Princeton University Press.

James, William (1960) *The Varieties of Religious Experience*, London: Collins.

Jenkins, Timothy (1999) *Religion in English Everyday Life: An Ethnographic Approach*, Oxford: Berghahn Books.

Kee, Howard C. (1980) *Christian Origins in Sociological Perspective*, London: SCM Press.

Kelley, Dean (1972) *Why the Conservative Churches are Growing*, New York: Harper and Row.

Kellner, Hansfried and Frank Heuberger (eds) (1992) *Hidden Technocrats: The New Class and New Capitalism*, London: Transaction.

Kidd, Colin (1999) *British Identities Before Nationalism: Ethnicity and Nationhood in the Atlantic World, 1600–1800*, Cambridge: Cambridge University Press.

Kleiner, Art (1996) *The Age of Heretics: Heroes, Outlaws, and the Forerunners of Corporate Change*, London: Nicholas Brealey.

Laborde, Cécile (1999) 'French Politics 1981–97: Stability and Malaise', in Malcolm Cook and Grace Davie (eds) *Modern France: Society in Transition*, London: Routledge, pp. 151–71.

Lasch, Christopher (1977) *Haven in a Heartless World*, New York: Basic Books.

Le Bras, Gabriel (1945) *Introduction à l'histoire de la pratique religieuse en France*, Vol. II, Paris: Presses Universitaires de France.

Lewin, Roger and Birute Regine (1999) *The Soul at Work*, London: Orion.

Luckmann, Thomas (1967) *The Invisible Religion: The Problem of Religion in Modern Society*, New York: Macmillan.

MacDonald, Margaret Y. (1988) *The Pauline Churches: A Socio-historical Study of Institutionalization in the Pauline and Deutero-Pauline Writings*, Cambridge: Cambridge University Press.

McGregor, Douglas (1960) *The Human Side of Enterprise*, London: McGraw-Hill.

Mahesh, V. S. (1993) *Thresholds of Motivation: The Corporation as a Nursery for Human Growth*, New Delhi: Tata McGraw-Hill.

Malina, Bruce J. (1982) 'Social Sciences and Biblical Interpretation', *Interpretation*, 3–6, pp. 229–42.

Martin, David (1990) *Tongues of Fire: The Explosion of Protestantism in Latin America*, Oxford, UK and Cambridge, MA: Blackwell.

— (1996) *Forbidden Revolutions: Pentecostalism in Latin America and Catholicism in Eastern Europe*, London: SPCK.

Marx, Karl (1977) (orig. 1848): 'The Communist Manifesto', in David McLellan (ed.) *Karl Marx: Selected Writings*, Oxford: Oxford University Press.

Maslow, Abraham (1965) *Eupsychian Management*, Illinois: Richard D. Irwin.

Meeks, Wayne A. (1972) 'The Man from Heaven in Johannine Sectarianism', *Journal of Biblical Literature*, 91, pp. 44–71.

Michelat, Guy, Julien Potel, Jacques Sutter and Jacques Marie (1991) *Les Français sont-ils encore catholiques?*, Paris: Editions du Cerf.

Milbank, John (1993) *Theology and Social Theory,* Oxford, UK and Cambridge, MA: Blackwell.

Miller, Donald (1997) *Reinventing American Protestantism: Christianity in the New Millennium,* Berkeley, Los Angeles and London: University of California Press.

Milner, Sue (1999) 'Trade Unions', in Malcolm Cook and Grace Davie (eds) *Modern France: Society in Transition,* London: Routledge, pp. 132–50.

Nevitte, Neil (1996) *The Decline of Deference,* Ontario: Broadview.

Nora, Pierre (1996) *Realms of Memory, the Construction of the French Past* (Introduction to vol. I), New York: Columbia University Press.

Pedler, Mike, Tom Boydell and John Bourgoyne (1988) 'Learning Company Project' (A Report).

Pickett, Raymond (1997) *The Cross in Corinth: The Social Significance of the Death of Jesus,* Sheffield: Sheffield Academic Press.

Pietersen, Lloyd (1997) 'Despicable Deviants: Labelling Theory and the Polemic of the Pastorals', *Sociology of Religion,* 58, pp. 343–52.

Poulat, Emile (1960) 'La Découverte de la ville par le catholicisme français', *Annales ESC,* 16, pp. 1168–79.

—— (1982) *Modernistica,* Paris: Nouvelles Editions Latines.

Pryce, Alison (1999) 'Post Feminist Spirituality', unpublished PhD thesis, Lancaster University.

Ramer, Andrew (1999) *Angel Answers: A Joyful Guide to Creating Heaven on Earth,* New York: Simon and Schuster.

Ray, Larry and Andrew Sayer (1999) 'Introduction', in Larry Ray and Andrew Sayer (eds) *Culture and Economy after the Cultural Turn,* London: Sage, pp. 1–24.

Rich, Frank (2000) 'Round Midnight', *The New York Times,* vol. CXLIX: OP- ED, 1 January, p. A31.

Richards, Jeffrey, Scott Wilson and Linda Woodhead (eds) (1999) *Diana, the Making of a Media Saint,* London: I. B. Tauris.

Rieff, Philip (1979) *Freud: The Mind of the Moralist,* Chicago and London: University of Chicago Press.

Robertson, Roland (1978) *Meaning and Change: Explorations in the Cultural Sociology of Modern Societies,* Oxford: Basil Blackwell.

Roof, Wade Clark (1996) 'God is in the Details: Reflections on Religion's Public Presence in the United States in the Mid-1990s', *Sociology of Religion,* 57, pp. 149–62.

—— (1999) *Spiritual Marketplace: Baby Boomers and the Remaking of American Religion,* Princeton, NJ: Princeton University Press.

Roth, Guenther (1987) 'Rationalization in Max Weber's Developmental History', in Sam Whimster and Scott Lasch (eds) *Max Weber, Rationality and Modernity,* London: Allen & Unwin, pp. 75–91.

Schleiermacher, Friedrich (1928) *The Christian Faith,* H. R. Mackintosh and J. S. Stewart (eds), Edinburgh: T. & T. Clark.

Schneider, Louis and Sanford Dornbusch (1958) *Popular Religion: Inspirational Books in America,* Chicago: University of Chicago Press.

Schumacher, E. F. (1980) *Good Work,* London: Abacus.

Schutz, Alfred and Thomas Luckmann (1973) *The Structures of the Life-World,* Evanston, IL: Northwestern University Press.

Scroggs, Robin (1980) 'The Sociological Interpretation of the New Testament: The Present State of Research', *New Testament Studies,* 26, pp. 164–79.

Shi, David E. (1985) *The Simple Life: Plain Living and High Thinking in American Culture*, Oxford: Oxford University Press.
—— (1986) *In Search of the Simple Life*, Salt Lake City: Peregrine Smith Books, Gibbs M. Smith, Inc.
Simmel, Georg (1997) (orig. 1918) 'The Conflict of Modern Culture', in Georg Simmel, *Essays on Religion*, New Haven, CN: Yale University Press, pp. 20–5.
Smith, Greg (1998) 'Religious Belonging and Inter-faith Encounter: Some Survey Findings from East London', *Journal of Contemporary Religion*, 13 (3), pp. 333–51.
Smith, Jonathan Z. (1975) 'The Social Description of Early Christianity', *Religious Studies Review*, 1, pp. 19–25.
Social Trends (1994, 1995 and 1998), London: HMSO.
Theissen, Gerd (1979) *Studien zur Soziologie des Urchristentums*, Tübingen: Mohr Siebeck (2nd edn, 1983; 3rd edn, 1988).
—— (1982) *The Social Setting of Pauline Christianity: Essays on Corinth*, John H. Schutz trans., Edinburgh: T. & T. Clark.
—— (1983) 'Christologie und Soziale Erfahrung. Wissenssoziologische Aspekte Paulinischer Christologie', in Gerd Theissen, *Studien zur Soziologie des Urchristentums*, Tübingen: Mohr Siebeck, 2nd edn, 1983, pp. 318–30.
—— (1993) *Social Reality and the Early Christians: Theology, Ethics, and the World of the New Testament*, Margaret Kohl trans., Edinburgh: T. & T. Clark.
Thomas, R. S. (1995) *Collected Poems 1945–1990*, London: Phoenix.
Thompson, John B. (1984) *Studies in the Theory of Ideology*, Cambridge: Polity Press.
Thrift, Nigel (1997) 'Soft Capitalism', *Cultural Values* 1 (1), pp. 29–57.
Tipton, Steven (1982) *Getting Saved from the Sixties: Moral Meaning in Conversion and Cultural Change*, Los Angeles and London: University of California Press.
Troeltsch, Ernst (1912) *Soziallheren des Christichen Kirchen und Gruppen*, Tübingen: Mohr.
Turner, Bryan, S. (1981) *For Weber: Essays on the Sociology of Fate*, London: Routledge and Kegan Paul.
van Kersbergen, Kees (1995) *Social Capitalism: A Study of Christian Democracy and the Welfare State*, London: Routledge.
Walsh, John (2000) 'So Hell is a Real Place after all: Thank Heavens for That!', *Independent*, Monday Review, 3 April, p. 5.
Walter, Tony (1999) *The Week Diana Died*, Oxford: Berg.
Warner, R. Stephen (1993) 'Work in Progress Toward a New Paradigm for the Sociological Study of Religion in the United States', *American Journal of Sociology* 98 (5), March, pp. 1044–93.
Watson, Francis (1986) *Paul, Judaism and the Gentiles: A Sociological Approach*, Cambridge: Cambridge University Press.
—— (1994) *Text, Church and World: Biblical Interpretation in Theological Perspective*, Edinburgh: T. & T. Clark.
Weber, Max (1951) *The Religion of China: Confucianism and Taoism*, Glencoe, IL: Free Press.
—— (1952) *Ancient Judaism*, Glencoe, IL: Free Press.
—— (1958) *The Religion of India*, Glencoe, IL: Free Press.
—— (1965) *The Sociology of Religion*, London: Methuen.

Weber, Max (1985) (orig. 1904–5) *The Protestant Ethic and the Spirit of Capitalism*, London: Unwin.

Whyte, William (1963) (orig. 1956) *The Organization Man*, Harmondsworth: Pelican.

Willaime, Jean-Paul (1996a) 'Laïcité en religion en France', in Grace Davie and Danièle Hervieu-Léger (eds) *Identités religieuses en Europe*, Paris: La Découverte, pp.153–71.

—— (1996b) 'Les Religions et l'unification européenne', in Grace Davie and Danièle Hervieu-Léger (eds) *Identités religieuses en Europe*, Paris: La Découverte, pp. 291–314.

Wilson, Bryan (1968) 'Religion and the Churches in America', in William G. McLoughlin and Robert N. Bellah (eds) *Religion in America*, Boston: Houghton Mifflin, pp. 73–110.

Woodhead, Linda (1999) 'Diana and the Religion of the Heart', in Jeffrey Richards, Scott Wilson and Linda Woodhead (eds) *Diana: The Making of a Media Saint*, London: I. B. Tauris, pp. 119–39.

—— and Paul Heelas (2000) *Religion in Modern Times: An Interpretive Anthology*, Malden, MA and Oxford, UK: Blackwell.

Wuthnow, Robert (1986) 'Religion as Sacred Canopy', in James Davison Hunter and Stephen C. Ainlay (eds) *Making Sense of Modern Times: Peter L. Berger and the Vision of Interpretive Sociology*, London and New York: Routledge and Kegan Paul, pp. 121–42.

—— (1994) *Sharing the Journey: Support Groups and America's New Quest for Community*, New York: Free Press.

Yerkes, James (ed.) (1999) *John Updike and Religion: The Sense of the Sacred and the Motions of Grace*, Grand Rapids, MI: Eerdmans.

York, Michael (1995) *The Emerging Network: A Sociology of the New Age and Neo-pagan Movements*, London: Rowman & Littlefield.

Zanders, H. (1993) 'Changing Work Values', in Peter Ester, Loek Halman and Ruud de Moor (eds) *The Individualizing Society: Value Change in Europe and North America*, Tilburg, Netherlands: Tilburg University Press, pp. 129–53.

Index